Last Landscapes

Last Landscapes

The Architecture of the Cemetery in the West

Ken Worpole

Colour photography by Larraine Worpole

REAKTION BOOKS

Published by Reaktion Books Ltd
79 Farringdon Road
London ECIM 3JU, UK

www.reaktionbooks.co.uk

First published 2003

Printed in China

British Library Cataloguing in Publication Data

Worpole, Ken, 1944–
Last landscapes : the architecture of the cemetery in the West
1. Cemeteries
I. Title
718

ISBN 1 86189 161 X

Contents

When we find a mound in the woods,

six feet long and three feet wide,

raised to a pyramidal form by means of a spade,

we become serious and something in us says:

someone was buried here. *That is architecture.*

Adolf Loos, *Architecture* (1910)

Introduction

In the earliest gathering about a grave or a
painted symbol, a great stone or a sacred grove,
one has the beginning of a succession of civic
institutions that range from the temple
to the astronomical observatory,
from the theatre to the university.

Lewis Mumford, *The City in History*[1]

Like many people, from childhood days onward,
I have always been intrigued and disquieted by
cemeteries, and other places where the dead are
evoked or commemorated. However, I only
became seriously interested in the subject in the
mid-1990s, when after researching and writing
a number of studies on urban parks, I was
commissioned by the Gulbenkian Foundation
(UK) to write a paper on the growing problem
of the loss of burial space in London.

What started off as a professional piece of
work on public policy (public policy being, in one
felicitous coinage, 'hopes dressed in uniform'[2]),
soon developed into a sustained personal interest
in the plight of the cemetery and funerary culture
in the modern world. It was clear that in nearly
all of the current literature dealing with urban
and planning issues for the twenty-first century,
the role and ritual space of the cemetery had been
ignored. Yet anyone who has visited a churchyard,
cemetery or crematorium garden – and we mostly
visit these places at times of distress or upheaval –
cannot but be overcome by the range of emotions
that occur there and nowhere else in the natural
landscape or the spaces of the city. Because these
emotions are so powerful, and indeed basic to

human identity, it seemed to me to be crucial to retain, and even enhance, the space of the cemetery in the city and the landscape.

This is a book about landscape and meaning, more than it is about death or bereavement. I do not subscribe to the commonly expressed view that modern societies have 'abolished' death or hidden it from view. In fact, I rather agree with the person who, compiling a bibliography about death in the 1970s, noted ironically that 'Death is a very badly kept secret; such an unmentionable and taboo topic that there are over 750 books now in print asserting that we are ignoring the subject.'[3] While I happen to believe that most people still treat death seriously, I do think that in its topographical, processional, landscaping and architectural aspects, commemoration has been poorly served in recent times.

One only has to compare the frequency in which images of cemeteries appear as key settings in films and television dramas, compared with the infrequency in which they appear in landscape or architectural magazines, to know that those ultimately responsible for cemetery design are out of touch with public concerns and interests. Furthermore, while many people are reclaiming aspects of funerary ritual back from professional and commercial interests – in the organization of personalized funeral services and even arrangements for the disposal of bodies – in matters to do with the public and architectural culture of death, innovation in design, landscape and architectural aesthetics remains rare.

One of the reasons for this is economic. The cost of dying may come only once in a lifetime, but it often comes unexpectedly, and it invariably comes in one go. Victorian cultures – within both middle-class and working-class circles – spent heavily on funerals, mausoleums, headstones, and commemorative rituals. The new cemeteries of the nineteenth century were profitable businesses, selling burial space at premium rates. However, once they were full, the flow of money ceased. In the second half of the twentieth century, with the rise of cremation (sometimes chosen because it is cheaper than burial), and with many people less prepared to spend large sums on funerals, the capital and operating costs of establishing and maintaining new cemeteries seem to be increasingly incompatible with good design and high-quality levels of maintenance.

This is particularly the case where burial is assumed or contracted to be in perpetuity, as is the case in Britain and North America. In many European countries burial is for a fixed period only, at the end of which the remains are excavated and placed elsewhere, and the grave space is then re-used. The re-use of graves in civic or urban cemeteries changes the economic basis of the cemetery entirely, enabling it to meet the burial needs of each generation anew. In time this may happen in Britain too, and possibly in North America. On the other hand, the growing interest in 'natural burial', particularly in Britain and other parts of northern Europe, may resolve some of these issues in other ways.

In the course of writing this book it has been interesting to note how very different are the attitudes and practices surrounding bodily disposal and commemoration in different countries, which otherwise appear to share similar lifestyles and cultures. Put crudely, there are three ways in which you can dispose of your loved ones and fellow citizens: burn them, bury them or build them a place of their own. All present distinct ethical and cultural challenges to the surrounding society, and that society's sense of its own identity and history. Unexpectedly, there is very little anthropological research that explains why there should be such dramatic differences among otherwise similar modern cultures, above and beyond specific religious requirements.

My own reading of the situation can be summarized as follows: northern Europeans are happy with cremation and any kind of earth burial, but find the re-use of graves unacceptable, and resist inhumation in vaults above ground; southern Europeans are more resistant to cremation but are happy with most kinds of burial, above or below ground, and are even relaxed about the re-use of graves, even after as little as ten years; Americans are generally unhappy about cremation, prefer burial (because resurrectionary beliefs remain strong), but find the re-use of graves and the idea of 'natural burial' unacceptable, at least for the time being.

WORDS AND THINGS

In this book the terms *burial place*, *cemetery* and *churchyard* will be the principal terms used to denote the vernacular, formal and religious places where the remains of the dead are interred or collected. One distinguishing feature of most cemeteries, historically, has been their 'gathered' morphology, in which clusters of graves are usually surrounded by a wall, or in other ways set apart. A powerful exception to this pattern occurred in ancient Rome, where tombs and mausoleums lined the roads in and out of the city.[4] The word *burial* derives from the Anglo-Saxon *birgan*, some of whose other derivations and related words include *barrow*, *burrow*, *borough*, *burgh* and even *berg*, bringing together implications of both a mound where the dead are interred, but also a place of origin or settlement.

The field, so to speak, is crowded with many other terms of a cognate meaning, such as *graveyard* (the term suggests smallness of scale, yard being etymologically connected to *gård* or *garden*), *burying ground* (common in the early years of North American settlement), *necropolis* (a large cemetery or literally 'city of the dead' close to a city, such as the Glasgow Necropolis), *mausoleum* (a monumental burial tomb, the name derived from the tomb built for King Mausolos in the fourth century BC, the plural of which employed in this book is *mausoleums*, now that the word has clearly been Anglicized[5]), *ossuary* or *charnel-house* (a place where bones are collected together with some degree of ritual meaning), *columbarium* (a building with niches or closed compartments for the formal retention of cremated remains, or in the case of coffins, *loculi*), and, rather further back in time, *catacomb* (originally the subterranean cemetery of St Sebastian near Rome, but also used to describe excavated passages and burial niches carved out of bedrock, such as can still be visited in Paris), and *crypt* (the underground vault constructed in many early church buildings, and used as a burial place for more illustrious corpses).

References are also made to pre-Christian burial stone constructions such as *cromlechs* and *dolmens* (stone chamber tombs), as well as burial mounds such as *tumuli* or *barrows*. In addition this book will also look at various kinds of memorial gardens, commemorative landscapes, memorial sculptures and *cenotaphs* (an empty tomb, memorial or monument to someone or many people who have died and are buried elsewhere, if known at all). Recent writers, such as James E. Young in his study of Holocaust memorialization, have sought to make a clear distinction between *memorials* and *monuments*, quoting Arthur Danto's corrective that 'we erect monuments so that we shall always remember and build memorials so that we shall never forget'.[6]

In earlier times there were two commonly used Latin words for a burial ground: *cœmeterium* and *atrium*. As Christopher Daniell has written, *cœmeterium* reflects the nature of resting and sleep, deriving as it does from the Greek word for bedroom. *Atrium* comes from the classical Latin, and originally meant a reception room in a house partially open to the sky, but it was used to describe an enclosed space, or cemetery.[7] The walled cemetery therefore captures this architectural ambiguity of being both a walled room and an open space in the landscape: shelter and exposure, absence and presence, at one and the same time. *Tumulus* and *tomb* both come from the same Greek root word, meaning a swelling, reminding us that bodies rarely entirely disappear from the earth's surface: their presence remains marked, naturally or culturally, by an irruption of some kind in the landscape.

Finally, in modern times, particularly in northern Europe, there is now a growing preference for what is generally termed *natural burial*, defined as the burial of a body within a biodegradable coffin or shroud in a naturalistic setting, with grave markings, if any, designed to return to nature. Other modern practices have now revived the use of the term *urn burial*, to describe the interment of cremated remains in containers in appropriate settings, and the term *secondary burial* refers to the procedure whereby after an agreed period, remains are excavated and stored elsewhere, usually in order to make the grave space available for re-use.

The landscapes and burial places dealt with in the chapters that follow are mainly to be found in Europe or North America. Furthermore, the belief systems which informed these sites come initially either from northern European pagan or Hellenistic traditions, and subsequently from the dominant Judæo-Christian culture of Europe and North America. I note on a number of occasions distinct architectural and landscape traditions between northern and southern Europe. In one case, that of the burial ground at the Mosque of the Tekka of Hala Sultan in Cyprus, brief mention is made of Islamic burial markers and their relation to the topography of the place. These landscapes and settings are of course special, if not always sublime, and there is a long history of practices and conventions in both architecture and landscape design (though its earliest practitioners would not have described it in such terms) about the most appropriate means of marking the places of the dead. An elaboration of these elements forms the main part of the book. *Last Landscapes* is an architectural and cultural history of burial places and cemeteries in Europe and North America, from pre-Christian times to the present day. It is also a summary of the distinctive landscaping and architectural features of these places, and the relation of these to the belief systems and social structures that underpinned them; an assertion that the places of the dead are pivotal landscapes, where past and future values and beliefs are held in balance or negotiated (as such, the cemetery exerts a moral power within the wider culture); a reminder of the importance of funerary architecture in creating 'libraries in stone', in which the beliefs and identities of past individuals and cultures are inscribed for future generations; a discussion about the different burial practices and cultures associated variously with cremation, burial and inhumation in monumental forms above ground, as well as a consideration of the contentious issue of the 're-use' of graves, which today marks major differences between otherwise quite similar countries and cultures, along with related architectural and landscaping implications; a consideration as to how, in modern societies and cultures, economic choices – whether enacted within religious, civic, or free market frameworks – increasingly shape funerary forms and cultures; an elaboration of a number of new ways of thinking about the relationship between life cultures and experiences, and those of the funerary rituals associated with death, notably through the enduring metaphor of the tomb or grave as the final home; and, finally, a plea to reintegrate the places of the dead into modern lifeworlds and social and physical geographies.

Although the practice of architecture is central to this book, I am not an architect; none the less, I am fascinated by the role that architecture plays in shaping human experience and emotion. The same is true of landscape and garden design. Understandably, such literature as exists about the creation of meaning through architecture and landscape in contemporary society is largely from the point of view of those professionals practising in these forms, not those experiencing them. The gap between the intentions of the designers and the received understandings of the users or spectators is sometimes great. In this book I try to appreciate both points of view.

THE CEMETERY AND SOCIETY

Furthermore, no single intellectual discipline or 'discourse' structures or shapes this book: it is the product of what the American anthropologist, Clifford Geertz, once called the increasing amount of 'genre mixing in intellectual life'. I share his opinion that this reconfiguration of social thought is to be greatly welcomed. Geertz states at one point in an essay on the modern hybridization of intellectual disciplines that, 'Many social scientists have turned away from a laws and instances ideal of explanation toward a cases and interpretations one, looking less for the sort of thing that connects planets and pendulums and more for the sort that connects chrysanthemums and swords.'[8] As it happens, both chrysanthemums and swords are to be found in this book, and indeed connections established between them. The former is a flower long associated with death, famously in the title of one of D. H. Lawrence's finest short stories, 'Odour of Chrysanthemums', and the latter is the bronze sword embedded in Reginald Blomfield's stone or granite Cross of Sacrifice, which became one of the most resonant and distinctive artefacts in British and Commonwealth war cemeteries, following the end of World War One.

In an earlier book – *Here Comes the Sun* – I argued that the iconography and design of the urban built form and public landscape was strongly linked to powerful belief systems that cities develop and enact, principally through the processes of design and planning. Such belief systems might be religious, political or social; or indeed any combination of these. In the design of cemeteries – no less than the design of parks, pleasure gardens, lidos and other public spaces (the subject-matter of that earlier book) – such belief systems sought to develop an appropriate symbolic and institutional form for these new public or quasi-public places. This the nineteenth-century secular or non-denominational European cemetery seemed to achieve.

As a result, the development of well-managed and often beautiful cemeteries and burial grounds in cities became associated with ideas of progress and even social harmony. As historians such as Richard Etlin and James Stevens Curl have pointed out on many occasions, the development of Père-Lachaise cemetery in Paris was a fulfilment of many of the ideas of anticlericalism and egalitarianism advocated during the French Revolution. Indeed, James Stevens Curl concludes that 'the official Decree of 23 Prairial, Year XII (12 June 1804) drew up the rules for French cemeteries that have essentially remained the same until our own day'.[9] In Scotland, and then elsewhere in Britain, the formal urban cemetery, which was developed to avoid the overcrowding and unhygienic conditions of the city churchyard, was largely the result of non-conformist, Dissenting or Protestant impulses to rid death and burial of its mystical and Gothic (especially Catholic) elements.

Such cemeteries were 'products of a radical reform movement just as significant in the history of the urban fabric as those other political and sanitary reforms that were features of the liberal climate of the epoch'.[10] In the twentieth century, the Stockholm Woodland Cemetery set the standard for a new era of cemetery design appropriate to a more democratic and self-conscious society. Committed cemetery professionals today, and there are thankfully quite a few, are still apt to quote the words of the nineteenth-century politician William Gladstone, who once said 'Show me the manner in which a Nation or Community cares for its dead and I will measure with mathematical exactness the tender mercies of its people, their respect for the laws of the land, and their loyalty to high ideals.'[11]

A great debt is owed in the pages that follow to the handful of European and North American historians and writers who have sought to understand the complex arrangement between the living and the dead in changing modern societies. While there is still too little material in many areas, there is one field where there has been considerable work done on the subject, notably in the many books and studies of the impact of mass slaughter in World War One, its effects on the home societies, on the landscapes of battle, and on the arrangements for the disposal of the remains of the many millions killed in war, and the commemoration of their memory. Because there is, relatively speaking, so much written about the cemeteries and war memorials of World War One (other than in Russia, where attention to the Second World War eclipses all other understandings of death and commemoration in the twentieth century), I have chosen to treat the matter fairly briefly, and in the Bibliography to point readers to far more detailed and exhaustive studies of this terrible human and social catastrophe. Readers will also notice that there is little here on landscape and architectural traditions relating to cemeteries in Eastern Europe – though some mention is made of the specific plight of Jewish cemeteries left to dereliction after the Second World War – and in future it is hoped that others will remedy this.[12]

On more than one occasion I have been asked if I haven't found the subject too depressing, even morbid ('unwholesome, sickly; marked by exaggerated or inappropriate feelings of gloom, apprehension or suspicion', according to the *Shorter Oxford Dictionary*). The opposite is true, I have found, and so have others working in this fascinating field of human culture. The subject is strangely uplifting, and indeed has its utopian aspects as well.[13] The 'sense of an ending' is a utopian trope, embodying a sense of completion. It was the renegade French writer Georges Bataille who noted that the major difference between nature and human society (especially late-capitalist society) was that the former didn't include the element of accumulation. Nature is based on growth and entropy, proliferation, but also on dissolution and decay. If death didn't exist, the nightmare of permanent (and increasingly unequal) material accumulation would never end. Sometimes one can only be thankful to death for acting as the last remaining brake on human concupiscence and vanity.

Finally, this is a book in which the images are as important as the text. For this book, Larraine Worpole and I went in search of images that actively shape the nature of the text itself, so that in writing I have endeavoured to respond to the 'felt' atmosphere of these extraordinary landscapes and funerary symbols. This is not without difficulties: keeping in one's mind's eye a set of images and visual relationships at times challenges the very intentionality of the act of writing itself. I hope I have managed to find the right balance between the two.

A Celtic cross looms above stony ground.

chapter one

Living with the Dead

Just in case you thought there was no distinction between representation and reality, there is death. Just in case you thought experience and the representation of experience melted into each other, death provides a structural principle separating the two.

Regina Barreca, 'Writing as Voodoo1'[1]

Some years ago I was invited to give a lecture in Ålesund, a small coastal town in Norway, where I stayed on for a few days, sightseeing and walking. Ålesund is especially memorable because the architecture there belongs not to Norway but to another world: that of the Austro-Hungarian empire. In 1904 the timber-built fishing village, as it then was, burnt down completely, leaving the majority of its population of 10,000 homeless. The German Kaiser, Wilhelm II, had been a frequent visitor to Ålesund, often sailing in the western fjords, and offered to send a team of architects to help reconstruct the town, which they went on to do in the then fashionable Jugendstil manner. And so it remains today: a pristine collection of townhouses, shops and public institutions in pastel colours, with ornate doorways, turrets and towers, with just a hint of fairy-tale.

From the window of the hotel in which I was staying, I looked out on three islands lying out in the fjord, one flat, and the other two rising precipitously from the waves: Giske, Valderøy and Godøy. On the day I arrived the weather was foul, with a dark sky enveloping the islands in a scrim of driving rain, while spray and the sea lashed at their shorelines. They looked formidably isolated and unreachable, though two mornings later the sun shone on them and they became tamed landscape again, poised, dreamlike and inviting.

Until only very recently, people travelled between such islands, and indeed to Ålesund itself, by public ferry or private boat. But large government grants have been awarded throughout Norway to connect the principal islands and routeways by tunnel, the monies being partly recouped by hefty toll charges, payable even by those who travel by bus. The tunnels that connect these small islands descend and ascend at vertiginously steep gradients, and some of the magic of travelling through the fjords and between the islands of the western archipelago – the gleaming paintwork of the ferries, and their smell of diesel oil, the hot coffee served, the changing skies and roiling of the water, which I remember from visiting and working in Norway in the 1960s – has now vanished, replaced by tunnels of brute concrete lit by sodium lamps and smelling of stale exhaust fumes. Nevertheless, I was able to visit all three islands, but found two of them dangerously impassable for casual walking, and so spent a day on Giske.

Giske was the island seat of one of the great Viking clans, and is today home to some 200 families. The houses are all made of wood, and painted in yellow, ochre or green – taking their hues and colours from many of the wildflowers which surround them – and are raised above the ground on stilts or large boulders. A number of the more recent houses have turf roofs, with grasses, herbs and wildflowers in full flower rising several feet into the upper air, rippling with each gust of wind from the nearby sea.

Most have balconies, porches and sitting out decks, and all have detachable ladders secured to the roof, a feature of most houses in rural Scandinavia. It was a fine June day, and the air was scented with the smell of the sea, wild grasses and woodsmoke. The bus had dropped me, by request, at the first stop on the island, and I was making a circular walk back to where I began. In a very short while I came to the church.

At the hotel, earlier that morning, I was told that the church on Giske was built 'some time in the twelfth century', but what hadn't been mentioned was that it was built entirely of white marble. There is no white marble in Norway, nor for many hundreds of miles. Nobody knows exactly whence the marble came, most likely Spain or Italy, but what is certain is that it was brought by open wooden boat over great distances, possibly in a large convoy, or after many return journeys, and certainly at great risk. Yet while admiring this extraordinary act of religious enthusiasm and piety, it was the small churchyard I found most intriguing.

The first reason was that most of the surnames on the headstones were identical, as if the churchyard were the final resting place of one vast extended family, and the name of this family was that of the island itself, Giske. Nearly all shared the same inscription: *Takk for alt* ('Thanks for everything'). I asked a young woman arranging flowers in the church if she would mind telling me something about the island and its history. Everybody born on Giske has always taken the name of the island as their surname, she said, and this was quite common in her part of Norway, especially on the islands. The place you come from provides you with your name and public identity. Her surname was Godøy, that of the next island, where she was born.

I also asked her about the inscription 'Thanks for everything'. This seemed almost casual in tone, the sort of thing one might say to friends who had kindly entertained one for a weekend, rather than a final wave from the far shores of oblivion. It seemed pleasingly generous, and not harrowing or exhortatory as many inscriptions are, particularly from Victorian times, or in areas of uncompromisingly austere religions, as I had assumed Norwegian Lutheranism to have once been. She agreed that it didn't translate well, and that its use on headstones might be better translated as 'Give thanks for everything'.

The village churchyard at Giske stays in my memory because it perfectly exemplified a state of human settlement of the most traditional kind: a place at one in name with its location and human community. It also evoked some of the psychological comforts (or pleasures) of miniaturization: the human world scaled down to its essential elements. Burial grounds and cemeteries somehow seem to fix a time and a place in a culture for ever, carrying the past into the present and even into the future in perpetuity. The anthropologist Robert Fortune once described 'the ideal village of Dobu (as being) a circle of huts facing inward to a central, often elevated mound, which is the village grave-yard'.[2] This form of spatial geography many believe to be settlement in its truest sense, where the dead share the same territory and identity as the living. Such spatial arrangements seem to suggest that death is not the end of the human story; in fact it shapes and defines that story. At other times, and in other places, especially in the

rural churchyards, or island cemeteries that Larraine and I have visited over the years – the lonely Irish monastic settlement and graveyard on Devenish Island on Lower Lough Erne in County Fermanagh, for example, or that on the island of Björkö in the Stockholm archipelago, where we wandered among several thousand grave mounds punctuated by birch and aspen trees, with purple loosestrife running riot in the grasslands – one is silenced by the elemental mystery of death. In such places, there is a palpable feeling of both extreme solitude and consolation. (Heidegger says of death that it is 'the shrine of nothingness and at the same time the shelter of being'.[3]) In such purified settings, one can often feel a melting sense of presence and absence simultaneously, together with the suspension of time. The enormity of the world shrinks to a small burial mound, or even to the space of a single grave. Death exercises a powerful grip on both landscape and the human imagination.

When, in the mid-eighteenth century, Edmund Burke deliberated on the notion of the 'Sublime', he included feelings associated not just with delight and beauty, but with fear, even terror.[4] There are few settings which conjure up this equivocating feeling of the Sublime more than the places of the dead. On occasions, death can also do its job too well, encroaching upon the living community, particularly in more remote parts of the world, to such an extent that it triumphs completely. The sociologist Tony Walter tells the story of a former student of his who came from the remote Shetland island of Foula, the inhabitants of which feared that one day soon they might have to vacate the island as their way of life was becoming unsustainable. The point at which that situation would be reached, according to the student, was 'When there are not enough men to carry a coffin.'[5]

In this book I try to elaborate on the way in which the places and practices of death and burial reconfigure not just the landscape, but our orientation to space and time, place and history. I continue to explore a growing realization of the degree to which people's lives are as much shaped by the rooms, houses, streets, cities and landscapes that form the backdrop to their lives as they are by the scripts of ideas, political ideologies and psychological traits and dæmons that they internalize or inherit. The anthropologist Christopher Tilley has written about these relationships at length, noting that, 'the meanings of landscapes become indelibly attached and unfolded in myths, stories, rituals and the naming of places . . . [and that they] form potent sources of metaphors for the social construction and perception of reality'.[6] The phenomenology of the familiar world – by which I mean the direct sensual experience of the textures, artefacts, sights, sounds and scents of our daily experience, especially those located in and around those places we call home – is one of the greatest of human consolations, and central to that phenomenology is the presence of these last landscapes of the dead.

ARCHITECTURE BEGAN WITH TOMBS

The burial of the dead creates dynamic shapes and force-fields in the inherited landscape: barrows, tumuli, stone circles, groves, windswept cemeteries and even burial islands. While successive generations, whether settlers, migrants,

raiders or colonists, may have often adapted or destroyed pre-existing settlements built for the living, burial places have often been left untouched, or even extended as the founding sites for new ones. A respect for the terrain of death, along with the individual grave site, seems to be one of the continuities of human landscape and culture, though there have been monstrous exceptions on occasions, where the vandalism or destruction of an enemy's graves or burial sites has been regarded as a final humiliation.

Not only has death reshaped the landscape; Howard Colvin has reminded us that 'Architecture in Western Europe begins with tombs.'[7] In more recent times the growth of archaeology has provided the modern world with much invaluable and fascinating material about past lives and cultures, while at the same time, ironically, breaking a long-standing and wide-spread cultural taboo against disturbing the dead. Archaeology presents us with the paradox of Schrödinger's Cat: by 'opening the box' we seek to discover the truth, but only at the expense of destroying the inviolability and mystery of the grave, which for many is its ultimate truth and meaning. Gaston Bachelard put it more poetically, noting that 'there will always be more things in a closed, than in an open, box'.[8]

The overlay between ancient and modern burial places can be seen, for example, at the great twentieth-century cemetery at Malmö East, in the Skåne region of southern Sweden, designed in 1916 by the landscape designer and architect Sigurd Lewerentz, sited and laid out around a Bronze Age burial mound (or *lund*). The beautiful early Christian church and churchyard at Gamla Uppsala, north of Stockholm, fits snugly into a

East, Middle and West Burial Mounds at Gamla Uppsala, Sweden, AD *c.* 550–600. The parish church, based on the remains of the 12th-century cathedral, forms part of the same spiritual geography.

long line of Viking ship-barrows. Likewise, in England at Ogbourne St Andrews, Wiltshire, there is a large bowl barrow in the churchyard in which evidence of a pagan Saxon burial was once found.[9] Not far away, at Knowlton in Dorset and Cholesbury in Buckinghamshire, churches were built within larger circular earthworks dating back to pre-Roman times, and while these do not necessarily imply that the earlier sites were regarded as burial places, they were regarded as having some kind of spiritual significance in the landscape.[10] It has been argued that in some parts of Britain 'the number of cemeteries or barrows located on, or next to, older monuments can reach staggering proportions: some 60 per cent of known seventh-century Anglo-Saxon cemeteries in the Upper Thames Valley are found in such locations.'[11]

Similarly, pre-Christian standing stones can be found erect in the churchyards of Brittany, Cornwall, Denmark and elsewhere. Likewise, in Rome, the catacombs first dug by pagan peoples were subsequently copied by early Christians, Jews and others, often constructed close to each other, and even, at times, sharing the same networks of underground corridors. When early settlers moved westwards across North America, even they felt obliged at times to bury individuals close to the burial grounds of Native Americans. This was the case of Benjamin

Nukerk, the first white settler in Onondaga County (in what is now central New York state), who, when he died in 1787, was buried 'a small distance away from a large number of unmarked graves of Onondagas'.[12] Differences in temporalities and cultures are often accommodated if not resolved in the very nature and form of the landscape itself.

In many burial places, ancient and modern cultures lie side by side, as the dead accumulate and settle in perpetuity. While several thousand years separate the first formal burial sites from the most modern of cemeteries, many practices and belief systems are common to both. Burial and cremation, for example, have coexisted in quite different cultures and at different times, as have practices regarding the orientation of the bodies to be laid in the ground; similarly, many cultures have practised individual, familial and group burials. Likewise the erection of marking stones, and the dedication of a particular site or area of settlement, especially for the disposal of the remains of the dead, are often common across time. In addition, certain kinds of herbs, shrubs and trees – notably evergreens – have been considered to possess particular properties or meanings appropriate to the rite of death and burial, while the association of life with the sun (and daylight) and death with darkness and the night, is also common to many cultures. Burial practices in relation to dead children have also been distinctive in many cultures throughout history. Later in this book I will deal with the many different architectural responses to these practices.

LANDSCAPE AND DEATH

The influence of the dead on landscape form and experience can be highly charged, even pervasive. The eminent geographer Yi-Fu Tuan has termed this relationship between burial, landscape and belief systems, 'geo-piety', a rather more pastoral version of the Durkheimian notion that space itself is socially (and religiously) constructed.[13] Ancestor worship and the respect accorded to human remains is common to most cultures and societies, and burial sites are often regarded culturally as 'a place apart', hallowed, respected, and at times even feared: landscapes that 'empower the mind'.[14] The anthropologist Bronisław Malinowski concluded that it was the very fact of death itself that was the principal source and inspiration for the many varieties of religious belief that have emerged from human societies and cultures throughout the history of the world, and from this assertion surely flows the related conclusion that this makes burial sites and practices especially important and symbolic in human place-making.[15]

However, to describe a burial site solely as a social or ritual space somehow seems rather too de-natured, since many people feel that the return of the dead to the earth is anthropologically a transition back from the social to the natural. It also relates to the wider anthropological understanding of the historic anomaly of the dead body, which Mary Douglas describes as 'our fear of the corpse, neither human nor waste'.[16] This, interestingly, seems to mark the latest wave of thinking about burial in advanced societies, through the espousal of 'natural' or 'woodland' burial in the interests of wider ecological and environmental concerns, as society in its latest mode of self-consciousness seeks to become more 'natural'.

An appreciation of landscape is largely based on a mixture of human imagination, learned visual responses, and social perception: part historical, part aesthetic, and part psychological. It is an active, dynamic relationship between the seer and the thing seen. Yet with regard to the emotions and thoughts that are stirred by the sight and experience of burial places, there is an obvious impulse that dominates all others: our sense that we too are destined for death, and that this 'ultimate form of phenomenological awareness', as the philosopher Françoise Dastur has written, 'is constant in our perception of the world'.[17] Thus the landscapes of the dead rightly exert a specific and compulsive hold on the human imagination, because they are reminders of the transience of human life, most particularly, of course, our own. Because they mix feelings of both beauty and anxiety – or even dread – they can rightly claim to be called Sublime.

For some, the presence of death in the landscape seem overwhelming. The late W. G. Sebald, in his agonized meditation *Austerlitz*, seems to suggest that not only is the gap between life and death wafer-thin and permanently immiserating, but that the world itself is one vast cemetery.[18] In the experience of Sebald's many post-war European exiles and émigrés – most commonly the principal characters and narrators of his extraordinary books – what lies beneath every great edifice or human settlement is most likely to be a mass grave, or the buried remains of some great atrocity. In this view, human history is a sequence of disasters, in which it is the secreted mass grave, the battlefield miasma, or the anony-mous pauper pit, which principally characterizes death in the modern era. His hero is Balzac's Colonel Chabert, who escapes from one of the vast burial pits at Waterloo, and whose life is lived as that of one who has emerged from the grave, rather than as one destined for it, like all others.

Significant remains of the storytelling element in landscape appreciation come down to people to this day. Much travel writing is in fact history, captured in the saying that 'geography is history'. To walk across the moors at Culloden is not simply to walk across turf sprung with heather. It is another kind of experience entirely, memoried in blood, betrayal and catastrophe. Not all writers about landscape are happy with the overlay between visual and historical cues and references. The doyen of naturalistic landscape study, W. G. Hoskins, in his classic *The Making of the English Landscape* (1955), remarked that 'the student of the English landscape therefore faces at times the possibility of underground evidence; though in this book I have striven to analyse what can be seen on the surface today as an end in itself. The visible landscape offers us enough stimulus and pleasure without the uncertainty of what may lie beneath'.[19] The fine line between landscape history and archaeology, that Hoskins refers to later in his book, is, in *Last Landscapes,* deliberately and frequently breached. For landscape is both a place and a story, and stories often start or finish underground.

Landscapes of the dead are always, simultaneously, landscapes of the living. It is this coterminousness of life and death that gives the burial site its salience and emotional power. Different societies, at different times, renegotiate the relationship between what anthropologists call 'life space' and 'burial space', depending on settlement patterns and the nature of livelihood. Indeed, it is salutary to remember that in some cities of the world, even today, burial space takes up almost as much ground as open space for the living. In Newham, an inner-city district in East London close to where I live, 61 per cent of the public open space there is made up of cemetery land; in Boston, Massachusetts, it is 35 per cent.[20] Over the years, when visiting my brother in upper New York state, I have taken the 'A' train to and from Manhattan out to Kennedy Airport through Queens: it has always seemed that the dead take up more room than the living in that vast low-rise urban conurbation, as the train rattles past mile after mile of cemetery land and cities of tombstones and memorials.

Thus the cemetery exerts a continuing influence upon the urban imagination, especially for children, for whom this walled world (a world literally turned upside down) is often a source of unease and superstition, as it is in so many neo-Gothic novels and films, from *Wuthering Heights* to *Easy Rider*, from *Great Expectations* to *The Night of the Living Dead*. It also has a benign aspect too. Historically, the churchyard enjoyed the legal status of a sanctuary in some countries, a place outside of taxation and the law, a place indeed where fairs and markets were sometimes held, according to Philippe Ariès, as well as a place where people courted and conducted their love affairs.[21] Today, such churchyards and historic cemeteries that remain in cities are still frequently used as sanctuaries from the frenetic pace and noise of the surrounding streets, sometimes redesigned and landscaped to fulfil this role.

Copperfield Street Community Garden, in Southwark, London, a modern urban sanctuary created from an old churchyard by the Bankside Open Spaces Trust.

The 19th-century municipal cemetery of La Certosa at Bologna, Italy, is based on an 18th-century Carthusian monastery. The remains of over 700,000 people lie here.

Only the popularity of cremation in the twentieth century has saved the living in many towns and cities from being outnumbered by the corpses of the dead. Even so, the relationship can, in some places, still be overpowering. In Patrice Chéreau's *Those who love me can take the train* (1998), for example, the film ends with a funeral at the Limoges cemetery, during which the narrator tells us that there are today over 180,000 graves in that cemetery, more than the population of the town itself. In the closing sequence, the vast cemetery is filmed in long sweeping shots from the air, revealing a city of the dead with its own roads and pathways between the endless rows of graves and monuments. Though not on quite the same scale, the cemetery of La Certosa in Bologna contains the remains of over 700,000 people (in a city with a population of 450,000), though the practice of re-using graves and mausoleums after a fixed period has allowed the space occupied by the cemetery to remain within the original boundaries. In many historic cities the dead seem to take up as much cultural space as the living, whether buried in churches, memorialized in buildings and squares, or monumentalized in public sculptures. In many modern cities today, however, this 'presence of the dead' hardly exists any more.

The scale of these landscapes devoted to the dead, compared with those devoted to the living, is largely unmarked in landscape or architectural thinking. When Sir Thomas Browne wrote his famous disquisition on death and burial, *Hydriotaphia: Urne-Buriall or, A Brief Discourse of the Sepulchrall Urnes Lately Found in Norfolk* (1658), he assumed that 'The number of the dead long exceedeth all that shall live. The night of time far surpasseth the day, and who knows when was the Aequinox?'[22] Hence the euphemism for death, still common in parts of North America, that when people die they go 'to join the majority'. While this still remains true, and despite a popular myth circulating in demographic circles in the 1970s to the effect that the numbers of living now exceeded the numbers of dead (a hot topic among demographers, with current estimates suggesting that between 5 and 6 per cent of all the people who have ever lived on this planet are alive today),[23] as the population continues to increase in many parts of the world, the issue of disposal remains an issue for public policy – as well as aesthetics and culture.

The vast majority of people who once lived are utterly anonymous. As Browne wrote, 'The greater part must be content to be as though they had not been, to be found in the Register of God, not in the record of man.'[24] Even so, formal burial sites remain among the most compelling sites of human topography: gathering places, if you like, of settlement and loss. When travelling, particularly in unfamiliar places, many people find themselves drawn to these resting places of the dead, feeling perhaps that these are the original and authentic settlements of the world, enduring and timeless, tying us even closer to the landscape and perceived humanity of the world.

Burial places can provide solace to the living, centuries, even millennia after the horrors of the deaths themselves, and the rites and rituals of various pagan or religious ceremonies or indignities, have passed beyond memory. In one of his most passionate sets of essays, *Etruscan Places*, D. H. Lawrence was in no doubt as to what Etruscan architecture and forms of burial had to say about the culture of the people themselves, and the cities they constructed, where death was regarded as a continuation of life, though in a separate realm:

The tombs seem so easy and friendly, cut out of rock underground. One does not feel oppressed, descending into them. It must be partly owing to the peculiar charm of natural proportion which is in all Etruscan things of the unspoilt, unromanized centuries . . . And death, to the Etruscans, was a pleasant

One of the circular tombs at the Etruscan city of the dead at Cerveteri, dating back to the 7th century BC.

Entrance to the Neolithic burial chamber at Pentre Ifan, in west Pembrokeshire, Wales, over 4,000 years old.

continuance of life, with jewels and wine and flutes playing for the dance. It was neither an ecstasy of bliss, a heaven, nor a purgatory of torment. It was just a natural continuance of the fullness of life.[25]

Much of this is emotional projection on the part of Lawrence, since so much remains unknown about Etruscan life and culture. Even so, many visitors have experienced similar feelings to those of Lawrence when visiting some of these extraordinary necropolises in the Italian hills in the regions of Lazio, Umbria and Tuscany, or indeed ancient burial sites elsewhere.

A detailed account of the history and present state of the tombs at Cerveteri is given in chapter Four on 'Cities of the Dead'.

SOME ANCIENT FORMS

The fascination with the burial ground or cemetery suggests that it represents a corner of the world that seems inviolable and timeless, possessing a moral order of its own, and exerting a corrective to the preoccupations of daily life. The Neolithic burial chamber at Pentre Ifan, in west Pembrokeshire, Wales, is one such early house of the dead, with its stern uprights (orthostats) and giant capstone offering not just an entrance into a large communal grave, but with its orientation to the beautiful Afon Nyfer valley (and beyond that, the Irish Sea), anchoring the land itself to the human condition, acting as a watchtower, monument and resting place simultaneously. For over 4,000 years now it has surely been impossible to think about this undulating, coastal landscape without

acknowledging the austere, abiding presence of the burial chamber at Pentre Ifan.[26]

The same is true of Sutton Hoo, the Anglo-Saxon burial site on a bluff above the River Deben near Woodbridge, Suffolk. Like all rivers on the east coast, the Deben was an early site of settlement for Iron Age farmers, Romans and then, eventually, for Anglo-Saxon invaders. Around AD 500 a colony of Anglo-Saxons established itself in that part of the Iceni tribe's land that later became Suffolk. The colony was headed by an elite group of nobles known as the Wuffingas, whose graves these are. They form a now familiar sight of low grassy mounds in a clearing surrounded by woods. As is so often the case, such ancient, and sacred, burial sites were located on a bluff or promontory overlooking a river or the sea. The name Hoo is derived from the Old English word *haugh*, meaning a high place. The continuing presence of these graceful, scattered mounds still has the power to mediate death, to assert its power over the landscape at the same time as drawing its sting.

The two most spectacular graves at Sutton Hoo are those of the most important warriors, who were buried separately *circa* 625 in full costume, surrounded by household and royal artefacts, and in – though in one case beneath – their great sea-going wooden ships. While a number of the other graves had been opened and robbed, and even levelled some time in the Middle Ages, these two had escaped pillage. Ship burials have only ever been found, so far, in Suffolk and in Sweden, at Gamla Uppsala. At Sutton Hoo, the main ship excavated – or at least its physical impression in the soil, as the clinker-built boat itself had dissolved completely in the acidic soil – revealed

Burial mounds at Sutton Hoo above the River Deben at Woodbridge, Suffolk, close to the coast. Created around AD 600 and related to those at Gamla Uppsala.

Another view of the three main burial mounds at Gamla Uppsala, though there are hundreds of other smaller mounds close by.

a proper sea-going boat capable of journeys to distant countries in the Baltic and even to the Mediterranean. Other burials found at this site included a nobleman in one grave, alongside a grave containing his horse, a woman of rank, a child with a silver spear beside it, and some cremated remains in other graves.

Several centuries after *circa* 625 this site was used for the burial of a number of people who had been executed there, either by hanging or beheading: one small group of bodies close to a group of post holes suggests to archaeologists that an early gallows had been established. Two of the grave mounds at Sutton Hoo have been left unopened, in the hope that future generations, supported by more advanced technologies, will be able to ascertain whether there is anything significant inside these two mounds without having to physically disturb them. That seems a singularly honourable thing to do, though whether anyone has a right to disturb any grave or burial place, no matter how ancient, remains open to question, and is now a subject of considerable debate among archaeologists.

The astonishing grave mounds, or tumuli, at Gamla Uppsala are of roughly the same date as those at Sutton Hoo in Suffolk, and belong to the same elite Viking tribe. Yet in Gamla Uppsala, of the two out of three main royal mounds (as they are called) opened up for investigation, all that has been found are the cremated remains of a young woman in one, and those of a young man in the other, with a few burned remains of pottery and metal. It is clear that these high status individuals were cremated along with all their grave goods, rather than buried with them, as they were in Sutton Hoo. Their impact on the landscape is

more impressive than their contents. To the south of the three royal mounds is an Iron Age cemetery containing the remains of several hundred people. To the north of the royal mounds is a stone church dating in origin from the middle of the twelfth century, and churchyard, within which is also located an equally beautiful wooden church. Furthermore, evidence has been said to have been found beneath the stone church of some kind of pagan hall. This, more neatly than any other example I've seen, shows how each successive religion frequently locates around the same place, for either religious, magical or opportunistic reasons.

Equally impressive are the many grave-mounds at Birka on the island of Björkö, close to Stockholm, established around 760 as a centre for trade routes connecting Scandinavia to the Carolingian empire, Byzantium and even further east. For several hundred years it was the most important settlement in Sweden, if not the whole of Scandinavia. At its most established, Birka may have had a population of over 700 inhabitants, a remarkable size of settlement for this period. It was a fortified town, whose ramparts are still evident. But, more astonishingly, its people slowly filled large parts of the island with graves, creating several distinct cemeteries. Over 3,000 burial mounds are preserved on the island today, giving the landscape a strange appearance found hardly elsewhere in the world: a seemingly endless undulating pastureland and woodland composed of irregular mounds, dotted with large cairns and standing stones. The effect is eerie, even though it is also peaceful and beautiful.

Although Christianity had reached Sweden by this time, and there is evidence that Christian

The island of Björkö on inland waters close to Stockholm was once home to the prosperous trading settlement of Birka, established around AD 760, where over 3,000 burial mounds are to be found.

Burial mounds on Björkö.

beliefs and influences had touched the lives of the people of Birka, they remained basically a pagan people until the sudden decline and abandonment of the island in the 10th century. Today a Celtic Cross dominates the highest granite outcrop on the island, close to the small, natural harbour, ostensibly celebrating 1,000 years of Christianity, though in fact the religion never took hold. Archaeological evidence suggests most burials in Birka were pagan cremations, and those whose bodies were buried were likely to have been visiting traders. Also, most burials contain evidence of grave goods – weapons, beakers, jewellery, slaughtered horses – which characterizes pagan burial of this era, whereas Christians, like Muslims, always stood out against this practice (as they also did against cremation itself). The extraordinary mounds at Birka form the last of the great pre-Christian burial grounds, impressive forms in the landscape, which did not appear again until Asplund and Sigurd Lewerentz chose to evoke these great collective monuments in the landscaping of the Stockholm Woodland Cemetery at the beginning of the twentieth century.

THE CEMETERY IN THE CITY

The urban cemetery serves other purposes today. It is a reminder not just of another world, but of a different topography, not so much the country in the city or *rus in urbe*, but a vegetative, entropic, timeless world that is beyond human or bureaucratic control. The cemetery evokes a sleeping world, a horizontal world, a world of permanent darkness and rest. The contrast between the world of the cemetery and the footloose, upright, hurrying bustle of the streets around it is always affecting. Similarly, as dusk falls, the cemetery evokes quite other emotions and sensibilities, *entre chien et loup*, between dog and wolf, as the French say. While many may find ancient groves and burial mounds somehow comforting, and even uplifting, the dense, vegetated city cemetery can be intimidating. The Polish writer Gustaw Herling, in his *Journal Written at Night*, tells the story of Filippo Maria Visconti, the Duke of Milan who lived from 1392 to 1447, a man of acute paranoia, who strenuously attempted to banish every intimation, thought or symbol of death from his waking world, which filled him with irresistible dread:

> He did not allow people to die within the confines of the fortress; the mortally ill were sent outside the walls. And in the Duke's presence talk of death had to be avoided at any cost; it was driven out by an exorcism of silences . . . He could not abide ravens or crows, 'funereal birds', and he ordered them all exterminated. He was sickened by the sight of withering trees, and in the citadel it was understood that they must be uprooted at once and replaced by healthy ones.[27]

In the design of the tombstones and columbaria, in the epitaphs, photographs (especially in Mediterranean Europe) and sculptures, in the poignancy of the carvings and lettering, one is unsettled as well as intrigued by the strong sense of preternatural place that is exerted in these open-air galleries and museums of the human dead. Until quite recently it was not uncommon to come across a headstone in an English churchyard or cemetery marking a double grave, in which only one of the couple had died, yet both names were engraved on the headstone, with the year of death of the surviving partner left blank, waiting to be completed. The idea that his grave was ready and his headstone or monument already engraved would surely have driven the Duke of Milan to a frenzy.

That certainty of knowledge about the exact place of one's final corner of earthly geography is today much weaker. Partly this is a result of greater geographical mobility, though there is also perhaps a greater reluctance in a more agnostic and hedonistic society to make arrangements for an event that many would rather not think about and prefer to leave to others to resolve. Paradoxically, the exception to this trend can be found in many parts of North America, where 'pre-need' arrangements for burial have become part of consumer culture itself, to the extent to which it could be argued that death is more normalized, and even integrated into the domestic economy.

In general terms, the longstanding spatial relationship between 'life space' and 'burial space' is, in some parts of the world, becoming attenuated by the rise of cremation, modern funeral practices and the geographical displacement of new cemeteries out to the suburbs or urban fringes, though this trend is now being contested in some parts of Europe.[28] In London, many inner city districts have exhausted their land-holdings for burial space, and, as a result, people are often buried many miles away from where they lived, severing the geographical (and anthropological) link between the community of life and the community

of death. The same is true today in many cities of the world. Is this yet another characteristic of advanced modernity, that we now deny a space for death in the landscape or architecture of the modern city?

If this is the case, then this is a wholly new cultural phenomenon, for historically the cemetery was a vital part of the urban palette of public institutions and public open space. When Préfet Haussmann proposed to close the existing cemeteries of inner Paris in the late nineteenth century and remove the bodies to newly created cemeteries beyond the city in order to fulfil his remodelling of the capital's streets and boulevards, the crowds protested in the streets with the cry *Pas de cimitière, pas de cité!* No cemetery: no city. In London, most bodies remained where they were, and the city was developed around or over them. It is estimated that over 6 million people lie buried in churchyards and cemeteries laid out in London between 1600 and 1900, only a minority of which are still in use.[29] The remains of the majority of those buried are now beyond mem-ory, identification or reach. Wherever you walk in the City of London, the so-called 'square mile', you are almost certainly walking over the dead.

Even so, from time to time in central London towards the end of the nineteenth century, the remains of tens of thousands of people buried in churchyards were excavated and re-interred in mass graves in the newly created suburban cemeteries. Such large communal graves can still be seen in the City of London Cemetery, often with a monument erected over them detailing from which churchyard the remains were originally removed. The removal of bones from overcrowded cemeteries may well have been a common sight in cities throughout Europe in the nineteenth century. Thomas Hardy wrote rather witheringly about it in 'The Levelled Churchyard':

O Passenger, pray list and catch
Our sighs and piteous groans,
Half stifled in this jumbled patch
Of wretched memorial stones!

We late-lamented, resting here
Are mixed to human jam,
And each to each exclaims in fear,
'I know not which I am!'

In Jan Neruda's exquisite story 'The Three Lilies', one regarded as so beautiful by the Chilean writer Neftali Reyes that he changed his surname to Neruda (and his first name to Pablo) in honour of it, the Czech writer set the scene for a tumultuous sexual *coup de foudre* with the narrator sitting beneath the wooden arcade of the inn, staring at 'white piles of human bones by the garden wall at the end of the arcade'.[30] There had been a cemetery on the other side of the wall, and 'just that week they were digging up the skeletons for reburial. The soil was still in mounds, the graves open.' The normality of excavating graves for re-use, and the reburial or storing of the bones elsewhere, was common in many parts of Europe, as it still is today, though the process is now effected rather more discreetly. Even until quite recently in Russia, groups of boy scouts would be used to trawl through woodlands where there had been fierce fighting (or even massacres) in the Second World War to collect the unburied bones of the dead for formal interment. Catherine Merridale has

written a whole chapter, 'A Tide of Bones', about this grim subject.[31]

In recent times, especially in the neo-liberal economies and cultures, the intimate churchyard or cultivated civic cemetery has been replaced by the mass suburban cemetery, where land values and eschatological values can be had at reduced cost. Today, therefore, cities such as London, Paris and New York, along with many others, are literally losing contact with their dead, particularly the recent dead. Few, if any, modern urban planning models make reference to provision for burial or even memorial gardens, with some notable exceptions, such as the proposals for commemorating the dead of the World Trade Center terrorist attack of September 11, 2001, at the site now known as Ground Zero.

Yet unless planners, architects and landscape designers take seriously the issue of how to create new kinds of cemeteries within the weave of the modern urban fabric, there is a real danger of creating cities without memory, cities in denial of death and humanity. Hi-tech architecture hascreated many new kinds of buildings and civil engineering wonders in the modern city, but it has yet to create anything original associated with the abiding cycle of human loss, fortitude and renewal. As Robert Pogue Harrison has written: 'We dwell in space, to be sure, but we dwell first and foremost within the limits of our own mortality.'[32] The new materials of architecture enable the spaces of the city to be enlarged and spanned on an ever grander scale, but at a loss of intimacy and a sense of the numinous. Few landscape architects have tackled these themes successfully in the modern metropolis either.

The Stockholm Woodland Cemetery (1915–61) by Gunnar Asplund and Sigurd Lewerentz.

The exception is the Stockholm Woodland Cemetery (1915–61), perhaps the most successful example of large-scale landscape design in the twentieth century, or, to use the even more decisive words of the architectural historian, Marc Treib, 'the most perfect and profound modern landscape on the planet'. [33] It casts a serene shadow over much of this book, as it does over the author's own imaginative world. Nearly a hundred years after the first drawings were made, the Woodland Cemetery is recognized today as being as influential for our times as Père-Lachaise was for its historic era.

THE DESTRUCTION OF MEMORY

Elsewhere in Europe, the plight of the cemetery in the 20th century is rather more depressing. The history of the deliberate destruction of Jewish cemeteries, particularly in Eastern Europe during and after the Second World War, has been accompanied by similar measures taken by many Communist regimes against historic or religious cemeteries in a similar period, levelling them flat to create new building land or parks, and using the gravestones and masonry as building materials, or for foundations. In Britain, for different reasons, but with the same end results, many Victorian city cemeteries have been left to vandalism and neglect, and today present an equally dispiriting sight.

Historically, of course, burial grounds, city churchyards and cemeteries have not always been sacrosanct. As we have already seen in nineteenth-century Paris and London, the proposals to relocate inner-city cemeteries (and the remains of those interred in them) to the outskirts in order to remodel the city and plan anew created enormous public uproar. Nevertheless, the obliterated cemetery, the ruined cemetery, the vandalized cemetery and the neglected cemetery are perhaps uniquely evocative icons of political and philosophical nihilism or emptiness of the twentieth century. In Bohumil Hrabel's ironic, elegiac novella about a forgotten village of the 'old time' soon to be 'modernized' by Communism, *The Little Town Where Time Stood Still*, the narrator describes his father's walk through the town:

When he was passing the old cemetery, he stopped. As he could see, people had even got going on this old cemetery with picks, and block and tackle, and levers and jacks, even here it wasn't enough for people that time has stood still. Nearly all the monuments had been torn out of the ground, nearly all the graves and tombs were open, memorials had been dragged on skids and boards with chains on to open drays like heavy barrels of beer, monuments with inscriptions which for more than two hundred years had given addresses, status and age and favourite verses, all this hewn and carved into stone had now been carried off to

another town, where grinding wheels and chisels had blotted out the names of people from the old time.[34]

This poetic description of the brute process of eradicating memory and place is detailed more factually in Catherine Merridale's bleak history of death and funerary practices in Soviet Russia, *Night of Stone*, where she describes how the Soviets in many Russian cities 'drew up lists of their graveyard assets, reckoning their value in tons of stone and negotiable metal. Gravestones, especially any that were made of fine marble, were removed for building projects.'[35] A number of the older stations of the Moscow metro system contain large amounts of tombstone marble. Several monastery cemeteries in Moscow, such as those of Alekseyev and Danilov, were levelled and turned into workers' clubs and parks, and the Pokrovske cemetery became a football pitch. Grotesque though these acts were, there were many nineteenth-century precedents for building or creating parks on cemetery land in other European cities, though nowhere else was this process enacted with such brutal authority (and such malignity of intention).

The enormity of the deliberate destruction of Jewish cemeteries throughout occupied Europe has been slowly recorded since the War; one very fine book on this subject is Monika Krajewska's photographic record, *A Tribe of Stones: Jewish Cemeteries in Poland*, which also records and translates many prayers and epitaphs from the era prior to the Holocaust.[36] The despair and tragedy inherent in these acts of destruction is captured by the photographer Hannah Collins in her vast photographic composition, *In the*

A vandalized Jewish cemetery in Poland. Photographic work by Hannah Collins. Tate Modern, London.

Course of Time, now on permanent display in the section on History, Memory and Society at London's Tate Modern. There is something especially poignant and distressing about vandalized and abandoned cemeteries, as if the present had spat contemptuously on the past.

But even dereliction resulting from neglect rather than wilful destruction can have an equally disheartening effect. In the early months of 2001, a Parliamentary Select Committee in the UK undertook a study of cemeteries, inviting evidence from individuals and interested parties. The Committee was deeply shaken by the evidence of neglect that many witnesses claimed, writing of places that now look 'forlorn and unattended, the monuments are broken and misplaced. Graffiti is found on the walls, the gates are broken and the gate piers badly eroded. There is a general air of abandonment and neglect.' Other witnesses asserted that the 'overall state of the Cemetery was an affront not only to those

with family buried there but to all right-thinking people.' The Committee concluded that 'Unsafe, littered, vandalized, unkempt, these cemeteries shame all society in their lack of respect for the dead and the bereaved.' [37]

Yet the problems of the cemetery extend beyond just issues of neglect. Even newer cemeteries fail to convince most visitors of the moral or redemptive power once associated with them. One London survey found that people still preferred the idea of burial in a Victorian cemetery than in a modern one.[38] An architectural writer commenting on the parlous state of one London cemetery has commented that 'The cemeteries and churchyards of the past were created as morally uplifting oases, reflecting the ideals, the dreams and tastes of the times. What in heaven's name do these sterile stumps, relieved only by grizzly green and multicoloured marble chippings, reflect of our ideals today?'[39] The bleakness of the setting has been compounded

In Britain, but also in North America, a number of 19th-century urban cemeteries have lost their economic rationale, and often appear abandoned.

by the quality of ritual, described recently in that singular British document *The Dead Citizen's Charter*:

> The average British funeral is a miserable and disappointing affair. For those who are not well-known figures or members of churches – most of us – the contemporary funeral lacks meaningful symbolism, dignity, adequate time and comfort for those who mourn.
>
> Add these two elements together and it is possible to see how much needs to be done to restore a proper sense of ritual to disposal and bereavement in the modern world.[40]

One reason for the lack of thought or respect given to the cemetery in modern urban societies could be that people no longer possess or share a vocabulary for describing what these unsettling landscapes mean culturally, in the midst of their streets, towns and cities. Are they religious or secular, places of despair or places of hope and reconciliation? Does the reminder of mortality in the heart of daily life help to assuage the fear of death or accentuate it? In societies that now claim to celebrate cultural diversity more than the values of civic commonality, is the cemetery or memorial garden today a culturally exclusive territory, one of a number of new kinds of landscapes that privilege differentiation, while stressing the wholly personal nature of belief and mortality? What landscapes mean, and how their meaning has been developed, negotiated or constructed, is the subject of the next chapter.

Derek Jarman's garden on the Kent coast.

chapter two

Landscapes and Meanings

The very idea of landscape implies separation
and observation. It is possible and useful to trace
the internal histories of landscape painting, and
landscape writing, landscape gardening and
landscape architecture, but in any final analysis
we must relate these histories to the common
history of a land and its society.

Raymond Williams, *The Country and the City*[1]

THE GREAT DESIGN

For early Christians, Heaven and Hell were
real places, part of the geography and geology
of the actual world itself, as many medieval maps
reveal.[2] Thus the landscape, with its sacred places,
was a highly moralized terrain. Furthermore,
all the major world religions described the natural
world as a representation or culmination of
pre-ordained purposes and designs, some with
man at the centre, others not. If the Earth was
conceived as a divine creation, then the 'meaning'
of landscape must derive from the mystery and
gift of this extraordinary act of extra-human
intentionality, and for much of human history
that view has held sway. A good example of this
can be seen in the paintings of the Hudson River
School, where it is abundantly clear – not only
in the paintings but in the artists' letters and
writings too – that nearly all believed themselves
to be recording and celebrating God's great
purpose.[3] That Divine purpose was made
manifest in the majestic valleys, mountains, rivers
and plains of the American landscape, the wonder
of which was there for humans to record.

Even hardened atheists cannot but be overawed
at times by the grandeur of the natural world, or

appreciate how plausible it must be to assume a hidden hand or immanent purpose to the extraordinary variety of life on earth, and its breathtaking topography. All cultures have their foundation myths – stories of how the world came into being – which form the basis for much of the way in which they interpret the meaning of the landscapes they inhabit. Over time, and through the processes of colonization and other forms of cultural interpenetration, different belief systems get mixed up, despite astonishing internal contradictions and dissonances. The Inuit hunter-gatherers studied by the anthropologist Hugh Brody, for example, although having converted to Christianity, still retained their older, rather more animistic, attitudes to their landscape and its creatures. As one of them told Brody: 'The Innu religion is the religion of life. Christianity is the religion of death. We have to follow Innu ways in order to get our food here on our land, to live. But we have to follow the Christians in order to get into Heaven. When we die. So we need both.'[4] (This exchange recalls a rather more sceptical story told by the American writer Annie Dillard, in which an Inuit hunter asked a priest if he would go to Hell, even if he didn't know about God and sin. No, the priest replied, of course not. 'Then why did you tell me?' asked the Inuit.)[5] Thus landscape, mortality and destiny are invariably linked.

For most cultures, religion has provided the principal explanation as to why the world takes the form that it does, and how human death might be embedded in this topography. Today we have to arrive at the meanings that landscape appears to demand from us by cutting through layers of religious, ethnographic, genetic, artistic,

political and psychoanalytic explanations, all of which have something plausible to tell us about how landscapes and places cause the effects they do. These effects are very powerful, often creating intense attachments and loyalties to places and terrain, as well as being a source of reassurance, even consolation. This chapter can only briefly deal with some of them, particularly those that deal with matters of death and commemoration.

THE CROSS IN THE LANDSCAPE

One of the most powerful and enduring of human embellishments inscribed on the vast natural canvas in Western culture has been the cross. Yet even the ubiquitous Christian stone cross, a defining feature of so many churchyards, and landscapes, shares some origins with the pagan menhir or standing stone.[6] In an area rich with pre-Christian monuments, such as Cornwall in the Celtic south-west of Britain, many ancient standing stones, some carved with crosses to represent the sun, were adapted by Christians; during the Reformation, however, many of these were vandalized or put to other uses.[7] There are many crosses within the Christian tradition. The most common one, with a tall upright and a shorter horizontal bar, is known as the Latin Cross. There is also the Celtic Cross, which has an upper circle connecting the smaller horizontal to the main vertical; the Greek Cross, where both are of equal size, as well as various other adaptations, such as the Orthodox Cross, with two parallel cross-pieces at an angle, similar to the Cross of Lorraine. This longstanding continuity of architectonic form continues down to the present, even into secular cemeteries and memorial

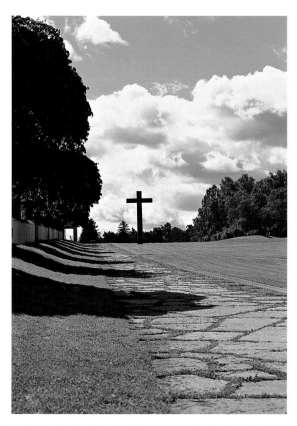

The path that leads from the entrance of the Stockholm Woodland Cemetery to the Memorial Hall was from the beginning described as 'The Way of the Cross'.

A single cross in a reflecting pool dominates Tadao Ando's 'Church on the Water' at Tomamu, Hokkaido, Japan, completed in 1988.

landscapes. The vertical column in the landscape can be read as a sign of human presence on earth, as well as an icon of our lonely humanity.

The resonant power of the cross, even in modern times, can be experienced most notably at the Stockholm Woodland Cemetery, where a large granite cross marks the rising path from the cemetery entrance to the complex of chapels and crematoria. This path was already being described as 'The Way of the Cross' in Lewerentz's competition drawings of 1915, and has since become the signature landmark of the Cemetery. As Caroline Constant has noted: 'There are several northern European precedents for this idea. The crucifixes in Caspar David Friedrich's landscape paintings, like those still seen in the German countryside, are both religious symbols and elements of nature. Moreover, a rough wooden cross was occasionally used in eighteenth-century Swedish gardens as a symbol of reintegration with nature.'[8] A single, plain metal cross is also the main feature of one of the other most remarkable pieces of spiritual architecture of the twentieth century, Tadao Ando's 'Church on the Water' (1988) at Tomamu, Hokkaido, Japan, where the cross stands in the centre of a flat, square artificial lake, frozen over during the winter, ruffled by wind in the summer, against a forest and hill background.

The cultural overlay between the cross and an assumed state of nature comes in the religio-cultural tradition of the verdant cross, the Christian adaptation of earlier pagan tree cults, portraying the wooden cross as capable of flowering into life again, and thus a sign of resurrection. It is therefore seen as an organic part of the landscape, as well as a human intervention.

Simon Schama has noted this series of cultural adaptations and transmigrations, in which the 'scriptural and apocryphal traditions of the Tree of Life were grafted onto the cult of the Cross [so] that a genuinely independent Christian vegetable theology came into being.'[9] Throughout the history of Christian theology and imagery, the cross that buds into life, along with the dead tree that brings forth fruit again, become important underlying images of the 'vernal resurrection'. The tree, the cross and the upright human figure are variations on the same elemental pattern in the visual field.

Many of Friedrich's paintings show crosses in deserted or mountainous landscapes – symbols of hope and resurrection in what is often portrayed as solitary and unforgiving terrain. The painting that first brought Friedrich to widespread attention was *The Cross in the Mountains* (1807), an overtly religious work showing the crucified Christ on the cross looking down towards a setting sun, but surrounded by upright fir trees, eternally green. Other paintings that centre on the motif of the cross include *Morning in the Reisengebirge* (1811), *Winter Landscape* (1811), *Cross and Cathedral in the Mountains* (1812) and *Cross on the Baltic* (c. 1815). This last painting, unlike the others, no longer features a human figure on the cross, but simply the cross itself. Friedrich's work has exerted a particular influence on cemetery design and landscape.

Almost one hundred years after Friedrich, D. H. Lawrence, another devotee of the cult of death, became equally intrigued by these crosses in the landscape in the more mountainous parts of central Europe. In 1912, shortly after eloping with Frieda von Richthofen, Lawrence walked

A roadside wooden cross in the Troödos Mountains, Cyprus.

from Bavaria across the Austrian Tyrol into Italy. His short essay, 'The Crucifix Across the Mountains', is one of the most spirited and combative of his travel writings. Today these roadside crosses can still be found in the rural or mountainous landscapes of many Catholic countries, evincing a religious attitude towards landscape, and suggestive of the penitential nature of the lonely traveller's journey. Even Antony Gormley's Angel of the North sculpture near Gateshead in the north-east of England functions as a vertical marker in the landscape, and is exactly cruciform in its representation of the human body with outstretched wings.

There are also clear connections between the crucified body on the cross and very early formulations of architectural form, scale and measure. A number of historians have pointed out the many similarities between representations of the crucified Christ and to the drawings of the Renaissance artist Cesar Cesariano in his representations of the ideas of the Roman architect Vitruvius, particularly in the famous drawing of a man stretched out against the background of a square to show perfect human proportions. The idealized figure of Vitruvian man and the wracked, but perfectly shaped, body of Christ on the cross, were at times almost interchangeable in Renaissance painting and architectural drawings.[10]

The granite cross at the Stockholm Woodland Cemetery.

The Angel of the North, a giant public sculpture in cruciform shape by Antony Gormley, was erected as a symbol of renewal near Gateshead, north-east England, in 1998.

Over time, the cross has also become a secular icon of hope, if not salvation, and today architects and landscape designers feel able to make reference to it in cemetery design, even in otherwise secular settings. Its emblematic use recurs in the new cemetery complex (designed by Andreas Meck and Stephan Köppel) for Riem in Munich, adjacent to a historic graveyard, which makes a point of guiding mourners out of the chapel, by a pool and canopy to a ceremonial bell, and from there along a gravel path towards the large cross of the old cemetery, adding as one approving critic has pointed out, 'to a distinguished northern European tradition of making buildings in which rites of passage can be observed'.[11] Chapel, pool, path and cross seem to be key architectonic elements in the modern funereal landscape, even those designed for a secular world.

Wood and stone are often interchangeable in the interplay between nature and architecture, most notably in the long accepted belief or assumption, first outlined in an essay on Strasbourg Cathedral written by Goethe in 1773, that the piers and vaulting of Gothic cathedrals mimic the tree-supported canopy of the forest clearing. This concept of the 'cathedral forest' became part of the common currency of architectural debate about the nature of the Gothic in the eighteenth and nineteenth centuries, referring to earlier beliefs that the ancient forests, and forest clearings, were once the dwelling places of the gods.[12] Indeed, Friedrich once sketched a plan for a chapel whose oval shape was exactly echoed in a large elliptical grove of trees, acting as an ante-chamber to it.[13] In so many of Friedrich's paintings, cathedral and grove replicate each other's shape exactly, as the skeletons of winter trees do those of the ruins they surround. In the twentieth century the Finnish architect Alvar Aalto gave this concept fresh life when he described the internal spatial flows of buildings such as the celebrated Villa Mairea as 'forest space': space that transmits light from outside in uneven and surprising ways as one moves through an irregular floor plan, as if walking through woodland or forest.

Such symbolic transliterations are not just an element of Christian cultures. They can be seen in the way that certain Muslim grave markers share the same shape and form as the palm trees surrounding them (as do the wooden grave boards to be found in many Hungarian cemeteries, which take on an almost identical tree-like form). This is evident in the grave markers of the cemetery adjacent to the Mosque of the Tekke of Hala Sultan, near Larnaca in Cyprus, for example. This small, dusty mosque, the third most important pilgrimage site in the Muslim world after the Kaaba at Mecca and the Shrine of Muhammad at Medina, today lies in the Greek, non-Muslim, sector of the divided island, and is now little visited as a result. The rounded pillars of the Mosque are painted green, and resemble the trunks of the palm trees that surround the building, as do the handful of gravestones, shaped like rounded columns with 'outgrowths' at the top, like large stone pegs. 'Green', said the elderly man who looked after the Mosque, patiently showing a small company of us around it, 'is the colour of paradise in the Islamic world.' The word paradise itself comes from the Persian word for garden, *pairi-daeza*, which became *pardes* in Hebrew and *paradeisos* in Greek.[14]

Grave markers in the cemetery adjacent to the Mosque of the Tekke of Hala Sultan at Larnaca, Cyprus.

HOW LANDSCAPES SHAPE HUMAN EMOTIONS

These symbolic configurations are crucial to human design, and need to be understood in some detail if we are to appreciate what makes the landscape such a compulsive and recurring area of human interest and source of pleasure and consolation. Not all landscapes and designed gardens have to do with death, of course, and burial sites and cemeteries are only elements in a much wider human pattern of imbuing place and design with cultural meaning.

While many religions encourage people to feel gratitude for the beauty of the divine gift of the natural world, attitudes to landscapes associated with death are another matter. In contrast to the sense of joyous release that Lawrence felt when he visited the pre-Christian tombs of the Etruscans, if he had travelled fewer than 100 miles further north from Cerveteri or Tarquinia to Pisa, he could have visited the Campo Santo, where a vastly different view of the ecology of death and transfiguration is still evident. This thirteenth-century cloistered cemetery contains a giant fresco, the *Triumph of Death*, in the Capella Ammanati, painted in the aftermath of the Black Death. I remember visiting it one heat-dazed afternoon, when cycling in Italy in 1991, and rather wished I hadn't. The original fresco continues along the walls of the cloisters for nearly a quarter of a mile, and it is filled with graphic illustrations of fires, snakes, devils with pitchforks, babies torn limb from limb, women eaten by monsters and crushed beneath rocks, men flayed and cut into pieces. It is a work that, like the sun, cannot be looked at continuously.

The contrast between the representation of death as a place of happiness and a place of terror seems to run through all cultures and religions at different times and with varying emphases. Furthermore, the frescoes in Pisa made the very notion of underground, that which is to be found beneath the Earth's surface, a place of terror. This binary relationship of above and below ground, of open skies and immuring depths, is basic to funerary culture. Apart from these extremities of religious and topographical excess, there are many other, more nuanced, ways in which nature and human belief systems are thought to echo or replicate one other's patterns and sensibilities.

There was in England at one time, for example, a widely shared conviction that nature and society were simply different representations of one and the same organic process. This 'Tory View of Landscape', as Nigel Everett terms it, is based on what became known in the seventeenth and eighteenth centuries as analogy theory, the subject of a Anglican text, *The Analogy of Religion*, by Joseph Butler (1692–1752), which sought to demonstrate how Christian society, when properly administered, replicates the values of the natural world in terms of its relationships, processes and forms of self-regulation and life-cycles.[15] In this view, the principles of tradition, continuity, natural hierarchies of size, scale and pecking order, which were seen to operate in the natural world, ought therefore be considered equally appropriate to human affairs. Many other religions assume something of the same correspondences.

Modern ecological thought has, interestingly, resurrected similar ideas or analogies, this time based on the belief that unless society and nature are more closely integrated once again, catastrophe threatens. Indeed, the continuing interest in Gaia – a concept coined in the 1960s by the NASA scientist James Lovelock to explain how life on earth is a naturally self-sustaining system – is a clear expression of the view that social and cultural systems ought somehow to be in harmony with the natural ecology of the world.[16] In such a view, death is not a punishment, or a casting out into dark oblivion, but a reconciliation with the natural world, through a return to earth.

A MATTER OF EVOLUTION OR BIOLOGY?

There are also a number of different theories that seek to explain how humans come to experience and interpret landscape as a result of innate or inherited dispositions. One advocate of neo-Darwinist or socio-biological theories is Jay Appleton, who argues that, in the wider human relationship to landscape, particularly that of the open field or woodland, 'the pleasure of environmental exploration derives ultimately from innate patterns of survival behaviour'. Thus, it is in the open fields of the savannah that even modern people can experience the boundless plenitude of nature, while in times of danger they feel that they can seek refuge and safety in the shelter of the woods.[17] In this view – widely promulgated today in the name of evolutionary psychology – differences of landscape type attract or repulse because they evoke atavistic feelings of security or fear, which are in turn derived from innate animal instincts and habits. Thus it could be said, for example, that the walled cemetery represents a human response to the dangers of

The walled churchyard at Gamla Uppsala, showing the wooden and the stone churches enclosed within a high wall.

a hostile and predatory natural world, a place of retreat and sanctuary, as well as a place where people can stay in touch with their ancestral spirits or forebears.

Similar versions of this approach can be seen in quasi-biological theories of architectural design that map subjective human responses to built form through an understanding of sightlines, light and shade, height and massing, and proximity to other people or human activity. Certainly, one's feelings, whether in cities or rural landscapes, are very much shaped by colour, form and human presence, though since different people can experience the same landscape in equally different ways, we have to assume that

meaning is the result of the interaction between subjective apprehension and material reality. Yet the subjective reactions themselves can be learned: those who find themselves unexpectedly in wilderness landscapes, with only a minimal knowledge of the flora, fauna and weather conditions, are likely to have a much more disturbing and disconcerting experience than those for whom the terrain is both familiar and loved. The anthropologist Hugh Brody describes how he was as disoriented and apprehensive when he first arrived in northern Canada, as one of his Inuit friends was when he visited London.[18]

More recently, the environmental movement has turned its attentions to the concept of ecological design, asking how 'we weave the human presence into the natural world' again.[19] Place-based solutions to economic and social processes are urged. So far, however, few ecologists have paid much attention to issues of memorialization and the spaces of interment and loss, preferring to pay more attention to the mechanics of ecologically sound 'disposal' through natural burial. If the human attachment to the Earth is hard-wired, as some suggest, then natural burial seems the pre-ordained and proper thing to follow. But humankind is rather more complex and reflexive in its understandings of its relationship to the world than that. Nevertheless, the fact that some configurations of earth, sky, trees and rock bring about a sense of release, while others induce feelings of uncertainty or even terror, suggests that there are atavistic impulses at work wherever, or however, we encounter a landscape or a setting for the first time. Architecture can either amplify such feelings of awe or anxiety, or assuage them.

Caspar David Friedrich, *Cemetery at Dusk* (*c.* 1825).

THE PAINTERLY TRADITION

The dominant way of understanding the inter-relationship between landscape and human meaning in Western culture in modern times has, however, principally derived from the visual arts. Three paintings in particular, Jacob van Ruisdael's *The Jewish Cemetery* (*c.* 1670), Friedrich's *Cemetery at Dusk* (*c.* 1825) and Arnold Böcklin's *Island of the Dead* (1880), have all exerted a power on the European aesthetic imagination regarding the mystery of death and burial far beyond their original context. (We know for certain that Lewerentz and Asplund were greatly influenced by Friedrich's paintings as well as by Böcklin's *Island of the Dead* and Prince Eugen's *Forest*, 1899.) There has also been the enormous influence of painters such as Claude and Poussin, both of whom concentrated on portraying classical scenes and themes in some imagined Arcadia, so landscape came to be associated with mythology, a certain kind of architecture, and a certain kind of heroic or mythological life. This tradition itself may owe something to even earlier forms of animism, in its suggestion of mischievous gods and spirits at large in the woods and forests.

Jacob van Ruisdael, *The Jewish Cemetery* (*c.* 1670).

Arnold Böcklin,
Island of the Dead
(first version, 1880).

The inter-relationship between landscape painting and landscape design: the view through the picture frame overlooking the principal lawn at the Botanical Gardens, New York.

These paintings influenced the very design of contemporary gardens and private landscapes to fit this ideal, replicating the dreams of perfection evinced in these classical landscapes in the very soil and uneven terrain of England itself. These highly ordered ways of seeing landscape, with foreground, middle-ground and distance clearly delineated, also arose, as Raymond Williams has remarked, at the same time as theatre scenery, 'where the proscenium frame and the moveable flats were being simultaneously developed'.[20] The framing of the landscape, along with the framing of the canvas and the rules of perspective, implied a singular, and usually powerful, viewpoint – notably that of the designer, painter, estate owner or invited viewer. This was a kind of Look but don't Touch attitude. The classical temple, or the grand mausoleum or tomb, provided an essential element in this tradition, adding an aura of melancholy as well as symbolizing the passing of time.

Likewise, an important architectural feature of the English landscape garden was the folly, ruin, temple or grotto, memorializing a lost world of classical antiquity and a culture still thought able to exercise a judicious and enlightening influence on the modern sensibility. One of the most famous of these exercises in formal landscape design is to be found in the gardens at Stourhead in Wiltshire. Here an artificial lake forms the centre of an entirely self-contained world, with a circular walk at its perimeter leading in and out of copses and lawns, past waterfalls, grottoes, classical temples and across bridges, with each short section of the walk presenting new vistas and prospects, in which it is almost impossible not to surrender to the reveries of mortality and antiquity – as long as you get there before the crowds of other visitors. Over the door of the Temple of Flora (built 1744–6) is carved a line from Virgil's *Aeneid*, 'Procul, O procul este

A classical garden in the English landscape style: bridge, lake and Pantheon at Stourhead, Wiltshire.

profani' (Begone, you who are uninitiated! Begone!), which fortunately few visitors are able to translate on the spot.[21]

However, the educated individuals responsible for references of this kind are also the makers–financiers of such gardens. Their experiences are not necessarily shared by their visitors, although Marc Treib has suggested that both sets of 'meanings' are always in play. 'Any symbolic system', he suggests,

> demands education and the comprehension of both the medium and the message . . . We have lost the ability to read the original intentions,

but we can still decipher the original garden elements on our own contemporary terms. That these two worlds of meaning mutate over time suggests that meaning is indeed dynamic and ever-changing.[22]

Perhaps highly formal gardens – such as that at Versailles – leave much less room for subjective interpretation or ambiguity of meaning, but the more informal and 'natural' (even though artful) the landscape design becomes, the balance of power in interpretation and meaning begins to shift towards the beholder. With the rise of the 'public sphere' in the eighteenth century, as the middle classes entered the political and cultural domains, aesthetic issues suddenly become the topic of much heated debate, with the new interests rejecting, for both social and economic reasons, the idea that cultural values are simply the result of inherited rules and prescriptions. Even the Burkeian notion of the Sublime seems to dissolve all pre-existing formal conventions of the beautiful and the transcendent, instead hinting at danger and terror as being part of the new emotional aesthetic.

The Picturesque was from the outset quite heavily ideological in tone, and, for the English, quite nationalistic. In his seminal essay, *The History of the Modern Taste in Gardening*, first published in 1780, Horace Walpole commented that the new English preference for open fields, irregular tree-planting, serpentine paths and 'natural' lakes – all based on the premise that 'nature abhors a strait line' – reflected the English love of freedom and individuality. This he compared to the detriment of the French and Italian preferences for mathematical precision and geometric formality.[23] He evoked Milton's idea of Paradise as being a sylvan setting, with bowers, open fields and a variety of trees reaching their natural height and limit, rather than stunted, cropped or trimmed to geometrical proportions. This explicit correspondence between the aesthetics of representation and political values and allegiances was part of the burgeoning association between landscape and *mentalité*, which quickly became part of the language of Romanticism.

Thus, the more irregular, apparently artless and naturalistic a landscape or garden was, the more likely it would be able to promote ambiguities of mood and apprehension – melancholy, shape-shifting, a sense of the Sublime – whereas parterres, terraces, balustrades, knot-gardens, and trees, shrubs and hedges trimmed within an inch of their lives would be unable to achieve them. The employment of the haha, a trench that prevented livestock from straying into landscaped grounds, also allowed uninterrupted views from the garden out into the countryside. At the same time that the walls were coming down around the naturalistic landscape, they were going up around the graveyard and the cemetery, to formalize the separation of the place of the dead from that of the living. No longer would innocent shepherds stumble across an isolated tomb in an empty landscape, leading them to reflect on the transience of life and the brevity of their current happiness. Instead, pictorially, the cemetery became a forbidding walled and gated world apart.

STURM UND DRANG

Between 1830 and 1910 the artistic interest in landscape in Europe almost literally changed direction. The art historian Nina Lübbren has described how in this period, 3,000 self-styled 'artists' went to live in dedicated colonies established in various rural areas of Europe.[24] By 1900 there were over 80 rural artists' colonies firmly established in eleven different countries. This was a cultural movement of extraordinary significance, which over time had influences that reached out far beyond changing practices in the visual arts. To a significant degree it changed the sensibility of European landscape painting dramatically, for the majority of these new artists gravitated towards the Baltic and Celtic fringes rather than to the Mediterranean. Unlike many nineteenth-century poets who dreamed of 'a beaker full of the warm South', the new enthusiasm among painters was for flat moorlands, forest interiors, chilly streams and lakes, coastal villages and vast open skies. Nordic light, landscape and culture captured the early twentieth-century imagination, though there were already important new French genres of painting, including the *sous-bois* (undergrowth, or forest interior) paintings of the Barbizon school. As a result, evocations of the dead in twentieth-century Europe art and culture were as likely to take Nordic forms as those of the classical Mediterranean.

Despite the pull towards a 'Volk' romanticism, genuine artistic achievements did emerge from these rural colonies. Lübbren describes and analyzes the contribution a number of these painters – Carl Bantzer, Louis Eysen, Gari Melchers, Hans am Ende, Fritz Mackenson, Otto Modersohn and others – made to developing a new aesthetic of landscape painting, away from the Classical or Picturesque landscape tradition (with its 'elevated' perspective of ownership and power), towards an 'immersive' aesthetic where the wildness of the forests, the headlands or the dunes almost overwhelms the viewer, drawing them not only into these untamed settings, but at the same time forcing a new correspondence between the landscape and the inner self.

In some ways this immersiveness, starting out as an adherence to naturalism, ended up in the organic abstractionism of Henry Moore and Barbara Hepworth, again countering the received view that ruralist or naturalist sympathies and interests were inevitably aesthetically conservative. What many modern rural artists were trying to achieve was what Wilhelm Heinrich Riehl called 'reine Stimmungsbilder' (pure paintings of mood), which is precisely what supporters of Lewerentz's designs saw him achieving.[25] This new identification of landscape as an expressive representation of human feelings and cultural mores, a more Freudian version of the 'pathetic fallacy', has gone so far that one painter, the Dutch artist Armando, has expressed the view that he now regards the wartime landscape of his childhood as 'guilty' in its complicity in the atrocities of the Second World War.[26] But paintings of mood exercised a great deal of influence on architects such as Asplund and Lewerentz, who had begun to design a new kind of urban cemetery.

The size of the Stockholm Woodland Cemetery meant that the landscaping was conducted on a heroic scale, in order to evoke deeper attachments and subliminalities. In the second half of the twentieth century, such effects were also sought by artists who, escaping from the gallery, endeavoured to fashion landscape into memorable and memorializing forms. From Herbert Bayer's Earth Mound constructed at Aspen, Colorado, in 1955, to Robert Smithson's Spiral Jetty (1970) at Great Salt Lake, Utah, and Spiral Hill (1971), constructed in Emmen in The Netherlands, art and landscape, rather than standing at a respectful distance from each other around matters of proportion, perspective and the place of the viewer, tried in fact to fuse.[27] One of the most successful recent examples of land art on this larger scale was designed and completed in 2001 by Charles Jencks and Terry Farrell,

Landscape design by Charles Jencks and Sir Terry Farrell opposite the Scottish National Gallery of Modern Art, Edinburgh.

Stone circle by Andy Goldsworthy, created for the sculpture garden of Adelaide Museum of Modern Art, 1992.

immediately opposite the Scottish National Gallery of Modern Art in Edinburgh. Significantly, even when less heroic 'environmental artists', such as Andy Goldsworthy and Richard Long, have made their constructions in near or remote parts of the world, the forms they have often chosen – cairns, stone circles, braided flowers, woodland clearings – all have their traces in ancient memorializing or funerary traditions.

LANDSCAPE AND IDENTITY

We have seen how the English associated a certain kind of landscape with a quintessential English national identity, notably in the espousal of the Picturesque, more naturalistic landscapes that emerged in the eighteenth century. At the end of the nineteenth century, National Romanticism, a cultural and architectural mood that swept through many parts of northern Europe, distinctly allied the art, music and architecture of a specific nation or linguistic culture with a specific kind of landscape: the lakes and forests of Finland (Aalto, Sibelius), the fjords and fishing villages of Norway (Bojer, Grieg), the mountains, streams and forests of the Czech lands (Smetana, Plečnik), and so on. The landscape was part of the foundation myth of a new kind of nationalist spirit that emerged in this period.

Nowhere was this more true than in Sweden, where in the nineteenth century the writer Carl Jonas Almqvist chose to portray its society and culture through the image of the dog rose, 'formed of poverty, wild pleasure and chastity'.[28] The landscape architect and historian Thorbjörn Andersson has devoted much thought to this issue of the interpenetration of landscape form and national identity in Sweden. He has drawn attention to the prolonged dawns and dusks, along with the limited colour range of the natural flora, which together give the landscape at times a sombre mood and feeling. This, however, is often counter-balanced by the strength and crystalline quality of the light that occurs close to the many lakes and rivers. In brief, he writes, that 'These three qualities – clear light, limited natural typology, glacially modelled country – form the natural–geographical base from which the Swedish arts of gardening art and landscape architecture have emerged.'[29]

Andersson also observes that, for the Swedes, the Christian creation myth has little meaning: paradise is to be found in untamed nature, not in a walled, highly cultivated garden. The Swedish word for forest is *skog*, which has its etymological roots in the Early Icelandic word for shelter. In northern Europe the forest is not a wild place to which outcasts are banished, but the human world's original home. It is no coincidence that the modern ideal of woodland burial is a product of the northern, rather than southern, European imagination. In Italy, for example, the forest has historically been regarded as a place of fear and evil spirits, particularly those of suicides and criminals buried in the woods, as they are in Dante's *Inferno*.[30] The Italian word for foreigner is *forestiero*, someone from the forest.

Nowhere has the troubled association between landscape and national history been more apparent than in the post-war discussions as to how to respond in commemorative terms to the sites of the concentration camps in Germany and Poland, where millions died in conditions of appalling horror. One example has been the

Landscaping of mass burial graves at Bergen-Belsen concentration camp, Germany.

continuing debate about the landscaping of the Bergen-Belsen camp on the edge of Lüneberg Heath, north of Hanover, beneath which the remains of many thousands are buried.[31]

Immediately after the War, the British military government insisted that German officials make preparations to turn these sites into lasting memorials to the infamies that occurred there. Bitterest of ironies was that the natural topography – heathland, junipers, birches, pine forests and small farms – was exactly that which had been idealized by German Romanticism. The first two landscape architects appointed were quickly dismissed in succession, for not only were both subsequently proven to have had Nazi connections, but their design proposals in themselves 'directly related to Nazi "Blood and Soil" theory, which favoured native species, to the exclusion of foreign introductions'.[32] One recent writer on this matter has strongly argued against any 'design forged in harmony with nature' on

such a site, since such an ideal was itself strongly espoused by leading Nazi politicians, bird-lovers and naturalists almost to a man, it seems.[33] 'Ecological ideas', Joachim Wolschke-Bulmahn has asserted, 'are of no importance for the design of such a place as Bergen-Belsen. They are not relevant to its history or to its meaning for the future.' Any design, he seems to suggest, should disturb and anger, before encouraging contemplation.

The fact that this site is a burial ground as well as a place in need of commemoration has produced its own problems. Since it is forbidden by Jewish law to disturb any remains, leaving the site as it was, as some argued for religious reasons, could be construed as continuing the 'covering up' of history. Jewish opinion was also strongly against any figurative memorials. Furthermore, as a result of the Cold War, the Soviet prisoners-of-war cemetery was not included in the original commemorative landscape. Finally, while the conservationists and some landscape historians have argued that the agreed post-war designs that were implemented now have an aesthetic integrity of their own, and of their time, others have pointed out that subsequent generations will need to have the site interpreted anew. A seminar on this highly sensitive issue held in September 2000 concluded that the site indeed should be 'a place to mourn, to remember, to honour the dead, to understand (or at least to try to understand), to find peace, to make peace, to re-visit, to re-live, even to reorientate, to listen to oneself, to examine oneself'.[34] Such phraseology provides a helpful summary of the many reasons why the landscapes of the dead remain so important for the emotional needs of the living.

Similar themes have been explored even more recently in an essay on the contemporary landscaping of two other notorious concentration camp sites, Plaszow and Auschwitz-Birkenau in Poland.[35] In the former camp, which has been largely left untouched and unmanaged, overgrowth (or what the authors technically describe as 'unmanaged ecological succession') now threatens to erase the history of that terrible place altogether (it has been memorialized in film as the camp around which Stephen Spielberg's *Schindler's List* is based). Plaszow concentration camp itself was partly located on the site of two former Jewish cemeteries, which were levelled and erased to accommodate it. While many more of the original buildings and large parts of the camp infrastructure have been preserved at Auschwitz-Birkenau – where the issue is how to develop and manage a landscape ecology that 'frames the remains' in order to preserve or evoke something of their original bleak and pitiless atmosphere –

the essay's authors conclude that the project may be impossible. In such extreme places landscape design cannot but fail, simply because it can never emulate or simulate the death-pit miasma of the original setting. Any intervention is both simultaneously an embroiderment and a displacement of the historical truth. At the Treblinka camp a memorial designed by Adam Haupt and Franciszek Duszenko, consisting of some 17,000 granite shards set in concrete in a circle surrounding an obelisk, was dedicated in 1964, and it is regarded as capturing something of the scale and ragged brutality of the events it commemorates.[36] In strict architectural terms, it has been the fragmented, broken nature of Daniel Libeskind's work, notably in his designs for the Jewish Museum in Berlin and the Imperial War Museum North in Manchester, which have similarly managed to evince the incomprehensibility of the terrible disasters and occurrences they memorialize.

THE DEATH OF LANDSCAPE

Much of the literature of landscape and garden design deals with the relationship between the ownership of land and property, social status, the design principles and practices that flow from such patterns of power and the meanings they embody. In the strongly hierarchical symbolic systems of the past associated with royal prerogative, court power or established wealth, the 'meanings' immanent in landscape design were rather more clear-cut and instantly recognizable. This is not, however, so evident in the democracies and consumer societies of today, where design is frequently inflected to address complex social and cultural (and increasingly, multi-cultural) interests and traditions. In the case of the cemetery, this sensitivity to the nuances of cultural taste has been too little evident. Many modern cemeteries seem to be designed in the spirit of mass production, shaped and laid out not to inspire spirituality, but in order to accommodate the latest grass-cutting and leaf-blowing machinery and to achieve economies of scale. It is a paradox that as life becomes more heterodox and aestheticized in its daily forms, death becomes more mundane.

One such bleak place – though sadly it is only one of many hundreds – is the cemetery in Kent I passed while on a journey to visit the garden made by the artist and film-maker Derek Jarman at Dungeness on the coast, and in such marked contrast. Where Jarman had conjured up a magical landscape in an unprepossessing shingle wilderness, planted with wild flowers and set with old timbers and metalworks thrown ashore by the waters or left stranded by long-gone boats and trades, this great, dry grass desert with uniform

A 20th-century cemetery in southern England, devoid of any landscaping features or attempt to assuage feelings of grief. As life becomes more heterodox and aestheticized, death becomes more mundane.

rows of standardized graves seemed like a grim card-game of Patience left incomplete. There is no shelter from the sun, no trees lean over the graves to shade them, no slopes in the landscape lift one's eyes to the sky, or deflect from the endless monotony of what is less a place of consolation and more like a killing field, or a sports field hastily dug up for mass burials after some terrible atrocity.

James Stevens Curl suggests that 'At the end of the twentieth century . . . landscapes appear to be valued no longer'.[37] The landscape designer Martha Schwartz has on several occasions attacked modern architecture itself for denigrating landscape matters entirely, writing that, 'Architecture's myopic and self-serving attitude toward the landscape, as the passive, untouched setting for heroic objects, has been disastrous visually and ecologically.'[38] The sharp demarcation lines that are often professionally drawn between architecture and landscaping have disfigured cities and public spaces in many towns and cities throughout the world. Far too often, great works of 'trophy' architecture have been sited in the midst of second-rate utility landscapes, to the continuing detriment of both.

Marc Treib, however, detects signs of a renewal. In his view, the discussion of meaning in landscape design has 'resurfaced at the end of the twentieth century', after being absent for several decades, a silence he principally attributes to the *tabula rasa* elements of Modernism and its desire to start from the beginning again.[39] In reviewing more than twenty years of landscape architecture, as both designer and academic, Treib insists that landscape architects have rediscovered the importance of respecting local natural forms as well as the history of the places in which they have been commissioned to intervene. One principal influence has been the interest in natural ecology, notably in the work of Ian McHarg, elaborated in his influential book, *Design with Nature* (1966). Treib also highlights a growing post-war interest in phenomenology, and the renewed importance that philosophers such as Bachelard and Merleau-Ponty attached to the human significance of local form. There has also been, according to Treib, a revival of neo-primitivism, in the adaptation of ancient stone circles, spiral paths, mazes and hilltop copses and standing stones.

While Treib's observations are especially helpful in describing and elaborating on the current preoccupations of both landscape architects and land artists – particularly those at the forefront of the creation of new forms of meaning – it is important to remember once again that these framings are those of the producers of the landscape, not of those who view or experience them. It is still too often the case that advocates and practitioners of landscape architecture and design remain bounded by their sole interest in how their intentions have been realized in their own terms, rather than in how their intentions have been appreciated or understood. Too often they also seem to design for their peers rather than for the wider public, and as a result there is an over-reliance on latest forms and fashions and still too little responsiveness to the spirit of the place.

Architecture and landscape design embody human values. Richard Etlin cites a telling remark by Leslie Stephen, that 'the doctrines which men ostensibly hold do not become operative upon their conduct until they have generated an

imaginative symbolism'. Père-Lachaise in Paris was designed to do precisely this: stand as an emblem or symbol of a new world. Etlin also shows how some of the ideas that began to circulate at the time of the French Revolution enabled people to understand how both life and death might be perceived and responded to in less terrifying and degrading ways. In the words of Chaumette, the procureur-syndic of Paris, the new kind of cemetery should 'replace the images of sadness and despair, with sweeter, more philan-thropical ideas'. Out of such ideas grew, as we shall see, proposals for a different kind of burial rite and setting. In turn, the new cemeteries reinforced such ideas, and over time a quite new sensibility about death and the afterlife emerged, in which, as Etlin says, 'architecture and landscape played a role in crystallising nascent emotions and ideas'.[40]

RECUPERATIVE LANDSCAPES

It is important to understand the consolatory or therapeutic role which certain kinds of designed landscapes can play, matters that are surely central to the design and meaning of the modern cemetery or funerary setting. While some will gain a kind of melancholy *frisson* from contemplating an overgrown or neglected cemetery, others might profit spiritually and emotionally from landscapes and memorial forms that seek to build bridges between life and death. This is precisely why, from the late seventeenth century onwards, cemeteries have slowly acquired their own garden language and aesthetic. Indeed, early landscape designers and writers, such as J. C. Loudon in his influential book *On the Laying Out, Planting, and Managing of Cemeteries* (1843), foresaw a time when cemeteries would themselves become public parks and settings of moral uplift.

The many great joint-stock cemeteries that began to open in England from the 1820s onwards, heavily influenced by the success of Père-Lachaise, were designed with elegant carriageways, serpentine paths, artfully designed prospects and carefully planted copses of trees, and they 'incorporated many elements from the picturesque repertoire . . . further developed by the imaginative climate of Romanticism'.[41] Loudon, however, went further than this, regarding the well-designed cemetery as being as much, if not more, a place for the living as for the dead. Here, he surmised, people would stroll in agreeable surroundings, and have their fears of death tempered by artifice and elegant design.

The spiritual or 'healing' properties of landscape have, in recent times, begun to be re-absorbed into the vocabulary of civic culture. Yet this tradition is even older than that of the moralized landscapes of the seventeenth-century ruling elites. As long ago as the eleventh century, the French monk St Bernard wrote a treatise on the role of the monastic garden – in his case, that of the monastery at Clairvaux – as a place for contemplation and spiritual renewal:

Within this enclosure, many and various trees, prolific with every sort of fruit, make a veritable grove, which lying next to the cells of those who are ill, lightens with no little solace the infirmities of the brethren, while it offers to those who are strolling about a spacious walk, and to those overcome with the heat, a sweet place for repose.[42]

Around the world today, more and more hospitals, hospices and institutions for those suffering from forms of mental illness are creating gardens where patients can find solace and beauty – and, for some, the therapeutic pleasures of gardening itself – as an escape from their circumstance. Many such gardens, like many public parks, contain trees or bushes planted in memory of those who may have loved or used them. A number of influences on European and American garden design in this regard have come from the East, particularly Japan. New Age philosophies have also found their embodiment in garden and landscape design.

The most interesting, and very beautiful, adaptation of Japanese garden techniques to historic cemeteries I have seen was at the medieval church at Gamla Uppsala in central Sweden one Sunday afternoon. The blazing sun had driven most of the clouds from the sky, and the tree cover in and around the churches (there were two of them, one entirely constructed from wood, the other from stone) made it an idyllic scene. As Larraine and I went into the churchyard to photograph some of the graves, I realized that we were following a young woman with a rake. I further noticed that many of the graves, as well as all of the churchyard paths, were covered with a fine pink granite gravel, several inches deep. On each grave, sometimes mounded, sometimes enclosed with stone kerbs, the pink gravel had been carefully raked in simple patterns, very much in the Japanese manner. With just a limited repertory of basic rake marks – straight lines, cross-hatched squares, circles, quadrants and wavy lines – every grave in the cemetery had just been neatly restored and refashioned, and this

Gamla Uppsala. Many of the graves in this ancient Swedish churchyard are covered with fine pink gravel, which is regularly raked into different patterns, as in a Zen garden.

Prospect Cottage at Dungeness, Kent, former home of artist and filmmaker Derek Jarman.

From the 1980s until his death in 1994, Jarman created the most extraordinary garden for Prospect Cottage using only native vegetation and found objects.

was done regularly. Such a simple idea, and one that made the cemetery and its graves look pristine, almost like a open-air gallery or Zen garden. I have never seen such an exquisite example of 'renewable design'.

The memorial garden is in itself a hybrid genre of landscape, halfway between a public garden and a cemetery, but most certainly a place of reflection and tranquillity. While in twentieth-century Britain the memorial garden has been in danger of languishing in the rather stultifying shape of a formal, sunken rose garden, with associated steps, terraces and memorial plaques, Derek Jarman, perhaps unwittingly, created

something quite spectacularly new at Prospect Cottage, Dungeness. There, in one of the most unpropitious settings to be imagined – a vast, flat shingle beach, exposed to the high, bitterly cold winds that tear in from the English Channel, and with little undersoil to speak of – he created a garden that is now visited and loved by people from all over the world. In his small book about it, Jarman recalls the beginnings of the project:

When I came to Dungeness in the mid-eighties, I had not thought of building a garden. It looked impossible: shingle with no soil supported a sparse vegetation. Outside the front door a bed had been built – a rockery of broken bricks and concrete: it fitted in well. One day, walking on the beach at low tide, I noticed a magnificent flint. I brought it back and pulled out one of the bricks. Soon I had replaced all the rubble with flints. They were hard to find, but after a storm a few more would appear. The bed looked great, like dragon's teeth – white and grey. My journey to the sea each morning had a purpose. I decided to stop there; after all, the bleakness of Prospect Cottage was what had made me fall in love with it. At the back I planted a dog rose. Then I found a curious piece of driftwood and used this, and one of the necklaces of holey stones that I hung on the wall, to stake the rose. The garden had begun.

I saw it as a therapy and pharmacopoeia.[43]

Later, Jarman recalled that his garden echoed one he once saw in Baku, Azerbaijan, created by an old power worker as a memorial to his daughter who had died in a swimming accident. The garden at Prospect Cottage is laid out within view of Dungeness nuclear power station.

Jarman's landscape has already become influential among garden designers and those concerned with how we might make new landscapes that meld found objects, cultivars and natural topography together in new combinations and associations. In this process we can compare the work of land artists such as Andy Goldsworthy, with his desire to assemble highly formalized constructions using only natural materials *in situ*, with that of a neo-Classical artist such as Ian Hamilton Finlay, who, at his pioneering garden at Little Sparta in the Scottish Borders has reclaimed the art of inscription for landscape design as the key element of memorialization. Both are now highly regarded, and their work is emulated throughout the world.

It is not true, therefore, that the aesthetic languages and forms for responding to death have been exhausted. Far from it. There is evidence from many new designs for parks and private gardens, memorial settings and other landscapes that there are rich new forms being developed that respond sensitively to issues of personal loss and matters of public memory. The problem seems to be that the worlds of modern architecture and landscape design, and the world of the civic cemetery in particular, have drifted so disastrously apart.

A rural church and yard with a yew tree in Kent: an enduring symbol of social and cultural continuity.

chapter three

Death's Compass:

The Society and Ecology of the Churchyard

In Brittany at the beginning of this century, according to Gabriel Le Bras, there still existed special cemeteries reserved for suicides, where the coffin was passed over a wall that had no opening.

Philippe Ariès, *The Hour of Our Death*[1]

THE RURAL CHURCHYARD

Historically, it is the rural churchyard rather than the urban cemetery that has dominated the popular imagination and iconography of death, particularly in Britain. With many church buildings dating back to the eleventh century and before, the parish churchyard has come to represent a deep and enduring emblem of social and cultural continuity. It has also provided many people with a pastoral vision of death, and even community. At times that long historical reach extends into pre-Christian times. The yews found in English churchyards often mark earlier burial sites – just as Christian rituals and calendars themselves incorporate earlier forms of pagan belief – and legend has it that on his arrival in Britain, St Augustine ceremoniously showered a symbolic yew tree with Holy Water in order to convert the entire species from its pagan origins to the new religion. Time and again, as we have already seen, burial places overlap and interleave historically and culturally.

The French historian Philippe Ariès dates the development of graveyards around churches back to the seventh century, when after a long period in which the dead were buried anonymously in fields well outside village limits or city walls –

as one can see so clearly at Birka on the island of Björkö, Sweden – the burial of certain saints within or beneath the church building encouraged a new attitude towards burial within the living community also: 'From now on, every church had tombs inside its walls and a cemetery next to it. The osmotic relationship between the church and the cemetery had been definitively established.'[2] Well into the eighteenth century, according to Ariès, it was still quite common to inter certain ranks of people inside the church – in crypt, vault, or table tomb – though increasing numbers of people, particularly the poor, as well as children, were buried outside within the walled churchyard. The great stone floor of the Oudekerk in Amsterdam, for example, is entirely made up of polished, black granite tombstones, each with a keyhole at one end for lifting. There are over 10,000 people buried beneath this floor, in a church that is also known as the great 'living room' of the city. Julian Litten's *The English Way of Death* deals comprehensively with all aspect of intra-mural burial over the past 600 years, and contains many rare photographs of chantries and mausoleums.[3] Although it tended to be the wealthier whose remains were interred within or below the church, it should be remembered that until the nineteenth century, common law affirmed the right of every inhabitant of a parish (certain specific prohibitions excepted) to be buried in the parish churchyard or burial ground. In this, the established church enacted its own version of universal citizenship.

Thus the village churchyard possessed a significant degree of social universality, even equality, as Gray's *Elegy in a Country Churchyard* famously evokes. In Christian culture the churchyard is commonly known as God's Acre. However, this popular image of a gently undulating pasture, broken up by random barrel vaults, slanting headstones and a handful of newly established graves where the freshly dug earth is still smothered by floral wreaths, all calmly shaded by yews, laurels, beech hedges and other established planting, is not the entire story. Even the arcadian spaces of God's Acre have not been entirely immune to geographies of status and power.

By the end of the seventeenth century, custom in England was beginning to favour burial outside the church itself, in graves marked by stones or 'steles', flat vertical stones sometimes ending in a circle enclosing a cross, bearing an inscription or some other symbol. Many such stones are often seen today stacked against the walls of the church or of the cemetery itself. Ariès hazards a guess at what an English churchyard might have looked like 'at the end of the seventeenth century and beginning of the eighteenth century: a kind of meadow in which the minister's animals grazed and which bristled with headstones, many of them richly decorated.'[4] The English were among the earliest to develop the outdoor churchyard with a distinctive tradition of flat headstones, of a kind that were copied in many other places, notably in the famous Jewish Cemetery in Prague.

Furthermore, when the Puritans first established themselves in what was becoming British America, they took with them the tradition of the outdoor cemetery, which was rarely rescinded in favour of indoor mausoleums or interment of any kind. In fact, in North America the funeral service itself is often conducted out in the open, by the side of the grave, rather than indoors, with temporary shelter and chairs provided if needed.

Until the mid-nineteenth century there would also have been large burial pits in some city churchyards reserved for paupers, and according to the historian Ruth Richardson, such paupers' pits could be twenty feet deep and not covered until they were completely full, and therefore the bodies were vulnerable to being stolen and used for dissection.[5] Such open pits also posed a serious threat to health. Ariès suggests that the use of very large common burial pits does not go 'further back than the sixteenth century', and that they were originally developed to cope with the large scale of deaths caused by plagues and virulent epidemics.

THE CHURCHYARD'S SOCIAL GEOGRAPHY

The consolatory and redemptive feelings that many people associate with these picturesque churchyards need to be tempered with a degree of realism about the relationship between the belief systems of those who established and maintained these places of burial (and who ordered the rituals and services that formalized the interments themselves) and the sometimes punitive and harsh social practices that accompanied them. Most early burials, for example, took place on the south side of the church; the north side was commonly 'deemed to be the domain of the Devil and was viewed with fear and superstition'.[6] In Britain, the north side was often reserved for those considered of lesser or even undesirable status, such as unbaptized infants, criminals and suicides: a place symbolically rarely visited by the sun. This was the dark side of the church's moral compass. Eventually, sheer numbers overcame issues of social distinction, as churchyards filled up from south to north; at which point the process started all over again.

Despite gradual overcrowding in many European and North American churchyards, social distinctions were often still adhered to, and consolidated. The Finnish anthropologist Juha Pentikäinen has in recent years published a large body of work on Scandinavian burial practices of the past two centuries, discovering that even in death the Christian religion was never as benign or forgiving as it might have been supposed. Until well into the twentieth century, Pentikäinen claims, 'Swedish–Finnish church law classified the departed and their funeral ceremonies in four categories, according to the manner of death: "public", "quiet", "shameful", and "depraved".'[7]

'Public' funerals were the norm, while 'quiet' services were for stillborn children, the unbaptized, alcoholics, those who had committed suicide while temporarily deranged and those who had given their bodies for anatomical research. The priest was present, but only in order to read the committal. 'Depraved' burials were for those who had killed children, killed in anger, died in prison or were unidentifiable at the time of death. According to Pentikäinen their graves were situated in the 'bad' corner of the churchyard (the evidence is still there in many churchyards today), without a priest or Christian ceremony, while the bodies of the 'shameful', such as suicides or those executed, were buried in unmarked graves in the forest. Nor were Jewish cemeteries spared from this kind of segregation: according to the Talmud, enemies in life should not be buried side by side, nor should 'the wicked

Burial at night was the rule in the early part of the 19th century in the Protestant Cemetery at Rome.

lie next to the righteous'. In many East European cemeteries, suicides and apostates were buried in remote corners'.[8]

When the New Haven Burying Ground in Connecticut was established in 1796 and its grounds laid out by Josiah Meigs, special lots were set aside for members of 'Yale College', 'Strangers' and 'Negros', while the majority of the plots were sold for family graves.[9] There is hardly any evidence left of any burials of black people in colonial New England, as most were buried without headstones and 'the black graveyards of Boston and Providence are scattered if not

virtually destroyed'.[10] Many North American towns in the seventeenth and eighteenth centuries also allocated grounds known as 'potter's fields' (a term used in the Book of Matthew 23:7) for the burial of the very poor or 'strangers'.[11]

Burial at night was another way of marking low or excluded status. In the Protestant Cemetery in Rome (also known variously as the English Cemetery, the Non-Catholic Cemetery and even the Strangers' Cemetery), for example, the Roman Catholic Church required that all burials be undertaken at night until well into the latter half of the nineteenth century, while at the same time any kind of religious inscription on headstones intimating the possibility of life after death or hopes of Heaven was refused, as the Catholic Church insisted that outside its own faith there was no possibility of salvation (*extra ecclesiam nulla salus*, was the papal interdiction).[12]

The same requirement for night-time interment was also made in the American slave-owning states in the nineteenth century, as it was felt that daytime burial would interrupt the pattern of work; night-time burial also allowed slaves from neighbouring plantations to attend the ceremonies and rituals.[13] Racial exclusion clauses were also common to many early twentieth-century private cemeteries, such as Forest Lawn, whose rules insisted that 'no interment of any body or the ashes of any body other than that of a human body of the Caucasian race shall be permitted'.[14] Such exclusion clauses did not finally disappear until well after the Second World War.

It is not surprising in a city (and a culture) as deeply divided along sectarian lines as Belfast that funerary customs and practices are also highly differentiated, one element of which is the existence of separate cemeteries for Catholics and Protestants. Even in those districts where there is just one municipal cemetery for both, then a strict division of space into distinct and separate areas is evident. Within those areas there are often sharp divisions between different Protestant sects, such as Anglicans and Presbyterians. Lindsay Prior provides examples of maps of different cemeteries in the city, showing how the spaces have been allocated by period, by religion, but also by 'social worth' in other respects. In the map of Carnmoney Cemetery, not only are there different areas for Catholics, Anglicans, Jews and Dissenters, there are also common graves for the poor. As Prior says, 'In the existence of these discrete areas we can see something of the power of religion in organising and structuring both the world of the living and the world of the dead. Though it is a political religion which rules here as much as any eschatology of the soul.'[15] In Carnmoney there is a public plot in which the poor were once buried, and although the last interment of an adult took place in 1969, the plot is still used for the interment of stillborn children in unmarked graves. One informant told Prior that the public plot was 'on the bad ground near the dump'.[16]

The positioning of the bodies of the dead, both good and bad, during the act of interment was equally rule-governed. Yi-Fu Tuan, developing ideas first raised by Kant, dwells much on the somatic nature of geographical orientation, putting the body and its knowledge of itself at the centre of all forms of directionality, so that, for example, when upright we assume that 'the future is up and ahead, the past is below and behind'.[17]

Even in the burial chambers of Neolithic sites, bodies were positioned in relation to the sun, which in Christian cultures was assimilated into the relationship to the cardinal points of East (the Holy Land) and West. In Sir Thomas Browne's early disquisition on the culture and customs of death, *Hydriotaphia: Urne-Buriall*, he noted that 'The Persians lay North and South, The Megarians and Phoenicians placed their heads to the East: The Athenians, some think, towards the West, which Christians still retain.'[18] As Yi-Fu Tuan has pointed out, the ancient Egyptian word for face was the same as for the south.[19] For most of the Christian era graves were oriented in an east–west direction, with the head to the west, awaiting the second coming of Christ from the east, according to Matthew 24:27.[20]

In her study of cemeteries in the Orkney Islands, Sarah Tarlow notes that until the twentieth century the majority of graves were aligned in an east–west direction, but more recently, in the newer cemeteries, the graves are laid out in avenues, with many back to back, in order to maximize the use of space: thus traditional orientations have been abandoned.[21] Some religions, though, keen to distance themselves from anything that may be thought to have its origins in pagan ritual, locate gravestones in various directions. The Liberal Jewish Cemetery in Willesden, north London, for example, has graves facing in both easterly and westerly directions, though this is now much more common elsewhere too.

The churchyards of the Moravian Church are particularly interesting in this regard. They were originally laid out by 'Choirs' to reflect the seating arrangements inside the church during services.

The four 'Choirs' consisted of married men, single men and boys, married women, and single women and girls, and consequently the burial grounds were divided into four quarters and people buried according to their 'Choir'. In recent times this practice has been discontinued, as separating members of families from each other is no longer regarded as acceptable. Within the Moravian faith the churchyard was regarded as a garden in which the earthly body was sown: modest flat stones and the use of trees and shrubs contributed to the Gardenesque quality of the burial ground, which can still be seen in London's Moravian cemetery on the King's Road, Chelsea. The Moravians traditionally held a liturgy in the burial ground on Easter morning, sometimes at dawn, celebrating the resurrection with those already departed. A circular procession, accompanied by music, also occurred. In 1753, one such Moravian service in Yorkshire attracted an estimated 10,000 people.[22] Thus the cemetery became a significant place for public occasions.

Issues of status and manner of burial are of course germane to the social structure that informs the design and locations of burial sites. This is one of the reasons that originally made the Stockholm Woodland Cemetery such a radical departure from the traditional culture of burial, since the allocation of burial places was made irrespective of wealth or status, and elaborate or expensive grave markers were eschewed in favour of small headstones and wooden crosses. When the ashes of the film star Greta Garbo were finally interred in June 1999, nine years after her death, her family chose to bury them at the Stockholm Woodland Cemetery, 'a long way from the hustle and bustle of the world', with only the simplest of gravestones. Her niece, Gray Reisfeld, said that 'She had a deep love of Nature – typical of any Swede – and now she has come home to the beautiful Skogskyrkogården (Woodland Cemetery).'[23] In Sweden the notion of a 'good grave culture' now predominates, tending to limit the size and ostentation of individual grave markers in favour of the overall cemetery effect.[24] The one innovation that now distinguishes many Swedish cemeteries from those elsewhere in Europe is the ubiquity of 'grave lights', introduced in the 1940s. It is not uncommon to visit a Swedish cemetery at dusk, particularly in winter, to find that many of the graves are indeed marked by flickering lamps.

One final point needs to be made in relation to the geography of death, notably the disturbing proximity of many cemeteries to hospitals. This is very much an aspect of nineteenth-century institutional geography, though pre-figured in medieval times by the adjacent location of monastic infirmaries and burial grounds. The Glasgow Necropolis is next to the Royal Glasgow Infirmary, while the main Leeds Cemetery is directly across the road from St James' Hospital. The same is true of the 'Hietaniemen hautausmaa', the main Helsinki Cemetery, located opposite the Maria Hospital. In *Austerlitz*, W. G. Sebald's eponymous narrator describes a winter stay after a mental breakdown in St Clement's Hospital in London's East End, where he frequently found solace in 'staring out for hours through one of the dirty windows at the cemetery below'. There, in the grounds of the Tower Hamlets Cemetery, he could watch foxes, squirrels and even owls go about their business among the 'mausoleums, marble crosses, stelae and obelisks, bulbous urns

The municipal cemetery at Malmö designed by Sigurd Lewerentz, where what is called in Sweden 'a good grave culture' is maintained.

The Glasgow Necropolis with the Cathedral and Glasgow Royal Infirmary in the background. The proximity of hospitals and cemeteries goes back to monastic times.

and statues of angels, many of them wingless or otherwise mutilated'. The connection owes as much to the nineteenth-century attachment of workhouses (institutionalized residential wards for the elderly unable to support themselves) to many hospitals, as it does to the high death rates of the clinically sick patients themselves. It was for this reason that one radical coroner of the Victorian era called workhouses 'Ante-chambers of the grave'.[25]

THE SECRET GARDEN

In time the churchyard came to occupy a place in the artistic and cultural imagination. 'There is a man who has discovered the tragedy of landscape', the French sculptor David d'Angiers is reported to have said after visiting Caspar David Friedrich in Dresden in 1834. Friedrich was influenced in his early years by the pantheistic ideas of the German poet Gotthard Ludwig Kosegarten, who saw in the 'ancient oak groves, moonlit Nordic landscapes and heathen burial sites' a world of ideas and values inherent in the landscape forms and ancient stones and grave markers. Religious and political beliefs were often symbolized in art through the use of tombs, cemeteries and ruined abbeys as devices to represent or allegorize them.

Yet, so often these worlds of the dead are separate worlds, self-contained worlds, which we view but cannot enter. In a number of paintings by Friedrich, the living are portrayed standing at the gate of the cemetery, anxiously peering in, afraid to enter, unsure as to which world they truly belong. In Friedrich's *Cemetery at Dusk* (illustrated on page 46), a couple stand at the towering gates of a cemetery, looking in at the grave of a child they have buried there, but afraid to enter that other world. In *Ulrich von Hutten's Tomb* (1823), Friedrich's support for German national identity and liberalism took the allegorical form of portraying a tomb to von Hutten, a revered patriot of the Reformation, which in reality had never been built. The tomb is set into the floor of another ruined abbey, with a headless statue of Faith in a niche on the wall. From a crack in the tomb a butterfly is emerging into the light, representing, no doubt, the survival of freedom's ideals.

Friedrich's defining originality lay in seeing and painting the landscape as a place haunted by death and memory, rather than as a form of idyllic reassurance and celebration. Living and working in Dresden, he would have known the version of Jacob van Ruisdael's *The Jewish Cemetery* of c. 1670, that still hangs in that city, in the Dresden Gallery. This great melancholy landscape painting electrified the early German Romantics, especially Goethe, who devoted an essay to a detailed consideration of three of van Ruisdael's paintings, including *The Jewish Cemetery*. In this painting, he pointed out enigmatically, 'even in their ruined state, the tombs point to a past beyond the past; they are tombs of themselves'.[26] They are not literal, but allegorical, he insisted.

Ruisdael's painting is an exercise in mood rather than literal transcription, as no such specific cemetery existed, and he made the painting from elements of other landscapes, ruins and tombstones sketched in different places. One of these places was the Portuguese–Jewish cemetery Beth Haim at Ouderkerk near Amsterdam, which was first bought and used

The Portuguese–Jewish cemetery, Beth Haim, at Ouderkerk, near Amsterdam, opened as a graveyard in 1614, and sketched in its early years by Jacob van Ruisdael.

as a graveyard in 1614, and is still in use, despite the near-annihilation of the Jewish community in The Netherlands during the Second World War. Even today it retains much of Ruisdael's isolated melancholy.

Traditionally, cemeteries have always been walled landscapes, partly for anthropological reasons to do with creating boundaries between polluted and unpolluted space, or between secular and religious space, as well as for eminently practical reasons. Most notable of all cemetery walls is the one that surround the Protestant Cemetery in Rome. In some sections it includes sections of the original city walls from pre-Christian times, as well as the celebrated

Cestius Pyramid. But along the northern flank there is a beautiful section with high openings to the sky, its interior facing painted pink. A similar wall, with the same distinctive openings towards the top, can be found at the Memorial Gardens in Walsall designed by the British landscape architect Geoffrey Jellicoe.

The high, yellow-painted wall which encloses the extensive Assistens Cemetery in central Copenhagen was erected in the eighteenth century to keep cattle and other grazing animals from disturbing the graves. Many Jewish cemeteries are not only bounded by high walls, they have equally high solid doors that are locked when not in use for funeral services, and so the cemetery itself is

The high walls are a distinctive feature of Rome's Protestant Cemetery and many other cemeteries.

The walled Jewish Cemetery at La Certosa, Bologna.

totally hidden from general view; a secret garden (*giardino segreto*) or forbidden city in all but name. Walled, locked and hidden cemeteries are, like secret gardens, a part of the landscape of religious persecution or retreat. As Jane Brown has written of the secret gardens in the great houses of sixteenth- and seventeenth-century 'old Catholic England', these were 'the landscapes of recusancy', of belief systems and ways of living (and indeed dying) that had been excluded or declared forbidden by the mainstream religious culture.[27]

Today the country churchyard, like the church itself, has become as much an icon of heritage and past manners and styles as it is a functioning institution. Churches continue to be preserved, rightly, because of their architecture and their visual contribution to urban and rural placemaking, though many are locked up and services are no longer held with any regularity. In turn, the pastoral churchyard is today more often viewed as a sanctuary and secret garden, free of the horrors of recent death and mourning, though unlike many of their counterparts throughout the world, the British have largely

forgotten or dispensed with particular rituals associated with keeping the churchyard beautiful and maintaining it as a place for remembrance and ceremony. In Wales in the earlier part of the twentieth century the tradition of Flowering Sunday, when people cleared and cleaned graves and decorated them with flowers, was common. Not so any more. Yet elsewhere, even in highly secular societies such as Finland, as well as more Catholic countries and cultures such as Poland, not only is All Souls Day marked by large-scale attendances at churchyards and cemeteries, with

The imposing entrance and walls at Highgate Cemetery in London.

families and friends bringing flowers, gardening implements, food and candles, and sitting in the cemetery talking and reminiscing, but on other set days too, such traditions persist. The churchyard or cemetery is still regarded as a place of great cultural significance in the local landscape, and for this reason rituals and customs associated with its maintenance and good-keeping are upheld.

THE CHURCHYARD IN THE CULTURAL IMAGINATION

Since what distinguishes humankind from the rest of the animal world is an awareness that we live alongside the dead, the cultural marginalization of the cemetery is disquieting. For in literary, religious and philosophical terms, the place of the dead exercises an important power over the human imagination. Another writer who used the image of the churchyard as a setting for both public and private conscience, as well as a place of reconciliation, was James Joyce in his short story 'The Dead', which suggests that most human life is lived within the shadow of those who have passed away. In this story, it is the singing of a particular folk song at a party that suddenly reminds a woman of a young man who had loved her so much that he risked his life to be near her. Disregarding his own health he pursued her, courted her, and in the process died. She tells this story to her husband as they retire to bed at the end of the party, causing the husband to realize that he had never quite managed to fully know her innermost thoughts and feelings. After she falls asleep, bereft and unhappy, the husband looks out of the window

into the night sky, only to see the snow start falling:

It was falling on every part of the dark central plain, on the treeless hills, falling softly upon the Bog of Allen and, further westwards, softly falling into the dark mutinous Shannon waves. It was falling, too, upon every part of the lonely churchyard on the hill where Michael Furey lay buried. It lay thickly drifted on the crooked crosses and headstones, on the spears of the little gate, on the barren thorns.

In Joyce's story, the snow finally merges the landscapes of both the living and the dead, bringing them into a shared human community. Earlier than Lawrence or Joyce, Charles Dickens had written evocatively about the City of London churchyards in his essay 'The City of the Absent', where,

The illegible tomb-stones are all lop-sided, the grave-mounds lost their shape in the rains of a hundred years ago, the Lombardy Poplar or Plane-Tree that was once a drysalter's daughter and several common-councilmen, has withered like those worthies, and its departed leaves are dust beneath it. Contagion of slow ruin overhangs the place.[28]

Dickens's gloomy thoughts are later leavened when he comes across an elderly couple who are literally haymaking, scything and raking grass for animal fodder from between the tombstones, and even later still, when he chances on a couple of young 'charity children' courting among the ruins.

Some found these ancient churchyards picturesque, perhaps, but in North America there was apparently a strong aversion to this kind of cemetery, with its lop-sided gravestones and overcrowded conditions, leading to the widespread wish to create more spacious cemeteries away from the city. One commentator was particularly appalled by the way that 'the confused medley of graves seems like the wild arrangement of some awful convulsion of the earth'.[29] Surely this was as the Day of Judgment meant them to be?

The imaginative overlay between the living village and the dead one, or the inter-relationship between past and present communities, is one of the great tropes of imaginative literature. It comes across with exceptional power in Schubert's *Winterreise* (Winter Journey), a setting of poems by Wilhelm Müller, most notably in the song 'Das Wirtshaus' (The Inn). This is actually about the graveyard, although the poet imagines it as an inn, where the verdant funeral wreaths seem to invite the traveller to enter, though all the rooms are occupied, and the poor traveller is forced to continue his journey, though one feels that death would be a great release. Interestingly, in his essay on the history of the inscription *Et in Arcadia Ego*, Erwin Panofsky refers to another German *Winterreise*, dating from 1769, by Johann Georg Jacobi, in which is written that 'Wherever, in a beautiful landscape, I encounter a tomb with the inscription *Auch ich war in Arkadien*, I point it out to my friends; we stop a moment, press each other's hands, and proceed.'[30]

The village churchyard, or the city cemetery, is of course an inverted image or miniaturized simulacrum of the village, town or city itself, a correspondence beautifully imagined by Italo Calvino in his description of the 'invisible city' of Eusapia, where the inhabitants construct an identical copy of their city underground, where the dead go to live, though the dead in turn claim that in fact it was *they* who constructed the city above ground, resulting in an eventual confusion, so that 'they say that in the twin cities there is no longer any way of knowing who is alive and who is dead'.[31] Even more confusing is Calvino's city of Laudomia, where there are triple identical cities: one for the living, one for the dead, and one for the as yet unborn, each jostling for space and moral authority.

In Giske in Norway, the small churchyard could be regarded as a miniature version of the village itself, quintessentially evoking the spirit and continuity of life in the village, perhaps even more than that represented by the increasingly mobile living population. The cemetery and the town have always been in a close relationship to each other. When Sigurd Lewerentz was asked to design the new cemetery in Malmö in 1916, a commentator at the time, Ingrid Lilienberg, argued that the modern cemetery 'should have an entirely specific cemetery atmosphere (*stämning*), which only man's moulding and forming hand can provide. Further, the orientation must be clear. The cemetery's size and form must be perceptible in the planning. Its scale and atmosphere *should fulfil the destiny of an urban population*.'[32] In short, it was designed as another version of the city of Malmö, extended into the distant future.

CULTIVATED CHURCHYARDS

As many urban churchyards were filled to capacity, and in some cases the church closed, thought had to be given to how to manage the graves and protect these micro-environments (as they would be regarded by ecologists). There is now a renewed interest in these arcadian settings by environmentalists and gardeners. Churchyards have been found to be rich habitats for birds, butterflies and lichen, owing to the fact that many have been gardened or maintained without recourse to the use of insecticides, pesticides or other harmful chemicals. The Holly Blue, Orange Tip, Wall Brown, Common Blue, Skippers, Tortoiseshells, and many other butterflies are often found in English churchyards, where grasses, gravestones, walls and hedges in close proximity provide an ideal habitat for them. Somehow the presence of butterflies in proximity to tombstones – remembering Friedrich's painting of von Hutten's tomb – provides a comforting metaphor for renewal, and the fragile lightness of memory and being.

Likewise, the presence of lichen on headstones, walls and trees again might be thought to bring a form of natural encroachment and retrieval into the world of the churchyard or cemetery, and there is increasing interest among environmental organizations in focusing on ancient churchyards as a key site for the retention of biodiversity. Indeed, the naturalist Richard Mabey has entered a plea for ecological arguments to be now paramount in the discussion of the future maintenance of redundant churchyards, writing that:

At present, churchyards are regarded principally as resting places for the dead, where a respectful, sombre tidiness, clipped of all the excesses of nature, ought to prevail. That is an understandable feeling, but in the light of our growing sense of the interdependence of life, a more hospitable attitude towards the rest of natural creation might perhaps be an apter response.[33]

One enchanting example of the cultivation of an historic churchyard into a new kind of ecological garden can be found at Bolton Percy, near York, which has been managed and maintained by Roger Brook, a local gardener, since the 1970s.[34] Brook has created what has been called 'the country's most distinctive graveyard', where each grave has its own living floral tribute, while between and around the gravestones wild flowers – celandines, primroses, wood anemones and bluebells – proliferate. Much of the churchyard is taken up with the structural planting of hardy ground cover, undulating and flowing between the graves. The churchyard of Little St Mary's in Cambridge is also considered to be one of the finest gardens in the city, and it includes an admired collection of roses.

At Lambeth Church in London, now converted to the Museum of Garden History, where the Tradescant family – notable seventeenth-century plant-hunters and *virtuosi* – are buried, the churchyard has been planted and adapted as a knot garden and sanctuary for visitors. The knot garden, characteristic of the Tradescants' time, is designed using geometric shapes based on squares and whole or part circles that cleverly incorporate the letter 'T' into four symmetrical positions.

The exquisite garden in the churchyard of Little St Mary's, Cambridge.

The tomb of William Bligh at Lambeth in London. The churchyard – which is also the burial place of the Tradescant family of 17th-century gardeners – is now a public garden.

Plants inside the knot were all grown in Britain during the lifetimes of the John Tradescant the elder (*c.* 1570–1638) and John the younger (1608–1662). The holly spiral, bay cones, columns of myrtle and a flat-topped umbrella of rosemary contribute to the planting scheme, and the garden has become a delightful visitors' attraction as much for the planting as for the tombs of the Tradescants, and that of William Bligh of HMS *Bounty* fame, who is also buried there.[35] The epitaph for the Tradescants includes the lines:

> . . . when
> Angels shall with their Trumpets waken men,
> And fire shall purge the World, these hence shall rise
> And change their Gardens for a Paradise.

The Begraafplaats Te Vraag in Amsterdam, a 19th-century cemetery now maintained as a public garden.

In The Netherlands, a similar cemetery garden has also been created at a nineteenth-century cemetery in Amsterdam, the Begraafplaats Te Vraag, alongside the Schinkel Canal, where an artist was given permission to occupy the former coach-house there on condition that he maintained the cemetery in an appropriate fashion, and which is now designated as a public garden (*stadtuin*). This has been achieved by a more formal use of structure planting, with tightly clipped shrubs cut in formal rows, boxes and short hedges around the graves, to create a maze-like appearance in which the individual headstones still retain their discrete identity, yet are now threaded together by the planting into a vegetable community. Slowly, a standard, grid-based cemetery is taking on the visual complexity and beauty of an Elizabethan knot garden.

These are unusual attempts to transmute the historic churchyard into a new garden setting in the brittle, hard-edged landscape of the modern town or city, creating something rich and strange in the urban landscape repertory. Meanwhile, most churchyards continue to retain their historic, if at times rather unyielding, formality, one softened by weathering and time. The landscape aesthetic of the churchyard was developed by default in many ways, though it is now lodged deep in the modern psyche. The idea that the landscape of the dead might require the development of a garden aesthetic of its own was developed in retrospect. The conscious design of cemeteries was yet to come.

Begraafplaats Te Vraag, Amsterdam.

Père-Lachaise Cemetery, Paris.

chapter four

Cities of the Dead

What makes Argia different from other cities is that it has earth instead of air. The streets are completely packed with dirt, clay packs the rooms to the ceiling, on every stair another stairway is set in negative, over the roofs of the houses hang layers of rocky terrain like skies with clouds . . . At night, putting your ear to the ground, you can sometimes hear a door slam.

Italo Calvino, *Invisible Cities* [1]

ETRUSCAN PLACES

In February 2002, Larraine and I followed in D. H. Lawrence's footsteps and went to Cerveteri, to the extraordinary Etruscan necropolis of Banditaccia (usually also called Cerveteri), some 48 kilometres north from Rome close to the Mediterranean coast. Lawrence travelled there in 1927 with his American friend Earl Brewster, specifically to visit the Etruscan tombs, and indeed wrote a book about it, *Etruscan Places*, published in 1932 after his death. He travelled there by train from Rome, and then walked the last five uphill miles, whereas we travelled on a very bumpy bus, rolling and braking hard at times across the sunny Campagna, on a warm, bright day with just a milky tinge of thin wispy cloud to the sky. Like Lawrence, we were captivated by this extraordinary city of the dead.

The sheer skills and artistry that went into the design of these tombs built in the sixth and seventh centuries BC, their profusion, and the overall effect of creating a city of homes for the dead, with its own streets, avenues and undulating rooftops, makes much of the rest of pre-Christian architecture elsewhere in Europe seem crude and haphazard. Lawrence was entranced by the Etruscans and, being close

The Etruscan tombs at Cerveteri, created during the 6th and 7th centuries BC. The early tombs were excavated from tunnels cut into the ground, becoming streets below ground level. Later on, above-ground terraces were created and, finally, circular tombs for the wealthy.

to death himself when he decided to make the trip to Italy, clearly found a reassuring spirit and culture there that brought him evident joy: his descriptions of the tombs, murals and artefacts, wildly unscientific and highly speculative, nevertheless brim with fellow-feeling and enthusiasm.

The plain mechanics of the necropolis are this. The hills are of a soft stone called tufa. Gullies were dug into the landscape to create trench streets, and off these sunken roads neat caves were cut into the tufa, with finely formed doorways and interiors made up of a number of small square rooms (sometimes called cubicles, at other times cells) containing stone beds or niches. The bodies of the wealthier Etruscans were laid in these niches, surrounded by familiar goods and artefacts, and thus they became houses of the dead. Over time, more elaborate ways of creating these burial homes were developed, although the principle of digging down into the stone and carving out square or rectangular rooms persisted. In two streets, now called via dei Monti Ceriti and via dei Monti della Tolfa, single-storey terraces (what Americans call row houses) were created, architecturally very similar to those one might find in a terrace of small houses in a mining village in northern England, each with a flat roof and a door opening. Inside, steep steps lead down once again into the deep underground rooms. The modern sign-post indicating these two streets of tombs points out baldly that 'These two roads prove that a normal town-planning scheme existed inside the necropolis.'

At a later stage of development, the design of the tombs took on the form of a series of large, perfectly round domes or tumuli erected over the grave entrance, creating an irregular series of what look like grassy beehives or spaceships, some as much as 40 feet high, with heavy retaining walls of dressed stone with braided carvings. Within these tumuli tombs, steps descend steeply into the earth from the ground-level doorway, leading into a large ante-chamber, which is then sub-divided at the end into three separate rooms. This 'tripartition', according to experts, distinctly reflects Eastern influences in domestic design and plan form. So on the same site, over a period of several hundred years, there is a clear development from a basic single-room, hut-type tomb, to a terrace of domestic tombs, and then, finally, to separate, self-contained villas. This is a residential urban quarter in all but name.

All of this development is of a piece with the development of domestic architecture, rather than sepulchral architecture. It was this, Lawrence was convinced, that made the Etruscan view of death seem to be less a dark journey into lonely nothingness, and more a continuation of life in its domestic – and more sociable – forms. Where there were murals or frescoes, these invariably showed hunting scenes or banquet scenes, again emphasizing the idea that, for the Etruscans, death was a form of translation into a world very similar to that of the living, but with a heightened sense of the more pleasurable elements of living pursued even more intently.

In his essay on the necropolis at Cerveteri, Lawrence wrote that

There is a stillness and a softness in these great grassy mounds with their ancient stone girdles, and down the central walk there lingers still a kind of loneliness and happiness. True, it was a still and sunny afternoon in April, and larks rose from the soft grass of the tombs. But there was a stillness and a soothingness in all the air, in that sunken place, and a feeling that it was good for one's soul to be there.

This is exactly what we felt, on our balmy, sun-dappled February day, with dozens of small finches and warblers singing in the higher branches of the trees, or flitting between them, while lizards darted across the stone walls of the tombs. There were hardly any other visitors to be seen on the day we were there, though to me these tombs are the equal of Stonehenge or the cave paintings at Lascaux in terms of their artifice and resonant archaeological beauty.

The Etruscans also developed a culture of the hut urn, more in evidence at Tarquinian than at Cerveteri. The hut urn is a facsimile of a normal dwelling place but on a smaller scale, and it was used to contain the cremated remains of the dead. These hut urns could be remarkably detailed, including gabled roofs, smoke openings, and even

doors that opened and closed. While not every Etruscan was honoured with such a permanent habitat, the sheer number of hut urns created a distinct architectural settlement within the built space of the living. The art historian Nigel Spivey has emphasized the distinctly urban feel of these settings:

> The Etruscan dead were not hived off into dovecotes, nor subdued beneath cenotaphs; they had houses. In due time the dead had not only their own streets, but their own town planning too. This is why the best term for an Etruscan cemetery is not cemetery at all, or graveyard, but 'necropolis' which means, literally, 'city of the dead'.[2]

The hill-top necropolis at Banditaccia, directly within view of the 'living city' of Cerveteri, is repeated over 2,000 years later at the famous Glasgow Necropolis, another hilltop burial ground within sight of the city, as it is in many other parts of the world. The cities of the living

The Glasgow Necropolis was one of the first self-styled 'cities of the dead' to be founded in Britain, and still possesses a strange imaginative power.

and the cities of the dead sometimes become twin elements of the same urban psyche.

Such cities of the dead represent a distinct tradition from that of the Christian churchyard, or the early Christian practice of locating burial sites within the church. In such cases, a hallowed building (often containing venerated remains or relics) is regarded as providing a separate nexus for the sacred geography of the community. The necropolis, or city of the dead, suggests a quite different relationship to the entirety of an existing settlement, more civic and inclusive, rather than a sacrosanct place apart. In this distinction can be traced elements of what Hannah Arendt once characterized as Christianity's 'hostility' to the public realm, embodying the idea that the early Christians tended to live a life 'as far removed from the public realm as possible'.[3] The Christian faith has often favoured retreat. Such attitudes can also be found in Christianity's longstanding belief that its communicants should be *in* the world, not *of* it. Thus while the Christian churchyard was literally open to everybody – at least up until the Reformation, when Catholic and Protestant rituals and ordinances went separate ways – it was often seen as consecrated ground and not part of the public landscape of the *civitas* or city.

THE CATACOMBS OF ROME

The catacombs in Rome, first quarried several centuries after the Etruscan tombs at Cerveteri, display some of the same architectural and aesthetic interests. Yet they have a different feeling entirely, much less public and celebratory, much more sectarian and exclusive, even though the catacombs were developed by pagan cults as well as by Christians and Jews. But they belong to a more mystical, grimmer eschatological tradition. While there are many separate networks of catacombs in Rome, nearly all are attached to a particular martyr, saint or ancient religious building.

The idea of extensive underground interment was first developed because the early Christians could not afford to buy or own land for burial; so they went below ground to solve the problem of finding sufficient burial space for the growing numbers of converts to their faith and community. In the case of the Catacombs of St Domitilla, the land for the original basilica (and entrances into the underground tunnels) was bought by a rich convert, Flavia Domitilla (martyred *circa* AD 90), niece of the Emperor Domitian, and a martyr for her beliefs. So while the space above ground only occupies enough room for a small basilica, below ground the network of burial chambers runs to nearly ten miles (fifteen kilo-metres) in total, though visitors are taken no more than 300 metres in all.[4]

The cult of Christianity derived much of its

Entrance to the catacombs of St Domitilla, excavated during the first century AD, and part of a network of underground burial chambers many miles long.

emotional power from the allegedly exemplary lives, as well as the gruesome deaths, of the early martyrs. The so-called relics (personal artefacts, bones, phials of blood) of these adherents took on a talismanic quality. To be buried close to where their remains were interred, or at least to visit the burial places of these heroic figures, became one of the most important activities and rites of the religion. Thus the catacombs in Rome became a place of pilgrimage for Christians throughout Europe, and by the sixth century, written guides (such as the Salzburg Itinerary or the Malmesburg Itinerary) to the catacombs and tombs of the early Christian martyrs were available to pilgrims, especially those from northern Europe.[5]

Largely as a result of the Reformation, and the bitter wars of faith fought between Catholic and Protestant adherents from the sixteenth century onwards, such relics gained an additional ideological power. By the early seventeenth century, groups of specialized workers known as the *corpisantari* (handlers of saintly bodies) were employed to recover relics for redistribution among the Catholic churches of the world, in what one historian has described as an 'attempt by the Catholic Church to block widespread Protestantism by rediscovering the roots of the Christian faith, which took their shape in the remains of martyrs buried in the catacombs'.[6] Architecture alone, it seems, could not create a church; it also needed the relics of ancient human remains to imbue it with power, just as pagan buildings had once required an act of human sacrifice to guarantee their success and longevity.

A visit to these catacombs today turns out to be not the least disturbing or unsettling. Those bodies that have not entirely returned to dust have all been removed, and the tunnels and chambers are well maintained. At St Domitilla's there is a small administration building directly over the main stairs down to the underground basilica, the Basilica of SS Nereus and Achilleus, fourth century in origin and rather beautiful, built to commemorate two Roman soldiers who converted to Christianity and were consequently martyred and later buried there. According to the most recent evidence, the popular image of these underground burial vaults as meeting places, and even homes, of fugitive early Christians is entirely wrong. The Romans always respected the burial customs of other religions, it is now thought, and many of the very earliest catacombs contained pagan, Christian and Jewish burials. In fact, the site of Domitilla's catacombs itself contained a pagan cemetery with a columbarium from the first century AD.

The catacombs were excavated by a trade of diggers called the *fossores* (*fosse* in Italian is both tomb and cave), who were not only skilled in digging, but in painting frescoes and contriving inscriptions. The principal corridors are all between two and three metres in height and one metre wide, and all along the walls horizontal niches (*loculi*) have been cut into the stone for the insertion of bodies. Many of these niches are tiny, as little as 50 centimetres long and just 20 centimetres deep, and were for children. The bodies were anointed with oils, wrapped in shrouds and left to disintegrate, a process helped by the damp atmosphere. The niches were sealed by marble slabs or large tiles. The guide on our visit assured the children who made up part of our small party that even human bones return to earth eventually, for 'if we think of all the dead birds and animals in the world – where are their skeletons today?' There are many larger cells, chambers and cubicles to both sides of the main corridors, which were likely to have been family tombs or places reserved for wealthier individuals. The rough, dark corridors are always dividing and meeting up again, side-alleys extend in all directions into the darkness, and it would not be a good idea to get lost. Some of the larger chambers still have their beautiful *al fresco* paintings intact. Close to the entrance is a large space cut into the tufa that was used for the rite of the *refrigerium*, or funeral banquet. The practice of holding a meal on the occasion of a burial was common to the Etruscans, the Greeks, the Jews and the Romans, and of course it is still common today in the notion of the funeral tea or wake. The cellular structure of the catacombs continues to inform much contemporary Mediterranean cemetery design.

Since the reason why people were so keen to be buried in these catacombs was to be close to the final resting places of the early Christian martyrs, over time this belief in the sanctity of place was transmuted into the wish to be buried in the crypts of churches (where saintly relics might also be located), a practice that, as we have seen, continued throughout Europe well into the eighteenth century. The Etruscan necropolis, and subsequently the European garden cemetery, expressed a rather different relationship to the wider pattern of settlement than that of the religious burial ground; indeed, both could be regarded as an important addition to the public network of streets, places and urban culture, rather than a private retreat or cloister. The very word *necropolis* itself embodies the term *polis*, which implies both the city and the civic culture which that city embodies, simultaneously.

THE MODERN NECROPOLIS

The idea (or ideal) of the necropolis re-emerged in Europe at the end of the eighteenth century, notably with the example of Père-Lachaise in Paris, which was opened in 1804. This new cemetery represented 'a turning point in one thousand years of Western history', according to Richard Etlin. Similarly, in James Stephen Curl's words, it quickly became 'world famous'; it was 'visited by many people interested in the problems of burying the dead in a civilised fashion, and its influence was enormous throughout Europe and North America'.[7] Yet while its impact was sudden and dramatic, and has remained so ever since, it was not conceived fully formed, as if nothing remotely of its kind had ever existed before. It was a triumph of symbolic integration: a synthesis of many different elements that were already in existence in some form elsewhere, but to date had not been brought together. Père-Lachaise drew on ideas and practices with regard to both landscape theory, and the dignification and humanization of death, which had been accreting in political and philosophical circles throughout Europe in the eighteenth century. These were political as well as aesthetic, and related to changing ideals of landscape as well as to refinements of city living.

Given that it is often difficult to distinguish hard and fast typological boundaries between the necropolis, the garden cemetery, or even the American rural cemetery, issues of taxonomy need further clarification. For even though *in extremis* these generic landscape terms can and did modulate quite suddenly into distinct landscape types and conventions, for the most part there has always been a large degree of overlap and, at times, conscious assimilation. One way of seeking to understand the cultural achievement represented by Père-Lachaise is to examine the pre-existing elements that contributed to its success.

There are at least five discernible elements that, combined, helped to produce the unprecedented success of Père-Lachaise and the widespread admiration and emulation it garnered throughout the world.

First, there was the element of radically transformed thinking about landscape influences incorporated into its original design, largely in response to the rise of the English 'Picturesque' movement in the seventeenth and eighteenth centuries. This represented a significant aesthetic break with the neo-classical tradition throughout Europe, especially in relation to the architecture and landscape of death, even though today the early planting schemes have been displaced by a proliferation of tombs and its naturalistic elements have largely disappeared.

Second, there was the growing – and not unrelated – influence of Romantic ideas, notably in the burgeoning belief in the self-dramatizing and expressive nature of life, along with the struggle to break free of the bounds of religious conformity. In this view, death was regarded as a final rest or eternal sleep after a life of remorseless (and sometimes debilitating) self-discovery.

Third, there was evidence to suggest that models of grand cemeteries and mausoleums that had been discovered and admired in India in the wake of imperial conquest were being brought back to influence architectural practices within the mainstream European monumental tradition.

Fourth, there was an architectural gravitation towards the 'hut' culture of the Etruscans, taking the form of a city of the dead made up of an increasing number of individual and family tombs or 'houses'.

Finally, there is no doubt that the egalitarian and rationalist principles espoused during the French Revolution, and which transformed both institutional and public life and culture in France and beyond for ever, were also being brought to bear on issues of death and memorialization. The Enlightenment belief in the dignity of the sovereign individual now needed to be carried on to matters of death and commemoration.

'NATURE ABHORS A STRAIGHT LINE':
THE INFLUENCE OF THE PICTURESQUE

To the modern visitor, Père-Lachaise may seem distinctly urban, and rather formal, with its cobbled streets and avenues of tombs and monumental mausoleums, and far removed from the sylvan image of the garden cemetery. Like most cemeteries, also, it feels very different on a fine Spring day, when the sun is shining and the many flowers are in bloom, than on a winter's day when the rain is sleeting down, the sky is overcast, and the only light comes from the rain glistening on the cobbles or reflecting the sky in the puddles. Yet it had been designed by Alexandre-Théodore Brongniart with significant Picturesque elements. Early prints reveal it to have been heavily planted with poplar trees and

Part of the cobbled, urban street pattern at Père-Lachaise cemetery in Paris.

shrubbery, with winding paths of gravel, loose stones and shingle, on what was a very steep site.

When first opened, Père-Lachaise was in the countryside, though today it is part of the urban fabric of the 11th *arrondissement*. Though designed as an Elysian Fields, like the society itself beyond the cemetery walls, it too quickly urbanized, as the trend for chapel tombs or ornate family mausoleums gathered popularity. In 1805 just fourteen new tombstones were built in the cemetery, whereas ten years later it was nearly 2,000 in a single year, resulting in this rural Elysium quickly coming to resemble the built-up town or city that the visitor encounters today.

For more than a century Père-Lachaise was regarded as the most influential cemetery in the world, a pioneer in landscape form, in the monumental quality of its many tombs and sculptures, and for its many famous dead. It occupies a unique place within French culture, and it was also probably the first cemetery to become an essential place to visit within the wider tourist and museum culture. Despite the graffiti, the candle-stubs and drink cans left by Jim Morrison fans, the many bouquets brought to the grave of Edith Piaf, Simone Signoret or Yves Montand, the cult votive offerings left behind by devotees of Chopin or Wilde, the cemetery

Monument in Père-Lachaise cemetery to French citizens who died at Auschwitz , one of many such grim memorials to the political catastrophes of the 19th and 20th centuries.

The unnerving tomb of Georges Rodenbach in Père-Lachaise cemetery.

transcends all these affective outpourings of twentieth-century popular culture and never seems anything less than a place of great historic significance and sobriety. Perhaps it is because the tombs of some of these great individuals and personalities of the past 200 years also have to share space with the graves and memorials of those who suffered from some of the most terrible atrocities of the same period – whether the victims of the brutal suppression of the 1870 Communards or those of the Second World War – Père-Lachaise manages more accurately to reflect the tumult and upheavals of history than almost any other kind of cultural space elsewhere in Europe.

ROMANTICISM AND DEATH: THE DESIRE FOR OBLIVION

On 10 January 1794 (or in the new calendar of the French Revolution, 21 Nivôse, Year II) Jean-Baptiste Avril of the Administration of Public Works outlined to the Commune proposals for four new cemeteries in the city, each to be known as a *Champ de Repos*, or Field of Rest. The Revolutionary ideal of the new kind of cemetery was one free of the trappings of excessive religious morbidity, as well as of the brutalizing effects of mass burial. Avril believed that Nature itself held the key to making the new places of burial more uplifting and enlightening, and Etlin summarizes the new aesthetic thus:

> As for the vegetation in the cemetery, traditional signs of melancholy – cypresses, yews, weeping willows, and poppies – were to be combined with fragrant plants and flowering bushes whose perfumes would inebriate the visitor so as to fill him with a sense of calm. Soon you will forget the loss that you have sustained, mused Avril, and before you realise it, you will find yourself envying the dead.[8]

In this new culture of the cemetery, death was now seen as an eternal sleep or rest, rather than the transitional stage between life on earth and another world elsewhere, suggested by the precepts of formal Christian religion. Death as a form of sleep or oblivion, after a life of struggle and self-realization, is very much a part of the Romantic world picture. This idea was taken to its extreme in the case of the Marquis de Sade, who ordered that at his death, his body be collected on a cart by the local woodseller, taken into the woodlands on the Marquis's estate, a grave dug, the body interred, and

> Once the grave has been filled in, it will be planted with acorns so that in time to come the site being covered over and the copse being once again as thickly wooded as it was before, the traces of my grave will disappear from the surface of the earth, just as I am pleased to think that my memory will be erased from the minds of men . . .[9]

The desire for oblivion was never expressed more passionately, and, some might argue, deservedly.

EASTERN INFLUENCES

In recent years new evidence has emerged to draw attention to the considerable influence exercised on European cemetery provision – and the design of imposing mausoleums – by examples in India. The landscape and architectural historian Robert Williams has investigated in some detail the 'lost years' (1682–5) of the playwright and architect Sir John Vanbrugh (1664–1726). He discovered that, as a young man, Vanbrugh worked as a textiles manager at Surat in the province of Gujarat for the East India Company. While there Vanbrugh became familiar with Surat's cemeteries, where English, Dutch and other colonial traders, not having churches in the city within which to bury their European dead, developed woodland cemeteries on the outskirts, and in them frequently built formidably large mausoleums. Williams describes these as 'remarkable for their size and commitment to Mughal forms and details, the English and Dutch evidently working in competition with one another to best dazzle the city's rulers and perhaps win trading advantages'.[10]

The Mughal forms that Williams refers to arise out of the culture of the great Indo-Muslim rulers in India, who developed an extraordinary series of great monumental tombs or mausoleums. These included that of the thirteenth-century Sultan Shams al-Din Iltutmish in Delhi constructed in red sandstone; the sixteenth-century Humayun's tomb and water gardens, also in Delhi; the early seventeenth-century tomb of the emperor Akbar on the outskirts of Agra, again with extensive ornamental gardens; and, of course, the Taj Mahal ('a vast allegorical anticipation of the Day of Resurrection as imagined in Muslim cosmology'), completed in 1647.[11] These great architectural wonders, complete with formal gardens and water features, astonished early European visitors, and helped sow the seeds of a mausoleum culture back in the heartlands of empire.

Some years after Vanbrugh returned to England, he advocated these 'new' practices – the laying out of woodland cemeteries and the design of impressive tomb architecture. These ideas did gain credence, and the development of impressive family mausoleums on big aristocratic estates is largely credited to his influence. As Williams writes: 'In the course of the eighteenth century, the free-standing family mausoleum was to become a significant component of the English landscape garden, almost a commonplace. The origin of this development can now be traced

back to Vanbrugh, the result of his years abroad.'[12] Continuing this interest, James Stevens Curl refers to other, subsequent, cemeteries established by Europeans in India, such as South Park Street Cemetery in Calcutta, founded in 1767 (many years before Père-Lachaise), which was filled with temples, tombs and large-scale mausoleums, interspersed with palm trees and shrubs. The interest in other models of burial places and tombs was part of a wider two-way traffic in architectural ideas and styles (the adoption of the bungalow was another) that came out of the colonial experience.

THE HOUSE OF THE DEAD

Many modern visitors to Père-Lachaise are initially overwhelmed by its street-pattern layout, especially those more used to the garden cemetery tradition. There are whole roads full of family 'houses', elaborately designed and constructed, with many fine architectural and sculptural details, as if the occupants are still in the process of displaying their wealth, status and good fortune to enjoy a smart address. These houses are largely one-room dwellings, however, no matter how ornate, and in this sense they could also be described as elaborate versions of the Etruscan huts. There is often something particularly intriguing about such diminutive houses, the door of which leads not from one space to another but of one world to another – or of one world to oblivion. And the hut, like the one-room house, seems made for shelter and hiding in, rather than sociability.

In another context, Ariès once described the typical French cemetery as 'a little stone village

Avenue of family tombs at Green-Wood Cemetery in Brooklyn, New York.

with houses crowded together, where two transplanted cypresses are as conspicuous as feather dusters'.[13] A slightly grander version of this can be seen, for example, in the 'mansion on the hill' effect produced in Brooklyn's wealthy Green-Wood Cemetery, where elaborate family mausoleums line the wider avenues as if belonging to some exclusive residential neighbourhood. If the gravestone, tomb or columbarium niche is seen as a final house or home, which it often is, symbolically, it is also of interest to note that in research conducted in Britain about attitudes towards graves and their possible re-use, it was found that not only did women tend to visit graves more than men,

it was regarded more likely to be 'women's work' to clean and maintain them: another aspect of the traditional domestic role, extending from life to death as well.[14]

A more vernacular 'hut' tradition still survives in rural parts of the American South, where one can still find small gabled buildings in cemeteries designed to shield graves and protect them from damage by scavenging animals or harsh weather, especially the rain.[15] Sometimes known as grave sheds, grave houses, shelter houses and even spirit houses, the practice was widely adopted in the first half of the twentieth century, as well as being part of the Native American tradition, notably amongst the Cherokee tribes. These houses could be built of wood, brick or even stone, and sometimes their internal walls were painted. Although the practice has largely come to an end, existing grave huts can be found in cemeteries in southern Kentucky, east Tennessee, the Ozarks and east Texas.

Yet while the ideal of Surat in India, Père-Lachaise in France, the Glasgow Necropolis in Scotland, Highgate Cemetery in England and many other elegant early cemeteries was one of a different kind of utopian community, there are many more modern cemeteries that, devoid of any architectural or sculptural quality or inventiveness, appear bleak and deeply conformist. As Sebald's eponymous narrator, Austerlitz, by profession an architectural historian, insists in his long, sad story, one of the lessons of history is that what start out as model communities or ideal cities invariably end up as barracks. The same has also been true of cities of the dead. One of the bleakest modern cemeteries has to be Moscow's Khovanskoe, opened in 1972 and some 206 hectares (500 acres) in size. For point of comparison, London's Hyde Park is a mere 360 acres, while New York's Central Park is 843 acres. In Catherine Merridale's description, it is a vast city of unmarked alleys and paths, poorly maintained and liable to flooding, yet in which people have still tried to individualize the graves with photographs, plastic flowers, tables of ritual food, and even little roofs.[16] Yet the overall effect is numbing.

Scale is of the essence. Large cemeteries and monumental designs possess the power to instil fear rather than offer solace, as the pyramids of Egypt certainly did. The most ambitious and grandiose designs for buildings commemorating death in Europe were those of the French architect Étienne-Louis Boullée (1728–99), most famously in his drawings for a cenotaph for Sir Isaac Newton, as well as in his plans for vast walled cemeteries – on the scale of large cities – set in rural landscapes. Such plans only ever came near to being realized, in size at least (but certainly not design), in the monumental cemeteries and memorials to the dead of the First World War, most notably in the Ossuary at Douaumont (France), and in the Sacrario di Redipuglia (Italy). In Germany, an architectural culture based on creating 'fortresses of the dead' began to develop in the 1930s, one example being the heavily fortified 'Free Corps Memorial' in Annaberg, Silesia, built between 1936 and 1938 to a design by Robert Tischler.[17] During the Nazi era in Germany, many designs were commissioned for the eventual construction of great heroic mausoleums, cenotaphs and memorials to Germany's fallen soldiers, but following utter defeat in 1945, none was realized.

In the modern era, the most radical attempt to create a necropolis in the modernist – or more precisely, rationalist – architectural tradition, is that by architects Aldo Rossi and Gianni Braghieri, in their San Cataldo cemetery, completed in Modena, Italy in 1984.[18] The cemetery consists principally of a series of pastel-coloured medium-rise apartment blocks set among plain grass lawns, each block containing a large number of floors, corridors, rooms and individual *loculi*, in which the dead are sealed. At the centre of the site stands a taller building, at first glance another housing block, but which on closer examination is discovered to be roofless and empty, with many frameless window openings. As with his designs for housing for the living – which have been rather less successful than his houses for the dead, possibly because of their rigid formalism – Rossi affirmed the analogy of the house with the city: 'On the basis of this analogy, every corridor is a street, every court a city square, and a building reproduces the places of the city.'[19] San Cataldo is indeed a city of the dead, though it owes as much to the Surrealist reveries of De Chirico as it does to Le Corbusier and the purists of the CIAM.[20]

The success of Père-Lachaise consolidated the practice of giving each dead person a grave of their own, part of the growing social process of individuation at work in Enlightenment Europe, and which has since then served to undermine the monumentalist architectural tradition. The Decree of 23 Prairial, Year XII, issued in Paris in

1804, insisted on the principle of single burial, in which bodies were not 'superimposed but must always be juxtaposed'.[21] Not only was the cemetery moved to the edge of the city limits for reasons of health and hygiene, but also the mass grave came to an end and was replaced by the principle of individual burial, a kind of somatic anticipation of the electoral franchise achieved nearly 100 years later: one person, one grave. The acceptance of this principle also accelerated the development of the individual tombstone as well as the brief headstone biography, along with any sentiments or epitaphs that might be considered appropriate.

For a sociologist such as Lindsay Prior, the 'private plot is in many ways the prime monument to the modern way of death . . . a final

High-rise mausoleums at the San Cataldo Cemetery designed by Aldo Rossi and Gianni Braghieri in Modena, Italy, completed in 1984.

The cloisters of the 18th-century Carthusian monastery La Certosa in Bologna, which became popular as a burial place.

expression of that individualisation whose origins Tocqueville and Durkheim had traced to a modern "disposition to isolation".[22] In turn, as people became wealthier, the modest tombstone was sometimes transformed by the commission of quite extraordinary works of sculpture, particularly where the religious element was absent, culminating in works of astonishing kinds of expressionism rather than piety or resignation.[23] Furthermore, Père-Lachaise also enacted the principle of burial in perpetuity, though this was never offered in many other cemeteries, as we have noticed, where re-use remained the common practice.

An equally 'modern' approach to the creation of a new kind of urban cemetery was inaugurated at La Certosa di Bologna, established in and among the buildings of an eighteenth-century Carthusian monastery, some two years before Père-Lachaise. The buildings today include a relatively modern administration campus close to a very large church, which is the starting-point for a series of long cloistered squares and gardens, some of the cloisters and ambulatories being nearly 300 metres long. The cemetery was inaugurated in 1802, after Napoleon had ordered the monks back to France. Because burial within church walls had always

Wall tombs at La Certosa, Bologna, known in Italy as *forno* or oven tombs. Interment is usually for 25 years, after which the remains are taken out and the space re-used.

been considered particularly desirable, the paved areas of the dozens of cloisters were used for this purpose, so today one walks along and across miles of gravestones and tombstones set in the floors of the cloisters among the paving slabs.

In addition there are at least eight *campi d'inhumazione* (burial fields, including Protestant and Jewish burial grounds), large avenues given over to ornate *tombe di famiglia* (monumental family tombs), with many of the burial fields themselves surrounded by high white *tombe in edifice* (high concrete walls containing niches into which bodies are inserted and sealed). It is the last of these that are rare in northern Europe, where burial underground is considered culturally more acceptable. The individual wall slot is called, in Italian, the *forno*, or oven, which is what it looks like, open or closed. (Likewise, the columbaria for the interment of ashes take their name from *columba*, or dove, since the early Romans regarded them as similar in design to a dovecote.)

At the ceremony, usually following a religious service in church, the casket is put into the wall and the tomb cemented tight. Shortly after a marble plaque is added, often with a glazed photograph of the dead person and an ornamental holder for flowers.

What is surprising to some, perhaps, is that these forms of interment are not permanent. Buried bodies are disinterred after ten years (although there is the opportunity to secure another ten years of undisturbed settlement, if paid for), and the bones given back to the family or reinterred in a smaller space along with others. Those sealed in the walls get 25 years before the remains are removed and the space used for further interments. In Bologna, as in many other parts of Italy, people accept the idea of a finite period in which the body remains undisturbed, and many of the graves are immaculately tended and adorned with fresh flowers. But after a fixed period the sovereign grave or burial space is dispensed with, ready for the next occupant; and that is the end of that. (The highly sensitive issue of the re-use of graves, commonplace in many parts of Italy, is dealt with more fully in a later chapter.) So these are quite functional places, formally laid out, heavy and ornate with marble, along with the filing-cabinet efficiency of the *tombe in edifice*, but they are not landscapes or places of meaning in their own right. In this, there is a substantial difference in spirit and ethos to the English Gardenesque cemetery or the north European woodland cemetery, both of which are intended to evince the values of harmony with nature and permanent repose.

Few Italians would dream of visiting a cemetery simply out of interest, I have often been told, even to look at the statues or reflect on the place as an historical monument or setting. The power of death seems to nullify all other perspectives. The idea that the historic cemetery might be an invaluable educational resource or a legitimate setting for the study of local history largely remains unthinkable. The city of the dead, which started out as another homeland and as an integral part of the living community, in some places today remains something of a forbidden city – walled, cloistered, and still imbued with the ghosts of some baleful eschatology.

Memorial to the poet John Keats, Rome.

chapter five

Libraries in Stone

Here is a tribe of stones, a people of stones, an obstinate tribe which is ever marching and ever shouting and calling voicelessly. Against the background of native grasses, trees, nettles and blackberries, exotic Hebrew letters are still talking about those who lived here and passed away.

Anna Kamienska, *Time of Stones* [1]

PIVOTAL LANDSCAPES

The places of the dead are assemblages of signs: shifts in landscape form, openings and enclosures, arrangements of stone and sculptings, and, in more modern times, inscriptions and texts. We are able to read these signs in retrospect because they were designed and inscribed as messages to the future; indeed, many epitaphs make direct appeal to the sympathies and interests of future generations. This is why Panofsky argues that funerary art and architecture evokes both a sense of loss while, at the same time, seems to look forward to a different future, in this world or the next. In a sense the places of the dead are *pivotal* landscapes, places where life and death, past and future, the material world and the spiritual world are held in balance.

At the end of Thomas Hardy's *Tess of the D'Urbervilles*, Tess, having murdered her betrayer, is fleeing from the law, along with her husband, Angel Clare. In the darkness of the Wessex night they unexpectedly find themselves at Stonehenge. There the exhausted Tess sleeps on a flat sacrificial stone until the search party surrounds and captures her. She is taken to be tried at Wintoncester. Later she is hanged. In Hardy's day, Stonehenge was still widely regarded as a site of sacrifice in the midst of an barren landscape that 'bore that impress of reserve, taciturnity, and hesitation which is usual just before day [. . . where] the quivering little pools in the cup-like hollows of the stones lay still'.[2] To have arrived there is to have arrived at the end of the world, it seems.

While Stonehenge was not a burial site as far as is known, as a collection of standing stones it is part of a culture that placed large stones in the landscape as a means of connecting one world to another. When the young Henry Moore first visited Stonehenge in early October 1921, while a young student at the Royal College of Art, that first impression by moonlight stayed with him for the rest of his life. He later claimed to have visited Stonehenge 'twenty or thirty times'. His friend the poet Stephen Spender described Moore's early lithographs of Stonehenge as being deeply metaphorical, suggesting that the immense weight of one of the lintels etched by Moore seems 'poised there like a sarcophagus containing something sinister, a mummy or

Stonehenge in southern England, the largest and most famous of all European stone circles.

a body – ghostly . . . Below this figure there lies a flat slab in what seems a pool of water, like a prostrate victim.'[3] Clearly, both Spender and Moore had read their Hardy, and subconscious echoes of 'Tess' still haunted them.

The upright menhir or stele, the dolmen or lintel, along with the horizontal slab are the principal coordinates of much ritualistic or funerary architecture, combined, as at Stonehenge, or at nearby Avebury, in the form of a colonnaded circle, or henge. Moore's obsession with Stonehenge could be said to be largely responsible for his increasing commitment to sculptural abstraction, to the siting of his great works in open-air landscape settings, and to a conscious reconnection of mid-twentieth-century art to so-called primitive forms. In this sense he was an early explorer of what today is called 'land art': a body of artistic and sculptural expression that seeks to build on natural materials and natural forms in the landscape, but in a selective and heightened fashion, so as to bring the underlying morphology of natural forms to the surface. Moore also admired the totemistic role

Henry Moore was obsessed with Stonehenge throughout his life, and something of Stonehenge's brooding presence shows in this reclining figure in the sculpture park at Snape Maltings in Suffolk.

'The figure in the rock': a body shaped headstone on Devenish Island, Lough Erne, near Enniskillen, Northern Ireland.

The tomb of Oscar Wilde at Père-Lachaise Cemetery, sculpted by Jacob Epstein.

played by ancient forms of human representation, noting at one time, after seeing a head of a XVIII Dynasty Egyptian woman in the Archaeological Museum in Florence,

> I would give everything, if I could get into my sculpture the same amount of humanity and seriousness; nobility and experience, acceptance of life, distinction, & aristocracy with absolutely no tricks no affectation no self-consciousness looking straight ahead, no movement, but more alive than a real person.[4]

The very practice of sculpture itself is largely an attempt to represent the human body, figuratively or metaphorically, and in this sense funerary art often elides both architecture and sculpture in a single dynamic or melting form. This can most obviously be seen in the extraordinary headstone shaped like a human body in the cemetery on Devenish Island, or in the tombstone for Oscar Wilde designed by Jacob Epstein in Père-Lachaise, where the angel appears about to fly free from the stone from which it has been carved. It can also be seen in the expressive statuary art of Italian cemeteries.

INSCRIPTION AND RELIEF

The headstone and the slabstone were restored to common use throughout Europe in the sixteenth and seventeenth centuries, as the population, and its churchyards, expanded. With the headstone came new forms of inscription and sculptural flourishes, especially among the wealthy. In turn these followed or created new lexicons of scriptural phrases, aphorisms and apologias,

The Cestius Pyramid in Rome, erected as a tomb for Caius Cestius, who died in 12 BC.

The rear wall of the Protestant Cemetery in Rome, incorporating the Aurelian city wall of AD 300. The Cestius Pyramid can be seen in the distant background.

The beautiful and peaceful British War Cemetery in Rome, close by the Protestant Cemetery.

icons, emblems and other kinds of engraved motifs.[5] These lexicons are central to the aesthetics of death and memorialization, and Rome is a good starting-point for exploring how this tradition developed.

In that dream-like city one can still find in almost perfect condition the Cestius Pyramid, erected as a tomb for Caius Cestius (died 12 BC), 27 metres high and faced in white marble, and inscribed with details of his life and testament. The pyramid was later incorporated into the Aurelian city wall in AD 300, which in turn became one of the walls of the Protestant Cemetery opened in the eighteenth century: another example of the way in which successive burial cultures tend to cluster around the same site. (The British War Cemetery in Rome is only 400 metres away.) The pyramid was adopted by the Romans from Egyptian funerary architecture, fashionable under the emperor Augustus, and which from time to time is rediscovered again as an appropriate style, as can be seen in London's Highgate Cemetery and in other European cemeteries of the nineteenth century.

Much more important though, for our understanding of the early Christian world, and of life in Rome, are the inscriptions and frescos that were found in the catacombs, some of which can still be seen at St Domitilla's and other catacombs, once again open to visitors.

Without these brief words and tiny images, our understanding of those distant times would be severely diminished, as the authors of one of the most recent guides to the catacombs have confirmed:

Fundamental for understanding the Christian communities of the ancient world and one of the greatest sources for the history and chronology of the Roman catacombs is the contribution of the Christian epigraphy that restored tens of thousands of inscriptions in Latin and Greek to us. The epigraphic formulary is gradually enriched: if initially there is only the name of the deceased on the tomb and sometimes the date of burial, already by the III century the inscriptions are enriched with specific elements and symbols, mentioning the pax obtained, the duration of the life of the deceased, more rarely the consular dating. During the second half of the III century and throughout the IV the references to the pax, to the agape and to the new life in heaven are increasingly frequent. Moreover, magical formulae make their appearance as do words of wishing, prayer, sorrow, mentions of married life, the family and work.[6]

Here we have confirmation of the idea that burial places and cemeteries also function as libraries of past lives, beliefs, and artefacts, able to be read again and again by succeeding generations. Like libraries, cemeteries are quiet, catalogued and annotated. Furthermore, they also embody that expression of 'longing' that Susan Stewart suggests accrues from the processes of miniaturization and the formation of collections (cemeteries accomplish both).[7] The symbiotic and at times displaced relationship between libraries and cemeteries, or at a singular level between books and graves, is developed in James E. Young's study of Holocaust memorials. Young writes that 'The Yizkor Bikher – memorial books – remembered both the lives and destruction of European Jewish communities according to the most ancient of Jewish memorial media: words on paper. For a murdered people without graves, without even corpses to inter, these memorial books often came to serve as symbolic tombstones.'[8]

Inscriptions are only part of the story: icons and images are also invaluable too, though some religions – notably Islam and Orthodox Judaism – expressly forbid the use of imagery in religious ritual and culture. Yet despite this, one of the best records of gravestone imagery is that to be found in Arnold Schwartzman's extensive and beautiful record of European Jewish gravestones, which demonstrates that the prohibition concerning images was not as widely observed as one might have expected it to have been.[9]

Schwartzman travelled over 100,000 miles throughout the 1970s and 1980s visiting Jewish cemeteries in more than ten European countries, photographing and in other ways recording this once profuse and rich tradition. He was mindful of the thoughts of the great Russian painter and Constructivist, El Lissitsky, who had also studied Russian synagogue paintings and tombstones, with their

fish hunted by birds; the fox carrying a bird in his mouth; birds carrying snakes in their beaks;

a bear climbing a tree in search of honey; and all entwined with acanthus plants that bloom and move on the walls of the wooden synagogue. Beyond the mask of four-legged animals and winged birds, there are the eyes of human beings. This is the most characteristic aspect of Jewish folk art.[10]

Here, then, is another connection between religious and ritual imagery, and the folkloric expressionism of painters such as Chagall, Pisarro and Modigliani, as they brought a new figurative energy to the abstractionist aesthetic of modernism from such ancient forms.

The gravestones photographed by Schwartzman are richly carved in relief with figures from an astonishing bestiary: lions, dragons, eagles, griffins, scorpions, lobsters, storks, wolves and mythological beasts that are half-lion, half-fish. There are also many fruits and flowers as well as skulls and skeletons. Sometimes these adornments were identical to the emblem on the house where the deceased had once lived, since many people lived without street numbers in houses often marked by a symbol. As Chaim Potok notes,

A man of learning would have an open book on his stone. A scribe would lie beneath a stone on which a parchment and a goosefeather would be depicted. Chains and a crown marked the grave of a goldsmith. Shears for a tailor; a violin or harp for a musician; a mortar and pestle for an apothecary; a lion and a sword for a physician; a candelabrum for a pious woman; a charity box for a philanthropist or collector of charities; a sun and moon for a Kabbalist; an eagle with a circumcision knife for a mohel (circumciser).[11]

Truly these cemeteries were profoundly expressive places of culture and representation, in which ordinary lives, trades and human characteristics, were recorded for posterity. Yet, as Potok chasteningly remarks, 'Virtually none of the cemeteries in these pages exists in a viable contemporary Jewish community. The sun-splashed Mediterranean world of Sephardi Jewry – gone. The austere and learned northern realm of Ashkenazi Jewry – gone. Of what value to us are graven images in sites from which the quotidian rhythms and vitality of Jewish life have been erased?'

This is a troubling question, but it surely should be said that it is better that we still have these memorials from the past, than not to have them. There always remains the possibility that these landscapes and icons can still act on the human imagination in profound and redemptive

The famous Jewish Cemetery in Prague, founded in the first half of the 15th century in the centre of what was then a Jewish town.

Beth Haim, the Portuguese–Jewish Cemetery at Ouderkerk, near Amsterdam. View of graves with ceremonial hall.

ways, as they did before in the work of Lissitsky, Chagall and others. One such cemetery that has played this role as a cultural icon is the Old Jewish Cemetery in Prague, sadly damaged by the floods of 2002, one of the most austere and affecting historic settings of any city in Europe. This cemetery was founded in the first half of the fifteenth century in the centre of what was then a Jewish town.[12] The oldest tombstone dates back to 1439 and the most recent to 1787, when further use of the old burial ground, in what had become a residential district, was banned by Joseph II. This tiny space contains some 12,000 tombstones. Since religious custom forbid the re-use of old graves, earth was piled up, layer on layer, to allow for new burials, to the extent that in some parts of

the cemetery as many as twelve burial layers were added, one on top of the other. As a result, clusters of headstones or stelae protrude at all angles, at times resembling natural rock formations. Once seen, it is impossible to forget this dense, claustrophobic, intense garden or outcrop of the dead.

Over time, the Prague headstones followed the aesthetic funerary fashions of the day, with the early headstones being made of small squares of sandstone, followed by more expensive imports of white and pink marble, after which even more elaborate grave monuments were erected, with headstones carved with pilasters, half-columns, gable-tops, with images and inscriptions, and then finally chest-tombs appeared over the graves of

Four different motifs from headstones at Beth Haim: the hourglass, the skull and crossbones, the chopped-down tree and the splayed hands through which the radiance of the divine flows.

some of the most eminent citizens, known by their Hebrew name of *ohel* or tent, though many people referred to it as a *Häuslech* or 'little house'. Many of the later headstones exhibit animals carved in relief representing various names or trades. During the nineteenth century the Old Jewish Cemetery became a source of inspiration to many painters, who saw it as a key element in a new kind of Romantic portrayal of landscape suffused with apprehensions of mortality, as Ruisdael's painting of two centuries earlier contained.

Less well known, though very much larger and equally affecting, is Beth Haim (the 'House of Life'), the Portuguese–Jewish cemetery at Ouderkerk, a small village on the River Amstel some twelve kilometres from Amsterdam. This was sketched by Ruisdael soon after it opened, the land having been bought for this purpose in 1614 by Sephardic Jews driven out of the Iberian Peninsula. The cemetery takes up several distinct areas, or separate hedged gardens, according to period, and is immediately adjacent to the Amstel (and consequently subject to flooding and rising ground water). There is still a landing stage for boats carrying coffins, close to the elegant brick ceremonial hall that fronts the river, and where prayers were and still are offered for the dead (the cemetery is still in use). It is estimated that there

A finely detailed Tree of Life on a headstone at Beth Haim.

There is even a carved image on one tombstone of Moses carrying the Ten Commandments, one of which, as we know, expressly forbids the use of graven images. Another headstone offers a magnificent Tree of Life. Beth Haim must have at times seemed very forlorn, remote from the city, waterlogged, and then after the calamitous events of the Holocaust, almost abandoned. Today, however, it is regaining a sense of serenity as restoration work proceeds. Even so, the elaborately carved marble tombs, with their lettering in Hebrew and even Ladino (a Judaeo-Spanish language), look somewhat mystical and esoteric when seen beside the prim Dutch houses and bridges against which they are usually viewed.

LIFE STORIES

Sarah Tarlow's study of headstones in cemeteries on the remote islands of Orkney attests to a wide variety of motifs, decorations and vanities being used to decorate the stones in the second half of the nineteenth century (before then any form of decoration was rare), including floral borders, rope borders, Romantic symbols of hearts and flowers and Christian symbols of angels, books, scrolls, doves and the familiar cipher IHS (a Latinized version of a Greek inscription relating to Jesus, Saviour of Men).[15] Carvings of boats or anchors often adorned the gravestones of sailors and fishermen. This is also true in many other cemeteries serving sea-going communities, such as Southwold in Suffolk, for example, where the anchor is a common motif on a number of the graves, or in Paul, near Mousehole in Cornwall, where the headstone of one Master Mariner is inscribed

are nearly 30,000 graves, though very few of the older ones are still visible or marked. In fact, the oldest part of the cemetery today looks like a bucolic landscape with undulating pastures and woodland.[13]

The emblem of the skull and crossbones is to be found almost everywhere in the cemetery, in the ceremonial hall, and on many of the gravestones. The second most common motif is a pair of splayed hands touching the fingertips, representing the hands of the priest, through whose openings 'the blessed Shekhinah (radiance of God) streams down upon the congregants'.[14]

with lines from Tennyson's valedictory poem 'Crossing the Bar':

I hope to see my pilot face to face
When I have crossed the bar.

A number of gravestone inscriptions also tell a poignant local story. In Gorleston Cemetery near Great Yarmouth is to be found the grave of William Adams, the 'Human Fish of Gorleston', widely known along the East Coast of England for his remarkable feats as a swimmer and life-saver. His headstone reads:

In loving memory of Wm Adams who saved 140 lives from drowning. Died Oct 14th 1913. Also his wife Ellen Elizabeth Adams d. Feb 25th 1949 Aged 72. Also their son Graham Adams, prisoner of war in Turkey Aged 19.

In a churchyard in Brighton can be found the headstone with this inscription:

Motif of an anchor firmly embedded on the shore, on a gravestone at Southwold, a fishing village in Suffolk.

In Memory of
PHŒBE HESSEL
who was born at Stepney in the Year 1713
She served for many Years
as a private Soldier in the 5th Regt of foot
in different parts of Europe
and in the Year 1745 fought under the command
of the DUKE OF CUMBERLAND
at the Battle of Fontenoy
where she received a Bayonet wound in her Arm
Her long life which commenced in the time of
QUEEN ANNE
extended to the reign of
GEORGE IV
by whose munificence she received support
and comfort in her latter Years
she died at Brighton where she had long resided
December twelfth 1821 Aged 108 Years

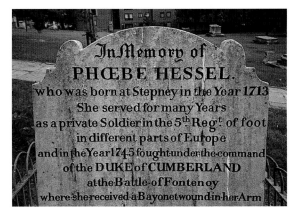

Detail of the headstone of Phoebe Hessel, whose extraordinary life is remembered in a churchyard in Brighton, Sussex.

Here are whole lives and epochs in the space of a few carved letters.[16] Few headstones, though, can tell such a devastating a story of loss as that in Kilchattan Cemetery on Colonsay off Western Scotland, a cemetery already mentioned:

To the memory of Richard Prior
Master Gunner R.N.
H.M.S. King Edward VII
Killed off Colonsay
eighteenth September 1912

Also his brothers
Charles, killed in Belgium
23 December 1914

Archibald, killed at Arras
3rd May 1917

Herbert, killed at sea
30th October 1918

And their cousins

James, killed at sea
22nd September 1914

Harry, killed on the Somme
7th October 1916 [17]

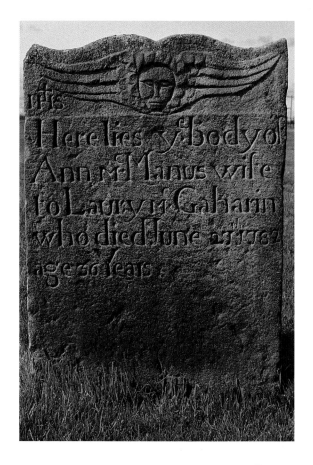

According to Tarlow, whilst religious imagery and wording still remained common in Orkney in the twentieth century, the gravestones more frequently began to reflect the emotional world of marriage and inseparability, with an increasing number of double graves commemorating life-long partnerships and epitaphs expressing either a deep sense of loss or the hope of eventual reunion, and sometimes both. Tarlow's study is particularly good on noting how the design and wording of gravestones and epitaphs reflected social and cultural changes in attitudes towards religion and the nature of personal love and affection. She also notes how increased wealth and the emotional investment in these double

Two headstones on Devenish Island, Lough Erne, movingly inscribed, with carved motifs.

graves, led to the importing of stone and marble from elsewhere, in preference to using the sandstone or limestone quarried locally, thus changing the look of the cemetery dramatically.

The modern preference for cremation, and now increasingly for 'natural burial', will bring to an end this long tradition of social narrative, poignant, despairing, tragic as it may often have seemed. This point is made forcefully by Douglas Davies and Alastair Shaw in the conclusions to their survey of British attitudes to death and burial, when they write that, 'we would anticipate that future historians might see some crematoria as centres where social identities were annihilated just as much as they were places where human bodies were removed from view.'[18] This is perhaps too harsh: the decline of meaningful inscriptions on gravestones probably started before cremation gained the upper hand, and it is the inscriptions which provided the social history more than the graves themselves. Nevertheless, it is difficult to refute the notion that modern funerary practices are leaving less and less of a historical trace within the wider social culture.

INSCRIPTION IN THE CITY

Today the inscriptions to be found in cemeteries are less effusive, and often minimal; the narrative work of the cemetery seems to be coming to an end. This is also happening in other, but still related, spheres of public life. The loss of inscription in the modern city was the theme of a project undertaken in The Hague in the 1990s, which resulted in a commission to the Scottish artist and landscape designer Ian Hamilton Finlay, undertaking two public designs celebrating the city's principal water source, the Haagse Beek, both of which involved elegant carved inscriptions, including the by now familiar 'Et in Arcadia ego'. The Dutch landscape historian Erik de Jong, in his essay on the project, stated that the commission itself grew out of a growing despair at the de-historicizing of the city through the displacement of meaningful public inscription by advertising signs and commercial lettering, and his thoughts deserve quoting at length:

The city scene also confronts us with texts of another sort that we hardly seem to pay heed to any more, given the pressure of modern urban life. In the Hague, for instance, there is the text of the first article of the Dutch Constitution that adorns the new building of the Second chamber of the Dutch Parliament. Or there is the simple name, 'SPINOZA', carved in red granite on the plinth that supports the effigy of the philosopher Baruch de Spinoza, on the Paviljoensgracht. Or the text 'EENZAAM MAAR NIET ALLEEN' ('lonely but not alone'), also carved in granite, by the sculptor Charlotte van Pallandt, as part of the monument for Queen Wilhelmina. These texts make up a whole with the plinth on which they are carved, or else they form an integral relation with the architectural composition they are part of. They are not a subordinate caption or subtitle; in symbiosis with the sculpture and the architecture, they convey an intrinsic message. Word and image combined mean that the raw materials of stone and bronze, as it were, speak to us. They are not the product of a culture of speed and transience; they originate in a will to endure.

Their material leaves us in no doubt about this: stone, bronze, marble or granite. Permanence, endurance also mean tradition. The letters are mostly done in Roman capitals, a script that we find in the architecture and sculpture of Roman times. In material and visual guise, inscriptions give form to what monuments were once intended to be – memorials. But the Latin word 'monere' conveys a double message. Besides 'commemorate' and 'remember' it also means to 'warn'.[19]

The inscriptions to be found in cemeteries, on memorials, and on memorializing buildings, still have an important part to play in the public culture of the historic city. Yet it is now a commonplace that the craft of lettering is today very poor indeed. Even worse is the occasional complete misunderstanding of the very tradition of the form itself. This emerged in the debate in the architectural press that surrounded the opening of the Metropolitan Police Memorial Garden in Hendon, north-west London, in October 2000, designed to commemorate the lives of those police officers who had died in the course

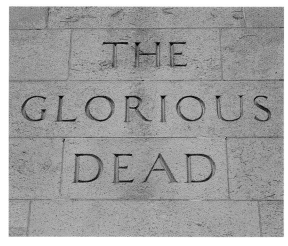

The famous inscription on the Cenotaph in London, commemorating the dead of two World Wars.

Commemorative stone and inscription marking a departure point of the D-Day Landings in June 1944.

Inscription on the pyramid tomb of Cestius.

of duty. While there was widespread approval for the garden design, there was also criticism of the lettering on the memorial stone, which rather than being carved, was made up of letters embossed in gold, which seemed singularly inappropriate to the task the letters had to do.[20] The reason for the carving or engraving of letters in memorial inscription is precisely because such letters embody a sense of absence, of hollowness, of something taken away.

Other forms of representation are beginning to

Detail of a landscape designed by Ian Hamilton Finlay in Hyde Park, London, near the Serpentine Gallery. Inscription is a central feature of Finlay's landscape designs.

Monument to Nurse Edith Cavell, shot by the Germans during the First World War as a spy. The inscriptions still have a resonance amid the noise and traffic of London's West End.

hold sway. In the twentieth century the popularity of photography offered an opportunity not only to use words or icons to represent the departed, but indeed provide a realistic image of that person taken in the fullness of life. The inclusion of photographs on headstones, either glazed, ceramicized or framed in glass, is, however, principally to be found in Catholic or southern European cemeteries, and is rarely seen in northern Europe (though this is now changing as a result of immigration). This is a real cultural boundary line in funerary culture, and certainly derives in part from the Protestant suspicion of iconography (equally shared in this instance with Jewish and Muslim cultures).[21]

There is a similar disapproval of taking photographs at funerals, even though this is one of the most important ritual settings of family life, when close and distant relatives and friends are brought together. Photography for christenings, birthdays and marriage celebrations is today almost *de rigueur*. But at a funeral, the appearance of a camera would be regarded as an unwarranted intrusion. The funeral is in some ways a private event in a public setting, whereas those other celebratory events are generally private events in private settings. Exceptions to this taboo are royal and show-business funerals, where celebrity and fame override the muted and mutable nature of the occasion. Even so, a number of cultural critics, including Roland Barthes, John Berger and Susan Sontag, often in reference to each other, have all drawn attention to the close relationship between the photograph – a moment frozen in time – and the moment of death, and have argued that it is photography of all cultural forms that is most responsive to the existential trauma of lost time and irrecoverable memory.

Nevertheless, the world wide web is also increasingly being used as an electronic memorial garden, where people can post inscriptions, biographies and photographs of loved ones. There are now a number of such sites. One of them, established in 1994 by Lindsay Marshall, a lecturer in computer science at the University of Newcastle upon Tyne, started out as a reference guide to published obituaries, but found that it was being sent new obituaries by the loved ones of those not famous enough to warrant a media obituary. So he established a Virtual Memorial Garden as a 'quiet place on the Net, if that does not sound too absurd'[22].

NAMING THE WORLD

It is no coincidence that so much poetry and prose in English literature of the past two centuries has been devoted to a celebration of nature and landscape, and our visual and mental senses have to a large extent been shaped and interpreted through such verbal constructs, largely of a poetic or epiphenomenal kind. No one has understood this better than the French philosopher Gaston Bachelard, particularly in his work on the Poetics of Space, where he explores the way in which the human psyche makes sense of the visual world, and at moments of heightened experience (as one often feels in the presence of the landscapes of the dead) or rapture, the duality of subject and object becomes 'unceasingly active in its inversions'.[23] We become the landscape and the landscape becomes us. For Bachelard, 'everything specifically human in man is *logos*. One would not be able to meditate in a zone that preceded language.' [24] We poeticize our feelings because we ourselves have been structured by poetry.

From this point of view, proper names are as important as generic typologies. 'Place names are among the things that link men most intimately with their territory', the English geographer Edward Relph has written.[25] The naming of roads, fields, hills, copses – right down even the smallest detail of the landscape – is a form of familiarization and human connectedness. Anyone who has read Flora Thompson's haunting trilogy, *Lark Rise to Candleford*, will recall that in the series of small Oxford villages where she grew up at the end of the nineteenth century, every field, copse, pond and even hedge possessed its own name; even the parts of some fields were named separately. The naming of the world is, in effect, the poetry of the world.

A reason why churchyards or cemeteries often appear to exert such an active presence is that they are full of names, biographical details, icons and epitaphs, further endorsing this notion that they truly do function as libraries in stone. The loss of inscription in modern urban architecture and design is part of the loss of identity and meaning. This is why Ian Hamilton Finlay's work has been so influential in modern landscape design, since it reclaims for inscription a central role in design and place-making. I often recall a conversation I once had with a planner from Stockholm City Council, during which we discussed what typologies of green open space were used in that city, and how topographers and planners distinguished wanted from unwanted open space there. He told me that if local people had a name for a piece of ground, it always signified that they had incorporated it into their affections or personal geographical schemas; those spaces that remained un-named usually indicated indifference or dislike.

Thus there is also a poetic impulse at work in the description and perception of landscape, the same kind of finely judged association and combination of forms, colours, species, mineral types, history and proper names that one finds in poetry. The more detailed – and at the same time precise – vocabulary one is able to use, the better are places and emotions conjured into being. Yet even if we steel ourselves against the temptation to project our inner psychological states onto the natural world, as so many poets have done, it would be hard to read the following without feeling the effects of these deep associations between language and emotion, particularly since they confront loss within the larger currents of human and natural change:

Divers have located the wreck of a second world war destroyer, HMS *Exmouth*, that was torpedoed and sunk with all hands off Wick in Caithness. The discovery is the result of a three-year underwater quest backed by the Ministry of Defence. A plaque of remembrance was placed on the wreck by the divers, and there are moves to have it declared a war grave.

'The wreck has become an underwater garden of stunning beauty, covered with bright hydroids, anemones and starfish,' said one of the divers, Alex Deas. 'I have never seen so much sea life on any other wreck in the world. It is most fitting the site has been transformed from one of death and destruction to a scene of tranquillity and life.'[26]

The very form of writing here, with its evocatory poetics, is a good example of what the theologian and sociologist Douglas J. Davies has referred to as 'words against death'.[27] By this he means the way in which nearly all cultures use liturgy, prayers, songs, blessings, invocations, eulogies, orations, poems and stories as a form of ritual language that allows death to be positioned, ordered and ultimately accepted. Strong echoes of such invocations are often to be found inscribed on park benches, or on plaques attached to seating erected at particular outlooks or scenic views, usually favourite landscapes or places associated with particular times of happiness, and often taking the form of memorial inscriptions, with dates of birth and death, along with short dedications or evocations of happy times gone by. The growing popularity of this form of landscape memorialization is not without its critics. In February 2002 a national newspaper in Britain reported that walkers have started complaining about the high number of memorial benches along the Pembrokeshire coastal footpath in West Wales, because 'so many reminders of dead people make them feel mournful'.[28]

THE CULT OF THE PANTHEON

The socially aggrandizing role of the urban cemetery, as a place with the potential to become a new elite setting, gained credence as an idea in the eighteenth century. Particular cemeteries became fashionable places in which to be buried, a means of accumulating status and prestige in bourgeois circles. When the radical M. Molé drew up the first great plan for the secularization of cemeteries in 1776, he argued that 'Ranks and distinctions will be preserved, and the hope of being laid to rest in the company of illustrious and useful men will exalt genius, promote patriotism, and glorify the virtues.'[29] This was an early outing for the view that the cemetery could become a moral force (as well as a religious force) in society. The process was taken to its extreme conclusion after the French Revolution, when the new administration decided to convert the great domed and porticoed building', completed under Louis XV in Paris, into a final resting place of the great. The Panthéon, as we know it today, was opened in 1791. Above the columns inscribed in gold on the architrave are the words 'Aux Grands Hommes La Patrie Reconnaissante'. A close look at the photograph of the building reveals that the original church windows were filled in, to give its interior greater solemnity.

The original Pantheon is to be found in Rome, and stands on the Piazza della Rotonda. The word *pantheon* implied that it was a temple dedicated to

The Pantheon in Rome, built AD 118–25 and a model for many subsequent forms of commemorative architecture: the famous oculus at the apex of the dome lights the whole building.

Wall fresco, the Pantheon, Rome.

The Panthéon in Paris, originally a church, but adapted as a final resting place for the Grands Hommes of France. The church windows were filled in to create a more sombre atmosphere.

all the gods, and its great dome a representation of the unity of the universe. Built in AD 118–25, the building still stands largely unchanged, nearly 2,000 years later, as a testament to Roman architecture and grandiloquence: its dome remained the largest ever constructed until the twentieth century. The breathtaking originality and boldness of the design influenced sacred and civic architecture ever after:

Hadrian's Pantheon is one of the grand architectural creations of all time: original, utterly bold, many-layered in associations and meanings, the container of a kind of immanent universality. It speaks of a wider world than that of imperial Rome, and has left its stamp upon architecture more than any other building. Its message, compounded of mystery and fact, of stasis and mutability, of earth and that above, pulses through the architecture of western man.[30]

A number of prominent Italian religious, political and artistic figures are entombed here, including the artist Raphael, and the Italian kings Victor Emmanuel II and Umberto I.

The Panthéon in Paris was intended to celebrate Republican virtues and heroes, though their stay was subject to increasingly political fluctuations in their reputations, as different factions gained control of the revolutionary process. The first occupant of the Panthéon, the Comte de Mirabeau, was interred inside the great dome on 4 April 1791, but when it was discovered that he previously had secret dealings with the King , his body was disinterred and taken elsewhere; the same happened to the second occupant, Jean-Paul Marat, whose body was interred in the Panthéon on 21 September 1791, and dug up and taken out less than a year later.[31] In fact, the long history of post-Revolutionary Paris, up to the present day, is also a history of the political uses of burial places as emblematic landscapes of the city: the 504 bodies of citizens who had died in the 1830 July Revolution, being buried beneath the Bastille column, while those of the Communards of 1870 who had been executed against the cemetery wall of Père-Lachaise, turned this Mur des Fédéres into a gathering-place and shrine of the Paris Left.

In 1818 cemetery officials had the twelfth-century remains of Héloise and Abélard dug up and re-interred in Père-Lachaise, along with the remains of La Fontaine and Molière. Since then, Père-Lachaise has become a cultural gazetteer of French, European and even North American culture. The jazz trumpeter Mezz Mezzrow lies only 50 metres from Maria Callas, Richard Wright almost next to Isadora Duncan; Gertrude Stein is only two blocks down from Oscar Wilde, while Jim Morrison is just across the street from Francis Poulenc. There is also a small Jewish quarter where one of the Rothschilds, Singer (a sewing-machine millionaire) and Camille Pissarro lie along the same small street. Some of the most emblematic figures of European and American culture are now to be found here, in the space of a single garden, itself acting as some great post-Enlightenment theatre of memory.

The talismanic quality of the remains of significant individuals – Christian saints, warring kings, political revolutionaries, film stars, folk heroes – seems to be an enduring feature of many societies and cultures. The most famous mausoleum of the twentieth century, that containing Lenin's embalmed body in Moscow's Red Square, paradoxically marks the death of a man whose political beliefs one might have thought demanded something rather more self-effacing. In fact it was conceived by its designer, Anastas Schusov, as being worthy of 'some great primitive chieftain on the Mongolian Steppes'.[32] Edwin Heathcote queries why the mausoleum 'is curiously absent from the many histories of modern architecture, though it is one of the most powerful buildings of the century and one of the most important works in defining a modern architecture of death'.[33] He further notes that 'the exploration of ideas of death, or more precisely, immortality, proved to be a fundamental cornerstone of Revolutionary art and literature'.[34] It is likely that a modern distaste for forms of heroic monumentalism are based on the often self-destructive illusions of twentieth-century political utopianism.

Even today, burials in the Panthéon are subject to various kinds of political chicanery: in 1989 President Mitterrand decided against the interment there of the remains of Marie Curie (she would have been the first woman to be thus honoured) as he did not want to be seen making a concession to feminism at that particular time. She finally secured a place there in 1995. In Britain something of this role is played by Westminster Abbey, where the remains of many of Britain's great poets and writers are now buried, though, on occasions, not without controversy. The Abbey refused to accept the body of Lord Byron, for example, on the grounds of his irreli-ous beliefs and conduct.[35] Others have had to wait a long time before opinion changed in their favour: Oscar Wilde, who died in 1900, was not finally memori-alized until 1995; D. H. Lawrence, who died in 1930, was admitted in 1985; while Dylan Thomas only had to wait 29 years after his death in 1953 before a plaque was mounted there.[36]

At one time there were plans to extend this hallowed national geography beyond the walls of Westminster Abbey. When the Swedish-born architect William Chambers arrived in London in 1751, the year in which Frederick, Prince of Wales, had suddenly died, he proposed building a mausoleum in the gardens of the Prince's palace at Kew. Later on, he went on to propose the erection of the tombs of British heroes along the Bayswater Road.[37] In Virginia, the Arlington National Cemetery plays something of a similar role, with many of the American nation's most illustrious war veterans buried there, along with presidents (William Howard Taft and John. F. Kennedy), a number of Supreme Court Justices, many famous explorers and literary figures, along with honoured members of minority groups. The Assistens Cemetery in Copenhagen, which began as a paupers' cemetery (the name derives from the Danish compound *assistancekirkegård* which means 'relief cemetery'), over time became the most desirable place to be buried in the city. Established in 1760 on a bleak piece of land outside the city, within four decades it was the favoured resting place for Copenhagen's bourgeoisie. Today you will find there the graves of Søren Kierkegaard, Hans Christian Andersen, Niels Bohr, Ben Webster and others.

The Protestant Cemetery in Rome is another burial place that has become a cult site. Close to the Cestius Pyramid is what is now regarded as the 'old cemetery' (*parte antica*), where Keats is buried, but which today is landscaped as a small park, where people sit and read. The main cemetery area, which you confront when the gate-keeper answers your ring at the doorbell, is much more formal and consists of rows of gravestones, headstones and marble statuary in rising terrace walks, all facing you as you enter

through the large portal, on which is engraved *RESVRRECTVRIS*. It is breathtakingly beautiful in the dappled sunlight, with hundreds of cypresses, pines, palm trees and even laburnum bushes canopying the rows of tombs. When Keats was told by his friend Joseph Severn that a burial plot had been secured for him, the dying poet replied that he 'already felt the flowers growing over him'.

This is another quintessentially European setting, in which there are imposing national communal tombs and mausoleums for various Swedes, Danes, Germans, English, Greek and Russian Orthodox citizens, whose governments or embassies have provided grave space for nationals who have died in Rome and had nobody to take responsibility for their burial. There are many American writers and artists who moved to Europe at the turn of the century, and many who have moved since. The American Beat poet Gregory Corso was buried in the cemetery in 2001, next to Shelley, though he only managed this by lying about his religion, apparently. The Italian Marxist Antonio Gramsci is also

The grave of the Italian communist and intellectual Antonio Gramsci in the Protestant Cemetery in Rome.

here. Within this walled cemetery, everything seems calm and peaceful, and it is beautifully maintained. It is hard to disagree with Christopher Woodward, who is convinced that 'This is the most beautiful cemetery on earth'.[38]

Not everybody is persuaded by the temptation to be buried in a cemetery that has acquired such status. The acerbic Austrian writer Thomas Bernhard wrote scathingly of this culture: 'To be an artist in Austria is a vile and false road of state opportunities, a road paved with grants and prizes and wallpapered with orders and decorations and ending in a mausoleum in the Central Cemetery.'[39] In Australia, a proposal to create a national cemetery in Canberra by ex-huming the remains of the famous from elsewhere in Australia to re-inter them all in one prestige cemetery was regarded as an act of cultural opportunism.[40] This was particularly the case when it was found out that several of those whose remains they wished to move – a wartime Labour Prime Minister, Ben Chifley, and an Aboriginal land rights activist, Eddie Mabo – were lying in graves that until then no one had bothered to tend or maintain for some years.

In like manner, the nationalist and counter-nationalist movements in Eire and Northern Ireland have always made a great play of the political funeral and the iconic geography of cemeteries in the larger cities. On 14 October 2001 the remains of ten Irish volunteers who took part in nationalist struggles following the Easter Rising of 1916 and were executed in Mountjoy Prison between 1920 and 1921 were given a state funeral followed by an oration by the Taoiseach (Prime Minister). The bodies were reburied in Glasnevin Cemetery with full military honours. In Northern Ireland during the violent period of nationalist and counter-nationalist unrest from the late 1960s onwards, matters of funeral practices, burial sites and associated rituals became deeply emblematic of wider political and symbolic forms of social organization.

In addition to the sensitive issues of political geography, there have been significant 'political uses of the dead' in Northern Ireland during this time, in which more than 2,500 people had already lost their lives by the time Lindsay Prior's study was published in 1989. In Prior's words, 'The worship of the political dead in particular, involving as it does marches and assemblies of large numbers of people, comes close to forming the elements of a civil religion.'[41] In the land-scape of Belfast itself, churches, cemeteries, memorial halls, public monuments, processional routes, all combine to give the city a highly partisan geography and ambience. During the worst of the Troubles, to be in the wrong place at the wrong time – and for some people, even in the wrong cemetery at the wrong time – could prove fatal.

Within both Protestant and Catholic cemeteries, elements of a 'Pantheon culture' are strongly represented, with the graves of notable political and religious militants occupying a place of honour, while providing the elements of a sacrosanct geography. These cemeteries also function as monumental libraries and texts of recent history, with names, dates, occupations, beliefs and manner of death, providing a material narrative and history of the city's turbulent and violent history. The power of these places to evoke strong feelings too often comes into play following the funeral of someone killed in political or religious conflict, as has been seen in Northern Ireland, but also in Israel and Palestine even more intensely in recent years, where funerals become occasions for effusive political emotions and calls for revenge, following which more killings occur, more funerals, and so the cycle goes on. In such scenarios, the cemetery becomes an amplifying chamber for those voices that conflate the call for justice with the call for revenge. The grave site has always acted both as a pulpit and a political platform.

THE CEMETERY AS GALLERY

More than one writer has observed that Père-Lachaise remains the largest sculpture gallery in the world, with over 100,000 memorials gathered in one place, reflecting many different periods and styles of sculpture: classical, monumental, Baroque, Expressionist, among others.[42] The growing preference for figurative sculpture reflected the secularization of funerary art and culture. In Britain at the time of the growing admiration for Père-Lachaise in the mid-nineteenth century, there was an equally strong religious reaction to this promiscuity of styles and symbols, many of them perceived to be either pagan or irreligious. The High Church architect and ideologue Pugin attacked in no uncertain terms the preference for 'urns, broken pillars, extinguished lamps, inverted torches and sarcophagi (rather than) recumbent effigies, angels, and emblems of mercy and redemption'.[43] One early nineteenth-century architect who was intrigued by the potential overlap between gallery and mausoleum was John Soane. His extra-ordinary building for the Dulwich Picture Gallery,

The tomb of the English architect John Soane in Old St Pancras churchyard in London. His design for his own family tomb is said to have inspired the later design of the famous red telephone box.

started in 1811 and completed only after several years as a result of financial problems, also houses a mausoleum for the bodies of Sir Francis Bourgeois, and his close friends Mr and Mrs Desanfans.[44] In fact Soane had some years before designed a domestic mausoleum, for Noel Desenfans, built in a stable yard in a terraced street in London in 1807. Soane's own extra-ordinary house at 13 Lincoln's Inn Fields in London is home to many funerary artefacts from the ancient world. His own design for the Soane family tomb in Old St Giles's burial ground at St Pancras, capped by a distinctive shallow dome, became the inspiration for Sir Giles Gilbert Scott's K2 red telephone box, which itself became an iconic feature of the British urban and rural landscape.

Other ecclesiastics attacked anything to do with Egyptian or Roman funerary forms and symbols. Not surprisingly, the strongest criticism was directed at 'the studied and elaborate representation of the naked human figure'.[45] The cult of representing the agony of death

Veiled woman on the Tomba Levi (1825) at La Certosa, Bologna, carved by Giovanni Putti.

Levi (1825) in the Main Cloister, the architect of which was Liugi Marchesini, and the sculptures by Giovanni Putti. This statue is one of four around the tomb, made up of two women (one representing Faith, the other Commerce), along with two putti (one mourning and the other praying). Another typical, but equally fine and mournful woman can be found draped on the Tomba Montanari (1891) designed by architect Attilio Muggia, with sculptures by Diego Sarti. The deep foldings of the clothes and the heavy hair, the languid and tender pose of the body are typical features of what is known as the Italian

and parting through the languid, eroticized, figure of a female nude, or of a naked couple entwined in love-making, reached its apotheosis in a number of the sculptures in the Staglieno Cemetery in Genoa, Italy.[46] Though not of this kind, many of the figurative statues in La Certosa, Bologna, mentioned earlier, are humanist rather than Christian, and express tenderness and loss rather than Christian piety or hopes for meeting in the next world.

Among the most well known of these sculptures at La Certosa is the exquisitely sculpted veiled woman, a detail of the imposing Tomba

Figure of a woman in mourning on the Tomba Montanari (1891) at La Certosa, carved by Diego Sarti.

The most beloved tomb at La Certosa, the Tomba Frassetto (1950), carved by Farpi Vignoli.

Detail of sculpture by Farpi Vignoli, of the Tomba Gnudi (1951) at La Certosa. Ennio Gnudi was a leader of a railway workers' union.

Liberty style. Another much visited and affecting sculpture is that of the Tomb Beretta, representing a small girl asleep in an armchair, draped in a heavy blanket. It was sculpted by Carlo Monari, another well-known sculptor in nineteenth-century Bologna.

In the twentieth century, two of the most famous and genuinely wonderful works of art are by Farpi Vignoli. The first is the Tomba Frassetto (1950), admired and famous throughout Italy, portraying Fabio Frassetto, an academic anthropologist, and his son, Flavio, killed in the Second World War, lying side by side, and gazing into each other's eyes with a searching familial tenderness. The father is dressed in his academic gown, the son in an army greatcoat. In reality, the father died before the son, but in this strange meeting they are reunited again. It is deeply affecting. The other is the Tomba Gnudi (1951), an ornate sarcophagus erected over the grave of

Ennio Gnudi, a leader of one of the railway workers' unions. The tomb consists of a heavy coffin being carried by the dead man's fellow workers, whose 'Guide in the labour struggle' he was, according to the inscription on the tomb. Both have a solidity and an emotional power equal to the great sculptures of the secular world beyond.

In a more abstract style, there is the fine Monument to the Pilots Fallen in Peace and War (1983) by Marco Marchesini, commissioned by the Bologna Air Force Association. The bronze sculpture stands on a travertine base and symbolizes flight in a controlled, expressive style,

Monument (1983) to the pilots killed in peace and war. Designed by Marco Marchesini, for La Certosa.

doubtlessly influenced by Italian Futurism (which had a serious preoccupation with the dynamics of powered flight). La Certosa is full of historical interest, including much fine nineteenth-century neo-classical statuary, a large First World War neo-classical memorial in the brutally nationalist style promoted by Mussolini, as well as a haunting memorial to the murdered partisans of the Second World War.

By contrast, most British cemeteries seem more sober and conventional in their statuary. Kensal Green Cemetery in London possesses a very large number of examples of Victorian statuary, a number of them by the same sculptor, E. M. Lander, one of several mason–sculptors who set up in London specifically to service the growing demand for funerary art, and whose company is still in operation, just outside the gates of the cemetery.[47] One of the finest sculpted monuments is that designed by Geoffrey Sykes for the painter William Mulready (1786–1863), in which the painter is shown lying serenely on a woven rush mattress beneath a canopy held up by six columns, all finely detailed. Around the base of the tomb are incised representations of some of Mulready's paintings and drawings. The cemetery is full of classically draped figures of women in mourning, of tombs decorated with military insignia, of broken columns and urns on pedestals, though sadly many of them have been vandalized or have had parts stolen. The most ornate tombs and sculptures adorn the graves of minor royalty, military men, diplomats and, surprisingly or not, artists and sculptors themselves. For an artist to be a member of the Royal Academy in the nineteenth century was fully to belong to the political and cultural establishment. If one really seeks to inhabit the Victorian consciousness, in the fullness of its foreboding and melancholy, then a winter's afternoon spent wandering around Kensal Green when the cloud cover is particularly low is as near as one can get to travelling back to that era.

The growing popularity of figurative sculpture within the cemetery largely comes to a halt around the time of the First World War, after which there is a general return to formalism and sobriety. One exception, of course, is with regard to war memorials, where figurative sculpture plays a very important part, especially in Britain,

Sculpture by Charles Sergeant Jagger at the war memorial at Hyde Park Corner, London.

where religious iconography has always been much weaker. Nearly every British city has at least one war memorial with a figurative sculpture, a number of them by Charles Sergeant Jagger, who produced the most memorable of them. While Jagger's sculptured soldiers are bowed beneath the weight of their greatcoats, weapons, backpacks and ammunition, elsewhere the iconic role played by the sculpted figure of the valiant soldier served other purposes. In Australia, according to K. I. Inglis, the lithe and proudly masculine figures which adorned some of the First World War memorials were also seen to attest to what one historian described as 'the supreme test for fitness to exist'.[48] The war was seen as representing a Darwinian struggle between nations, in which the Australian soldier acquitted his new country with pride. The war memorial thus became an important element in the culture of nation-building.

As figurative sculpture declined in the cemetery, it re-emerged in the sculpture park or sculpture garden, a secular version of the memorial landscape or garden. Two of the most famous, Vigeland Park in Oslo (developed between 1916 and 1930), and Millesgården (developed between 1908 and 1936) in Stockholm, were being established at much the same time. Vigeland Park has 194 sculptures containing more than 600 individual figures, most life-size, representing the cycle of life from birth to death, all sculpted by Gustav Vigeland (1869–1943). The focal point of the sculpture park is The Monolith, consisting of a raised podium with steps on all sides, down which 36 groups of granite sculptures are arranged in 12 radial rows. At the centre of the podium is a giant columnar sculpture, 17 metres high, and consisting of 121 human figures of all

Sculptures by Gustav Vigeland in Vigeland Park, Oslo, devoted to the human form through all the different ages of man.

Detail of the huge monolith sculpture that dominates Vigeland Park, a tower of 121 human figures piled on top of each other, eerily prescient of images that were to emerge later in the 20th century.

ages, piled on top of each other in prone and lifeless positions, eerily anticipating the images of piled bodies photographed at the time of the liberation of the concentration camps at the end of the Second World War. Vigeland Park provides an extraordinary setting for the sculptural evocation of the brevity and cycle of human life, just as the cumulative effect of the sculptures in a nineteenth-century cemetery, such as La Certosa, marked the same journey.

The sculpture gardens and terraces created by Carl Milles in Stockholm combine works by the sculptor himself, alongside replicas of ancient classical fragments and architectural pieces and details from ruins. They also, significantly, contain the remains of both Milles and his wife Olga, interred in the small Christian chapel to be found on the 'Little Austria' terrace. Many of the columns at Millesgården, a feature of the south-facing terraces, come from a variety of buildings, such as the old Stockholm Opera House.

The uppermost terrace at Millesgården in Stockholm, the home not only of Carl Milles's better-known works, but also the burial place of the artist and his wife.

Remains of the gardens at Hadrian's Villa near Tivoli, Italy, dating back to the pre-Christian era, and influential on 19th- and 20th-century landscape and memorial culture.

Carved water feature at Millesgården, reflecting the sky and clouds, but shaped like a sarcophagus.

The combination of sculptures, ponds, fountains, pergolas and colonnades is strongly reminiscent of such gardens as might be found at Hadrian's Villa near Tivoli in Italy, dating back to a pre-Christian era. The mood is one of antiquity, especially on the Upper Terrace, and lost civilizations. Milles himself collected a large number of ancient sculptures, including Greek and Roman marbles, and these are now exhibited in their own museum at the garden.

As the gallery moved out into the open air, certain modernists at the same time declared that traditional galleries had become cemeteries themselves – for art. This was a view entertained by the German cultural critic Theodor Adorno, who in one of his essays wrote that

> The German word *museal* (museum-like) has unpleasant overtones. It describes objects to which the observer no longer has a vital relationship and which are in the process of dying.

They owe their preservation more to historical respect than to the needs of the present. Museum and mausoleum are connected by more than phonetic association. Museums are the family sepulchres of works of art.[49]

In the twentieth century many figurative and sculptural arts increasingly moved out of the gallery and into the landscape, sometimes becoming the landscape itself. This can be seen in the rise of the sculpture park, or in new forms of public memorials, such as in Rachel Whiteread's seminal sculpture 'House', in the proliferation of public art programmes, and even land art. This aestheticization of the public landscape at times threatens to overwhelm or displace the funerary and ritualistic settings for memory and reconciliation. In the nineteenth century the cemetery was the most conscious public expression of an expressive architecture: landscape and sculpture that addressed the perennial issue of human mutability. Today the cemetery's aesthetic function has become almost non-existent, or invisible. An interesting exception to this trend is to be found in African–American communities in the USA, where some graves are still decorated as shrines, using a miscellany of natural and found objects such as shells, plant pots, hanging hub-caps, statuary, and household items.[50]

HOPE IN RUINS

The Picturesque tradition, though neo-Classical in its inspiration, also embodied Gothic elements, such as a taste for follies and ruins, grottoes and overgrown burial grounds. Ruins, like skeletons,

are, as Joseph Koerner has remarked, emblematic of a lost whole, whether it is a building, a body or an organic society. They represent the passage of time, decay and absence as much as physical presence: roofless and windowless creaking structures are about worlds and lives through which the winds now blow. Thus there is something doubly affecting and disturbing about a derelict or abandoned cemetery, as it becomes a ruin of a ruin.

In a letter to *The Times* published on 15 August 1944, T. S. Eliot, John Maynard Keynes and a number of other influential writers and intellectuals proposed that the ruins of a number of bombed churches should be retained as war memorials, and indeed a book was published with proposals and architectural drawings showing how this could be done.[51] Ruins retain the power to evoke and shock, just as tombs and gravestones do. Thus at certain moments in history, decisions have been made to preserve ruins (if that is not a contradiction) for memorializing purposes, and this did happen in some cases, such as St George's, close to The Highway in London's East End, where a modern church was inserted within the ruins of the bombed church, the remains of which were reinforced and kept intact. Part of the remains of the bombed Coventry Cathedral have been kept, and the cross on the altar is formed from two burned roof joists.

Yet people in modern societies are often deeply undecided about how to respond to the physical decay of the past, or what Ian Christie has called 'the landscapes of abandonment'.[52] The melancholy that drew painters such as Ruisdael to the places that fused in his painting *The Old Jewish Cemetery*, and which still draws people

The cross, made out of burned roofing joists, on the altar in the ruins of Coventry Cathedral.

to the abandoned cemeteries of certain European and North American cities, is being relandscaped and tidied up to meet the needs of modern urban lifestyles. The alternative is to do nothing, leaving behind what has been so graphically captured by the Cuban photographer José Vergara in his portrait of abandoned urban America as a psychic wasteland, inhabited by a residual population of the poor and marginalized, who cannot escape. Forsaken cemeteries feature prominently in these ruined landscapes. Vergara cites Marshall Berman on this phenomenon of abandonment: 'Urban ruination is serious; it is real; it is not a stage set; it has spiritual authenticity. Symbols of modern life have turned into symbols of death.'[53]

Certainly the failure to maintain many historic cemeteries – which often contain magnificent architecture and statues – has led to many of them looking abandoned: columns have fallen over, angels have lost their heads and wings, trees and shrubs sprout through stone and marble table tombs, wrought-iron guard-rails rust and crumble, and many heavy monuments have tumbled in on themselves. This image of the abandoned cemetery may be popular with photography students and *aficionados* of the Gothick, but to many others it represents a loss of meaning and a dispiriting source of disenchantment with the world.

On the other hand there are certain kinds of ruins that can represent the past, while offering something quite magical or contemplative. One of the most successful attempts to create a new kind of memorial landscape can be found at the Landscape Park, Duisburg-Nord, based on the site of the former steelworks in Duisburg, which had finally ceased production in 1985. Duisburg was once at the heart of Germany's northern Ruhr valley, one of the most heavily industrialized regions in the world. It is a vast site of some 230 hectares, including its own railway yard, administration buildings, sidings, electricity

The Landscape Park at Duisburg in the Ruhr Valley, Germany, created around the industrial remains of the redundant steelworks. Regarded by many as one of the finest new memorial landscapes in Europe.

station, storage silos and, of course, the giant furnaces and smelting towers that almost strike terror into the heart when you first see them, as they resemble the infernal machines and edifices of nightmares (or films such as *Metropolis*), blocking out the sky and casting everything around them into darkness as they do. The smell of sulphur still hovers in some places. Equally eerie is the factory compound itself, with its high security gates, guardrooms and shunting yard network, which has unfortunate echoes of a prison or concentration camp for some visitors.

It is difficult to visit ruins such as these and not fear for the past and indeed the future: the scale of operations seems beyond human control or sensibility. To have worked in the midst of these vast ovens and furnaces, enveloped in a permanent fog of smoke and gases, lost in the entrails of a rusting metal maze, must have taken its toll very quickly. Humans are like ants in such a landscape. Yet those who worked and lived here were reluctant

to see it levelled and erased from memory when the enterprise was finally closed. In 1989 a competition was held to find ideas for retaining much of the redundant infrastructure while making the site amenable to visitors, and in 1991 Latz & Partner, a German landscape architecture firm, was selected to turn the site into a park.

Along with many others, I share the view that the Landscape Park at Duisburg is one of the most astonishing landscape designs of the twentieth century. Although one enters the factory gates with a sense of foreboding and anxiety, many other emotions quickly come into play. The visitor soon realizes that this really is a genuine park, with the full range of park affects, from playfulness to melancholy, from the disruptive to the Sublime. Within a hundred metres of the gates, in the great yard leading to the first giant blast furnace reaching one hundred metres into the sky, one comes across a perfectly aligned, formal *allée* of pink lilac trees in full

Duisburg in the Ruhr
Valley.

bloom. Most of the plant-ing is sculptural,
filling the empty silos, sidings and open squares
with evergreens, shrubs and formal woodlands
of small trees. Those who climb the vertiginous,
Piranesian metal staircase – which weaves up
and around the blast furnace, and which when
the furnace was operating must have seemed
like climbing a volcano about to erupt – can look
back down on the whole of the site to witness an
extraordinary inter penetration of nature with
redundant industry, wild orchids with water
pipes, herbs with heating ducts, small forests
with railway lines.

Yet this is a park and a memorial garden in
many other senses. Some of the vast, reinforced
concrete coal bunkers, each one the size of dance-
hall, have been turned into climbing walls. Others
have been made into playgrounds, with slides
made out of large, twisting steel tubes, running
from one level down to another. Artificial lakes
are being formed from circular filter beds. This
park is, as one writer has suggested, both Arcadia
and Gethsemane, a garden of loss, as well as a
landscape of renewal. Its designer, Peter Latz,
has likened Duisburg to the Duke of Bomarzo's
decaying Renaissance gardens at the Villa Orsini
in Italy, and the comparison is not without
reason.[54] Sometimes such landscapes seem to
suggest that hope can flower again amid the ruins.

The Glasgow Necropolis.

chapter six

A Walk in the
Paradise Gardens

An obsession with one kind of garden – basically
the English landscape garden of the upper and
middling landed gentry – seems to have prevented
theory from addressing many other types of site
that the modern world has called for since that
watershed of 1800. The grounds of some English
country estates provided the model for all
nineteenth-century developments: the cemetery,
the public park, the golf course.

John Dixon Hunt,
'Modern Landscape Architecture and its Past'[1]

JOINT-STOCK AND GARDEN CEMETERIES IN ENGLAND

Less than a ten-minute walk from where I live
is Abney Park Cemetery in north London, where,
for more than 30 years, I, along with many others,
have regularly walked the grounds and overgrown
paths. The experience changes with each visit,
though it can at times be depressingly bleak,
particularly if a bout of windy weather has
collected up the neighbourhood's rubbish
and strewn it liberally among the graves, paths
and scrubland. Nearly 32 acres in total, it is still
a great, bounded expanse of open space in the
midst of one of London's most densely populated
districts. It is surrounded, today by high-rise
public housing blocks, crowded nineteenth-
century residential terraces – home to Britain's
largest Hasidic Jewish population, as well as
a large Muslim population – and synagogues,
mosques, churches, busy market streets,
nightclubs and all the rich mix of faiths, lifestyles
and social groupings that are now to be found in
big cities of the world.

The Cemetery remains a world apart from all
this bustling, cosmopolitan modernity. To come
across it unexpectedly is rather like coming across
a ruined monastery or outcrop of rain forest in
the middle of a great city. It is extraordinarily

fertile, with unusual flora and fauna, a home to plants and birds rarely seen elsewhere in the surrounding city. It is incredibly overgrown, at times choked thick and impassable with rank vegetation. Many people are reluctant to enter it, for religious reasons or because of deep-seated superstitions. There is also the rather more pragmatic fear for one's personal safety in this wild and gloomy terrain, which the modern world seems to have left behind.

Abney Park is a salutary example of the many great private garden cemeteries established by the early Victorians in London, one of the 'hoop of burial grounds that became known as "The Magnificent Seven". These are Kensal Green (1833), Norwood (1838), Highgate (1839), Abney Park (1840), Brompton (1840), Nunhead (1840) and Tower Hamlets (1841). London was thus ringed by landscaped funereal elegance in the tradition of John Claudius Loudon (1782–1843).'[2] From the 1830s onwards in Britain, the creation of new cemeteries became a major part of urban development and city-making. The formation of these cemeteries was often inspired by Nonconformist religious opinion, which argued for burial grounds where different religious sects could bury according to their own forms of service and ritual, separate and distinct from that of the established Anglican Church.

Before this proliferation of new cemeteries in London, a number of similar ventures had begun elsewhere. One such was founded at Chorlton Row, Rusholme Road, Manchester, as early as 1820, a joint-stock venture for Dissenters; at almost the same time, Rosary Road Cemetery in Norwich was laid out as a non-denominational public cemetery. Both still compete for the honour of being the first great civic accomplishments of the new funerary era. Several years later, in 1825, the Liverpool Necropolis was opened by Dissenters in that city, and in 1832 the first inter-ment took place at the Glasgow Necropolis, a self-styled garden cemetery with 'picturesque effect' modelled partly on Père-Lachaise.

The Liverpool Necropolis had a Greek Doric entrance, while the Glasgow Necropolis had so many works of architectural distinction that Curl describes it as 'constituting one of the most memorable compositions of townscape anywhere in the British Isles, and its name, a "city of the dead", is appropriate, for it looks like a splendid hill-town, embellished with grand tombs and monuments'.[3] As we have seen, Kensal Green Cemetery was the first of such cemeteries in London, opening in 1833. Abney Park was established as a joint-stock company in the same year as Highgate, though it opened a year later. All of Abney Park's Trustees were Congregationalists, though it was open to 'all classes of the community and to all denominations of Christians without restraint in forms'.[4] The enthusiasm for the new cemeteries was a mixture of Nonconformist energy and sound business sense, for many paid good dividends to shareholders in their early years. Stoke Newington, the district of London in which Abney Park is located, was home to many Dissenting and Nonconformist individuals and families, and both public approval and financial solidity were expected from the outset.

Abney Park Cemetery had been expressly designed as an arboretum, based on the collection of mature trees already planted, the legacy of several fine houses and gardens that had previously occupied the site, to which were added many new plantings commissioned by the Cemetery Trustees from the local – and famous – Loddige's Nursery in Mare Street, Hackney. At the height of its success as an arboretum, it had more than 2,500 different species of trees, more than the Royal Park at Kew, making it a genuine tourist attraction, as well as a place for burying the dead. It was enthusiastically supported by the then influential gardener and writer John Claudius Loudon, who indeed saw in it many of his own ideas successfully brought to fruition. For Loudon, a cemetery required a distinct landscape character that would make it recognizable as a cemetery immediately, largely through its formal avenues of trees, particularly conifers of the fastigiate (tapering) kind.

Loudon is a key figure in nineteenth-century landscape design; his influence is still evident today, not just in Britain but across the world. He had been a gardener and a farmer before he became a prolific and widely travelled journalist – visiting Moscow in 1814 and France and Italy between 1819 and 1820. His fame and success was perhaps owing to the fact that he shrewdly adopted the ideas of earlier landscape designers such as Humphry Repton – who had designed for the aristocracy and landed gentry – for the burgeoning and self-confident middle classes, whose cultural appetite for the family villa, the public park and indeed the public cemetery, in a style which he himself termed the Gardenesque, was increasingly influential in urban expansion.[5] Loudon's views and writings on the design of cemeteries were circulated widely before they eventually took the form of his famous treatise,

On the Laying Out, Planting, and Managing of Cemeteries; and On the Improvement of Churchyards, published in 1843, the year of his death. It was Loudon who was most firm on the subject of the moral uplift engendered by sympathetic design, writing that,

> Churchyards and cemeteries are scenes not only calculated to improve the morals and the taste, and by their botanical riches to cultivate the intellect, but they serve as historical records . . . The tomb has, in fact, been the great chronicler of taste throughout the world.[6]

Loudon was most certainly for evergreens – yews, cypresses, hollies – and against deciduous trees and flowers, most likely, one can only suppose, because deciduous trees shed their leaves each year, becoming skeletal in form; and flowers die. Evergreens, though, suggested the possibility of eternal life.

The handsome gates at the entrance to Abney Park Cemetery, restored in the late 1990s, were designed in the Egyptian style associated in this period with funerary architecture (they are remarkably similar to the gates to Mount Auburn Cemetery in Boston, inaugurated ten years earlier), and hieroglyphs engraved over the cemetery lodge-houses proclaimed 'The Gates of the Abode of the Mortal Part of Man'. The Cemetery also contains a Gothic style Chapel (now derelict), several war memorials, and many thousands of family chapels, mausoleums, tombs, tombstones and other grave markings. It is estimated that over 300,000 people have been buried there since it opened.

Over the next ten years Abney Park became

the final resting place of many distinguished Nonconformist families, including that of General Booth, the founder of the Salvation Army, whose hearse was followed by tens of thousands of mourners when he was buried in 1912. Not all the large headstones belong to local ministers and divines. Also buried in the cemetery are such notable nineteenth-century political radicals as William Hone (1780–1842), bookseller and author, once prosecuted for blasphemy, and whose funeral Charles Dickens attended, and James Bronterre O'Brien (1805–1864), the Chartist leader. One of the best-known sculptures – especially fascinating to children – is the giant white marble 'Sleeping Lion' marking the grave of Susannah and Frank Bostock, well-known Victorian menagerists. It is directly connected to a similar lion, called Nero, in the Western Cemetery at Highgate, overlooking the Circle of Lebanon. Nero marks the grave of another menagerist, George Wombwell, connected to the Bostocks in Abney Park by marriage. The famous Edwardian music-hall artists George Leybourne ('Champagne

Charlie') and his son-in-law, Albert Chevalier, are also buried at Abney Park.

There is a wealth of unusual and often very distinguished statuary in Abney Park, though its Nonconformist origins militated against excessive flights of sculptural extravagance and exoticism compared with other cemeteries in London (and certainly when compared with cemeteries elsewhere in Europe). Yet even at the time this kind of monumental art was not without its critics. One of them, Isabella Holmes, regretted that 'There are many sad sights but there are few as sad as one of these huge graveyards . . . can there be any more profitless mode of throwing away money? . . . the only people who profit by them are a few marble and granite merchants, and a few monumental masons – and they might be better employed!'[7] As the number of graves increased, so the trees were felled, and the woodland or Picturesque cemetery became another overcrowded city of the dead before it reverted to woodland again.

By the 1950s burials at Abney Park were restricted to groups of 'common graves' excavated along some of the main paths and driveways, and in this undignified manner what was once a wooded Elysium for a high-minded religious culture and its followers (and even for the many visitors who came to admire the landscaping), had become something of a dumping ground for those who had ended up in the workhouse or living on state charity. As income dwindled, the original cemetery company collapsed, and the site was acquired by the local council, which had no real choice in the matter of acquisition, since there was no serious alternative other than public rescue.

The greatly admired Sleeping Lion in Abney Park Cemetery, London, marking the grave of Susannah and Frank Bostock, well-known Victorian menagerists.

Today it is in places something of a forlorn, overgrown, entangled forest, used by dog-walkers and those with a Gothic turn of mind only. Many of the obelisks, table tombs and gravestones, particularly within the inner part of the cemetery, are broken, having fallen in on themselves or been smashed by vandals.. However, a Trust has now been set up to reclaim the cemetery, and is working to restore its lost grandeur.

Of this kind of cemetery, Curl has written that

I have always found the strange melancholy of graveyards and cemeteries peculiarly moving. The tombstones, mausolea and other monuments set among evergreens and mature trees have often intrigued, delighted and saddened me. The pious inscriptions, protesting too much about never-to-be-forgotten lives that are too patently forgotten, induce a profound mood of regret, of longing, and even of despair.[8]

A similar story can also be told about the even more famous Highgate Cemetery, which also came close to dereliction in some parts in the 1970s, after the company that owned it was forced to close the Western Cemetery, and the newly formed Friends of Highgate Cemetery won permission to begin clearing the undergrowth, felling invasive trees and restoring something of the original landscape design to view. In 1981 the freehold to the Cemetery was acquired, and since then the Friends group has worked tirelessly to restore many of the buildings and monuments, while developing an energetic programme of public tours and educational programmes. Meanwhile, the Eastern Cemetery, particularly

famous for being the part where Karl Marx is buried, remains a functioning, private cemetery.

THE EGYPTIAN REVIVAL

It is the Western Cemetery at Highgate that exhibits many of the most distinctive and characteristic features of the great era of Victorian monumentalism and funerary design, notably because of its many very fine private tombstones and monuments through to its justifiably famous and much admired Egyptian Avenue and Lebanon Circle. The gates to the Egyptian Avenue

Columns marking the entrance of the Egyptian Avenue at Highgate Cemetery in London, part of the Egyptian Revival in Victorian culture.

Family tombs in a circular terrace in the Lebanon circle at Highgate Cemetery, London.

appear exotic, even bizarre, to most people when they first see them, seeming more to do with a Hollywood film set than a discreet, sombre setting for Christian ritual. The Egyptian Avenue itself is flanked by a series of burial chambers, whose formidable metal doors bear the symbol of an inverted flaming torch, a traditional image of a life extinguished, and, even more unusually, contain keyholes that are also upside down, in line with the same reverse symmetry. The Avenue, also known as 'The Street of the Dead', leads to the Lebanon Circle, an extraordinarily remarkable piece of excavation and design, in which a ring of inner and outer catacombs were created around

an existing Cedar of Lebanon tree, which predated the cemetery itself by 150 years. This circle of tomb chambers echoes the terraces of Etruscan tombs at Cerveteri in Italy, though nearly 3,000 years separate them.

The elision between Victorian funereal culture and that of ancient Egypt, seen also at Abney Park, and in many other cemeteries of the period, is interesting, part of a stylistic enthusiasm known as the Egyptian Revival, stemming from the enormous archaeological interest in ancient Egypt in Europe from the eighteenth century onwards, with its associations with Freemasonry and repertory of symbolic forms and imagery, which became stock items in cemetery architecture, including pyramids, obelisks, flaming torches and sun motifs. Napoleon's campaign in Egypt in 1798 fuelled an enormous interest throughout Europe in the culture of this then little-known country, part of a wider Orientalism than grew from other imperial adventures and appropriations. It was known that the Egyptians thought rather more about death than life, as a number of Victorians also did. Herodotus had pointed out very early on that the ancient Egyptians regarded domestic dwellings as temporary items of architecture, and tombs as the permanent abode.

David Cannadine sees the rise of the joint-stock cemeteries as almost too comfortably expressing a Victorian self-satisfaction with their new found wealth:

> Likewise, those great mid-Victorian cemeteries – Highgate and Kensal Green in London, Undercliffe in Bradford, Mount Auburn in Boston and Greenwood in New York – were very much the Forest Lawns of their time, in both their expense and their status consciousness. For these romantic, rural retreats were essentially an analogue of romantic, rural suburbia. Their careful layout, with greenery, gardens, gently curving roads, and restful, contrived vistas, was exactly reminiscent of exclusive, middle-class building estates like Headingley or Edgbaston. Their precisely-graded plots, placing a premium on location, accessibility and view, reflected the same subtle social gradations of suburbia itself. And their family vaults, in which parents and children were once more re-united, reaffirmed that same middle-class belief in the sanctity of

family life (or death) that was embodied in that other great bastion of bourgeois values, the middle class villa.[9]

In this period, but particularly towards the end of the nineteenth century, the heavy monumental style of tombstone or mausoleum gave way to architectural arrangements of headstones, railings, slabs and even foot-rests that were designed to resemble not a house of the dead, but a family bed. The notion that death was one long, perfect sleep cast the family grave in a new mould.[10]

RURAL CEMETERIES IN NORTH AMERICA

In North America the first of the great rural or garden (sometimes known as 'rural romantic') cemeteries was established at Mount Auburn in Cambridge, Massachusetts, and consecrated in 1831, at the instigation of Dr Jacob Bigelow, a Professor at Harvard Medical School and the author of *American Medical Botany*. This was one year before the Glasgow Necropolis, and two years before Kensal Green, two of the pioneering Picturesque cemeteries in Britain. In many ways North America had absorbed the lessons of Père-Lachaise before Britain had, and indeed Mount Auburn was sometimes referred to as 'the Père-Lachaise of America' (as Kensal Green became known as 'the Père-Lachaise of Britain').[11] Bigelow invited other wealthy Bostonians to join him in setting up a private, non-profit-making body to develop and manage the cemetery, offering rights to burial in perpetuity. The cemetery was managed by a Garden and Cemetery Committee formed from elements of the Massachusetts

Horticultural Society, so it seems likely from the outset that horticultural and gardening elements were to the fore when considering the aesthetic of the cemetery itself, whether in its design, management or maintenance.

The managers at Mount Auburn, in common with those at many other North American rural cemeteries, frequently resisted proposals for over-elaborate family tombs, which were considered to be at odds with the pastoral setting originally envisioned. They continued to aspire to a woodland setting, with curvilinear paths, slopes, mounds and rolling pastures, water features such as streams, waterfalls and small lakes, and an uneven massing of shrubs and trees uppermost in the design: a 'garden of graves', in the words of one contemporary writer. The poet Emily Dickinson, who had a keen appreciation of the transience of life, and is rightly famous for her quizzical couplet 'Because I could not stop for Death / He kindly stopped for me', wrote of Mount Auburn, that 'it seems as if Nature had formed the spot with a distinct idea of its being a resting place for her children'.[12]

In addition to a shared interest with Europeans in Romanticism and its relation to the Picturesque or Gardenesque, the Americans brought two additional factors to the ways in which cemeteries were developed: a respect, sometimes bordering on awe, for the spectacular native landscape, together with a widely shared interest in what was termed Transcendentalism, a philosophy distinctly peculiar to America. American Transcendentalism was largely associated with Ralph Waldo Emerson (1803–82) who, borrowing from Kant, Schelling, Coleridge and Carlyle, developed an almost mystical form

of nature-worship, based on the idea that there were distinct forms of self-knowledge that could only be acquired through an immersion in the natural world. Such ideas were further developed by Henry David Thoreau (1817–62), who made a particular virtue of the simple, unadorned life – and death – at one with nature in the deep verdant woods. For the cultural critic Leo Marx, Nathaniel Hawthorne's seminal essay, 'Sleepy Hollow', written on 27 July 1844, sets the seal on pastoralism being one of the most significant forces in the American psyche.[13] It was not likely that with these influences so strongly admired and active in the religious and intellectual culture of North America, that cemetery designers and commissioners would take so kindly to the densely urban monumentalism favoured at Père-Lachaise, and which other, more Catholic, European, cultures found appropriate to their imaginative needs.

There were exceptions to this trend towards pastoralism, of course, particularly in the South. New Orleans is famous for its cemeteries and tombs. Topographical factors made a big difference. After two severe epidemics in the city (which also of course had strong French connections and influences) in 1832 and 1833, one cause of which was attributed to insanitary conditions prevailing in local burial grounds which were constantly subject to flooding – with freshly dug graves often filling with water before the coffin was even lowered into place – legislation was passed prohibiting burial underground. As a result, bodies were placed in sealed wall tombs or individual sarcophagi, many of which were elaborately designed, a number of them by architects and sculptors with strong connections back to French funerary and monumental culture. [14]

The success of Mount Auburn also popularized the use of the word 'cemetery' in North America for the first time, rather than 'burying ground' or 'graveyard'. The associations of the word 'cemetery' with sleep, rather than with death and decay, was part of a sea-change in American attitudes towards these landscapes and sovereign places. They quickly became popular visiting sites, and as David Sloane has pointed out, they were the first planned landscapes generally open to the public in the USA, before public parks even, and quickly gained a *belles-lettres* literature and a cultural cachet all of their own. The finest of the new cemeteries were visitor attractions on an international scale.[15] Ambitious, large-scale rural cemeteries proliferated rapidly throughout the larger towns and cities over the next 20 to 30 years, their names richly evocative of this arcadian, if somewhat saturnine, idyll: Laurel Hill (Philadelphia, 1836); Greenmount (Baltimore, 1838); Worcester Rural (1838); Harmony Grove (Salem, 1840); Spring Grove (Cincinnati, 1844) along with many other Cedar Groves, Pine Groves and Forest Hills that were founded over time in many different places.

A decade or so after Mount Auburn, the Brooklyn Green-Wood Cemetery was established, twice the size of Père-Lachaise, and for more than half a century, at 180 acres, the largest landscaped cemetery in the world. The Green-Wood Cemetery was created as part of the overall city plan for Brooklyn. From the outset it was not seen only as a burial place, for it was also a visitor attraction (there are reports of a constant stream of carriages to the cemetery, where people went boating on the ornamental lakes and studied the plants and shrubs).[16] By 1850 approximately 60,000 people annually took the organized Tour of Green-Wood. The cemetery occupied the highest point in Brooklyn, with views to the

Monumentalism and elements of the rural cemetery tradition at Green-Wood Cemetery in Brooklyn, New York.

Green-Wood Cemetery,
Brooklyn.

Atlantic to the east and Manhattan to the west.
There was much discussion at the time the
holding company was incorporated as to whether
it should be a wholly commercial undertaking,
distributing profits to shareholders, or not.
Many people found the idea of profiting from
death unacceptable, and it was eventually
established as not-for-profit company, though
still in private hands.

To the modern visitor, however, it now seems
to be almost exclusively used by the rich and
wealthy, and while heavily undulating in landscape form, and serpentine in its roads and paths
(Alpine Path, Cypress Avenue, Sycamore Avenue,
Ocean Avenue, *et al.*), with fine tree-planting,
several ornamental lakes and many thousands of
vast family tombs and mausoleums, the emotional
effect seems strangely impersonal, rather like an
exclusive residential development that might be
found occupying the better slopes of a naturally

favoured hill. It is certainly well-maintained, and
contains many fine views of the city, as well as
handsome tombs and family vaults. But it has lost
its vital connection with its ruralist, Transcenden-
talist origins: not a place for quiet reflection so
much as a place for ostentatious display.

THE NEW PASTORAL:
THE RISE OF THE LAWN CEMETERY

The now well-known American 'lawn cemetery'
dates from the redesign of Spring Grove
Cemetery in Cincinnati by Adolph Strauch in
1855. Strauch, a German-born horticulturist and
landscape gardener, had originally worked for
Prince von Pückler-Muskau at his estate in
Silesia, where Pückler-Muskau had developed
something of a particular interest in the
landscapes of death.[17] At his estate, Pückler-
Muskau had designed two grassed pyramids

on islands in a lake, for his wife and himself as tombs. On his wife's tomb he had inscribed the utopian edict that, 'Graves are the peaks of a far new world'.[18]

Arriving in the USA, Strauch had sought a more open, integrated cemetery landscape, where the individual plot-holdings were subordinated to the grand sweep of the whole setting. Strauch, who had worked in suburban estates before he came to Spring Grove, wanted more of a domesticated feel to the cemetery, with gentle, open vistas, and with expanses of closely mown lawn to provide the integrating factor in the overall aesthetic effect. In his plans for the development of the southern part of Spring Grove Cemetery, he imposed stringent rules as to the scale, design and acceptable symbolism of the individual tombs and grave markers, rejecting the eccentric individualism of many of the gravestones in other cemeteries, claiming that the total effect was more important than the individual monument. He was a collectivist *avant la lettre.*

Strauch also imposed his own team of gardeners and maintenance workers at Spring Grove, whereas previously many individuals had tended their own plots and memorials. He did away with most fences and borders, created grand open drives and carriage-ways that were not lined by trees, and made it known that only statuary in the 'Classical style' was considered fully acceptable under this new regime. As Sloane records, 'Strauch's ideas and innovations were central to the development of the lawn-park cemetery and the modern cemetery in general.'[19] Furthermore, Strauch not only designed the cemetery, he created the new role of the cemetery superintendent. For whereas, previously, landscape designers had drawn up their plans and then moved on, Strauch saw the whole process as being a combination of design and continuous 'artistic' management. In this sense it was more like a public park, maintained for daily use and pleasure, than a sequestered piece of American wilderness that might one day return to a state of nature, along with the remains of the inhabitants it contained.

By the beginning of the twentieth century, however, even this softening of the effects of death

Flat grave markers at Forest Lawn, Glendale, California, are set below the grass level to give the appearance of continuous lawn, punctuated by classical statuary.

through the employment of more suburban, domesticated landscapes, with their grassy knolls and pristine lawns, was felt to be too morbid, especially for those with money to spare. In 1913 Hubert Eaton established a memorial park called Forest Lawn in Glendale, California, where nearly all traces of the traditional and ritualistic culture of death and burial were landscaped out of existence. Eaton accelerated the trends established by Strauch, notably in rejecting the paramount visual role played by the individual family monument, headstone or tomb in creating the cemetery presence, in carrying the parkland principle to even greater effect, almost to the point of erasing all traces of burial processes, and, finally, in turning the cemetery into an aggressively marketed commercial enterprise, in full concordance with the practices and professional cultures of the real estate sales industry.

The cemetery thus became an extension of the exclusive, residential retreat. People, or 'customers' as they were increasingly to be called, were exhorted to buy their plot in this real estate nirvana, *pre-need*; that is to say, long before their death necessitated it, and especially while their finances were in good health, even if their mortal bodies were not. Eaton was an earlier exemplar of that extraordinary mix of fundamentalist Protestant certainty combined with an equally firm belief in business success as a reward for faith. Forest Lawn was not a traditional churchyard or cemetery open to all (not that Père-Lachaise or Kensal Green had welcomed the poorest of the dead particularly), but was specifically aimed at the respectable middle-classes, many of whom still fervently believed in a Second Life to Come, while remaining keen to

memorialize their achievements in the first. Thus the new lawn cemetery was not a universalist institution in the civic fabric of democratic America, but increasingly a private and privileged last haven, and in this way uncannily prefigured the exclusive 'gated communities' of late-twentieth-century residential America.

In 1917 Eaton published his religious and aesthetic creed for the new memorial park, which included the following:

I believe in a happy Eternal Life . . . I believe, most of all, in a Christ that smiles and loves you and me. I therefore know the cemeteries of today are wrong because they depict an end, not a beginning. They have consequently become unsightly stoneyards, full of inartistic symbols and depressing customs; places that do nothing for humanity save a practical act, and that not well.

I shall try to build at Forest Lawn a great park, devoid of misshapen monuments and other customary signs of earthly Death, but filled with towering trees, sweeping lawns, splashing fountains, singing birds, beautiful statuary, cheerful flowers; noble memorial architecture, with interiors of light and color, and redolent of the world's best history and romances. I believe these things educate and uplift a community.[20]

The cemetery ethos articulated here, an ironed-out mixture of picture-book philhellenism and Sunday School theology, represents a complete break with nearly all other traditions of burial culture. Nothing remains of the standing stone or upright stele, the yew tree or the forest

Forest Lawn, Glendale, California. Copy of Michelangelo's *David* and various classical sculptures.

circle, the burial mound or raised earth levels, the many and varied arcane sculptural and figurative symbols of loss, parting, fortitude, stoicism, epitaphs or inscriptions relating to family relationships, trades and occupations, religious beliefs, indeed the whole gamut of ambivalence about death and what lies on the far side of it so often represented in the morphology of the grave site and its markings. Here there was, and continues to be, no acknowledgement of entropy and decay, which the historic cemetery embodied through its weatherings of stone, its uneven growths of grasses, trees and hedges, its lichens, and slow aging of its buildings and structures. The new lawn cemetery was designed specifically to deny the processes of time or the landscape of ruins, both of which burial places have traditionally symbolized. At Forest Lawn nobody died, they simply got translated.

The lawn cemetery has continued to flourish in the USA, despite the caustic criticism and satire aimed at the original Forest Lawn, first in Evelyn Waugh's novel *The Loved One* (1948) and then in Jessica Mitford's acerbic *The American Way of Death* (1963). However, the model failed to gain hold in Europe. There are other features of Forest Lawn that also render it unassimilable in traditional landscape and burial culture terms. For example, it was rarely referred to as a cemetery, but nearly always as a 'memorial park'. The memorials chosen, often by the incumbent well before he or she died, had to be approved by the park administrators, and mostly came from a stock selection of replica neo-Classical or religious statues in white marble, which Mitford remarked looked 'like the sort of thing one might win in a shooting gallery'.

Nature was regarded as 'a passive backdrop to artistic memorials'.[21] The idea that burial could be separated from Nature, and the resultant assumption that death was not a part of Nature, seems strangely even more mechanistic than cremation. The coffins ('caskets') were not lowered directly into the ground, but were lowered into pre-cast concrete boxes, and then sealed with concrete, before being back-filled and turfed over. This is now common practice in the USA, where the use of steel caskets, inserted into thick concrete bunkers, symbolically ensure that the body will never be integrated with the earth, which some find very strange indeed.[22] Another result of using concrete is that once the earth has been impacted and turfed, there is little likelihood of any later subsidence, disturbingly suggestive of the interred body slowly decomposing and creating a small indentation in the lawn. Yet it is surely one of the archetypal features of the landscape of burial that small mounds, or indentations, of body length and size are precisely what gives the burial site its especial meaning, its somatic texture. Yet even Sloane talks about the need to alleviate 'the age-old problem of the sunken or mounded grave', as if this interruption in the landscape were unacceptable.[23]

The majority of burial plots were marked solely by a small bronze plaque, laid flush to the ground, and the plots were divided into sections with mellifluous names such as Kindly Light, Whispering Pines, Graceland, Eventide. Only evergreen bushes and trees were planted, as Eaton, like Loudon before him, was keen to avoid the sight of falling leaves, which might bring a horrible reminder of loss and decay into this blithe world of positive thinking. In his instructions to the architects who designed the great mausoleums in the park, he insisted that, 'insofar as possible all evidences of death should be eliminated and that this building should be a creation of art.'[24] In Eaton's aesthetic, neo-Classical art and architecture allowed people to forget the quotidian or the existential, creating

a kind of moral–material structure of uplift and future hope. He also introduced locked wall courtyards containing loculi where the remains of those who sought privacy could be interred, another early and prescient refinement of the 'gated communities' that today mark the new spatial geography of urban America at home. When Mitford wrote a chapter about Forest Lawn entitled 'Shroudland' in her book, she recorded that the year before publication, Forest Lawn had received over one and a half million visitors, many of them paying to see certain works of art or visit particular chapels, as well as spending large amounts of money in the Forest Lawn Gift Shop.

The memorial park, of which Forest Lawn was the principal progenitor, seems quintessentially American in the business acumen that inspired it, the design and marketing of its perfected landscape, and in its self-imposed isolation and detachment from the social complexities of everyday American life and culture. Its religious ethos was overwhelmingly Christian and simplistic, and the aesthetic was decidedly ahistorical, with little reference to traditional forms of funerary symbolism and landscape patterning. Nevertheless, Marc Treib has robustly defended some of its achievements. He has noted the original and explicit wish to design a 'landscape addressed to the needs of the living' rather than the dead, which it patently has done, given the vast numbers of visitors. It has also successfully factored in the costs of permanent maintenance (through the setting up of a separate not-for-profit trust), which ensures that Forest Lawn will never succumb to the dereliction and neglect seen so often elsewhere.[25] These are no small achievements, even if the chosen style is not to everyone's taste. Europeans may dislike the overly suburban, country club aesthetic, but, as Treib suggests, the lawn cemetery has established itself as a genuine part of American landscape culture. It has in its own way drawn the sting of death through the use of design, while contributing something original to the Western cemetery tradition.

THE FOREST CEMETERY

It was, however, the Stockholm Woodland Cemetery that brought the landscape idyll of the 'woodland' or 'forest' cemetery to international attention, as an exemplar of the shape and style of things to come.[26] This Cemetery was a unique collaboration between Sweden's two most famous architects, Erik Gunnar Asplund and Sigurd Lewerentz (who also trained as a landscape architect). It was begun in 1916 and not finally completed until the 1940s, by which time the two men had sadly fallen out with one other. Their joint interests and talents enabled them to design and construct a completely new kind of burial ground, neither a landscaped garden cemetery in the English tradition, nor a city of the dead in the Mediterranean or Islamic tradition. This was something uniquely new: an apparently natural forest setting in which the importance of the individual graves would be subsumed within the larger impact of the woodlands and sweeping meadows. The original design for the cemetery – which was based on open competition – was called 'Tallum' (*tall* is Swedish for pine tree).

Created on the site of a former quarry, this great cemetery occupies over 100 hectares, most of which is heavily planted pine forest, within which small graves are located at regular, though not mathematical, intervals. The first distinguishing feature of the design is that as one enters the main gate of the cemetery, one is confronted by a rising hill with a single great cross planted halfway up the incline, and beyond that, to the left, the austere columns of what looks like a Functionalist version of the Parthenon. This giant granite cross locks earth and sky together, though the symbolic meaning of the cross remains in dispute. It is based, as has already been noted, on the recurring wayside crosses seen in Friedrich's paintings, signifying hope in an otherwise abandoned world, though Asplund and Lewerentz insisted that the cross was open to non-Christian interpretations, quoting Friedrich himself: 'To those who see it as such, a consolation, to those who do not, simply a cross.'[27]

The path ascends alongside a walled garden and columbarium to the left; to the right there is just a great grassed hill and an open sky. No graves are visible at all until the visitor reaches the main chapel, and only then in the far distance, dotted among the columnar pine trees: just a vast rolling landscape, with deep forest beyond. On the top of the great grass mound is a grove of trees surrounding a small walled sanctuary. It is the sheer luxury of space that so impresses: a full third of the entire cemetery is given over to this imposing empty landscape with chapel, embodied in the long curves and high skies evocative of the ancestral, almost primeval, Swedish landscape with its barrows and sacred groves. The Swedish landscape architect Thorbjörn Andersson rightly draws attention to how absolutely different this cemetery is from the classical, highly formalized Père-Lachaise, where the visitor's emotions are highly regulated. In the Stockholm Woodland

Stockholm Woodland
Cemetery. Burial Grove.

Cemetery, he writes, there are 'feelings of landscapes of many different sorts, such as hope and happiness, sorrow and despair, death and resurrection. It is an environment full of feelings that facilitate contact between the inner and outer landscapes'.[28] Furthermore, Andersson is adamant that the success of the cemetery owes much to its espousal of a 'a central aspect of modernism: dissolved space, a fluid transition between contexts, a wish to accentuate movement'.[29]

The Cemetery is extensive and inviting: long forest paths cut through woodland, with distant views of columnar chapels and sudden openings with circular garden settings and running water. There are tens of thousands of small headstones in these woodland forests, all immaculately maintained. It is clear that severe restrictions on the size of headstone are imposed, and there are no sculptural monuments, as befits the rather austere Lutheran culture that still informs much Swedish architecture and design. Although at times there may be more than 50 gardening staff at work at the Cemetery – the scale of which suggests it was planned to act as the principal cemetery for Stockholmers in the decades, if not centuries, to come – it doesn't feel as if it was designed to be maintained as a landscape of 'mass production'. Quite the opposite: it has an intimate and other-worldly feel once one is alone in the woods.

There is no doubt that Asplund and Lewerentz were in close touch with the aesthetic and social movements of their time, and deeply influenced by them. One of these shifts was the rejection by many artists of the Classical or Picturesque tradition in landscape painting, in favour of wilder, more marginal landscapes and forms of representation. The shift was from manners to moods. As we know, forest interiors became a favourite subject in this period, leading to Nina Lübbren's notion of an 'immersive aesthetic', where the untamed representation of nature

Stockholm
Woodland Cemetery.
View towards the
Memorial Grove.

Monument Hall.

almost overwhelms the viewers, drawing them not only into these wild settings, but at the same time seeking a new correspondence between the shadowy woodland interior and the inner self. The Stockholm Woodland Cemetery quickly became a an international byword for this new immersive aesthetic, though others followed in its train.[30]

When the distinguished Swiss landscape architect Dieter Kienast began work on a number of cemeteries and cemetery extensions in Switzerland and Germany in the 1990s, he publicly stated at the outset that, 'The cemetery that unobtrusively subordinates itself to the landscape becomes an ideal image. The Stockholm woodland cemetery of Asplund and Lewerentz is the example to be emulated.'[31] Christian Vogt's haunting black and white photographs of Kienast's cemeteries, perhaps the best art photography devoted to exploring the architectural aesthetic of the cemetery in the modern era, recall the almost mystical stillness of Atget's early photographs of rural France, often taken at dawn or dusk, when the visible world seems to tremble on the brink of revelation. These carefully orchestrated emotions are a sign that the landscaped cemetery has always been a place of subtle and imperceptible changes, both of mood and atmosphere. These are, after all, places that should suggest something of the ineffable. Otherwise, what are they for?

opposite: Woodland
Chapel (1918–22) by
Gunnar Asplund.

above: Footpath leading
to the Woodland Chapel.

left: Resurrection Chapel
(1921–5) by Sigurd
Lewerentz.

Prospect Cottage garden, Dungeness.

chapter seven

The Disappearing Body:

Burial, Cremation and Landscape Form in the Twentieth Century

It may be improper to describe a grave mound as the commanding heights of ideology, but if the cause for which you would shed your blood seeks the last word in the interpretation of events, then you must ensure a controlling interest in the Four Last Things.

Peter Jupp, *From Dust to Ashes* [1]

COASTAL CEMETERIES

Early one morning in November 2001, a tourist walking on the beach of Juist, a small island off the coast of north Germany, came across a badly decomposed body washed up on the sands by the recent high tide. Police investigations revealed that the body had been in the water for nearly a year, and was that of a woman whose clothes and wristwatch suggested she had originally come from Britain, though continuing international police enquiries proved fruitless for identifying her. Her remains were buried in the island cemetery, and the grave marked with the name 'Juistine'. A local councillor who also acts as sexton and undertaker to the island, Wolfgang Zobel, when interviewed about the burial by a reporter from an British newspaper, said that 'If anyone is washed ashore in these islands and their identity remains unknown, then we feel that person belongs to our community. We say that since this person was stranded on our island, this should be her resting place.' [2] Villagers maintained the grave as if it were one of their own. A few months after this story appeared, DNA tests enabled a local detective to conclusively identify the body, following enquiries by family members who had read the original newspaper article.

After visiting the grave in Juist, the woman's son and daughter agreed that the body should remain where it had been interred: 'It's perfect', the daughter was quoted as saying. 'It's just the place she would want to be. She's buried among the dunes, flowers and wildlife. It is the most beautiful cemetery I have ever seen.'[3]

Coastal and island communities are replete with such stories, and seashore cemeteries provide much evidence for this, where people live closer to the arbitrary and often cruel nature of death than elsewhere. In Colonsay, a small Hebridean island off the west coast of Scotland, villagers continue to maintain the graves of three Italians whose bodies were washed ashore in August 1940 from the ship, *Arandora Star*, which was sunk by a German torpedo on 1 July 1940 carrying 1500 people, the majority of them Italian internees, from Liverpool to Canada. In an exchange of letters on the Colonsay island website in April 2002, one Italian journalist who came across the story, wrote about 'how the people of Colonsay have shown extraordinary kindness and respect for the remains of the Italians who were washed ashore'. Another Italian who read this story in the Italian weekly journal *Diario*, wrote to 'thank the people of Colonsay for all they have made and are still making to honour the memory of those three unlucky Italians'.[4] In Kilchattan cemetery on Colonsay there are also many other graves of sailors, known and unknown, British and foreign, mostly victims of Second World War naval battles, washed ashore days, months, sometimes even years after their deaths, but buried with dignity and care.[5]

It is not surprising that coastal or maritime cemeteries have provided some of the most powerful settings in the literature of place, for example in Paul Valéry's sun-dazzled epiphany, 'Le Cimitière marin', or Robert Lowell's ferociously gloomy and guilt-ridden 'The Quaker Graveyard in Nantucket', sited as they are, literally, on the boundary between earth and sea, life and death. In these poems the narrator's consciousness alternates constantly between the boundless, shifting sea and the fixed order of the cemetery, in a series of reflections on formlessness and finality, quiddity and nothingness. Nor is it surprising that so many ancient burial places are located within sight of a river or the open sea, as we have already seen in the case of the Neolithic burial chamber at Pentre Ifan in Pembrokeshire and the Anglo-Saxon ship graves at Sutton Hoo, where the spirits of the dead are assumed to keep permanent watch on the shifting sea. In one of the most architecturally astonishing new cemeteries in Europe, Finisterre, on the far western coast of Spain, the simple granite cubes containing the burial niches face outwards across the Atlantic from their lonely promontory.[6]

The respect accorded to a dead body, and a powerful feeling that no matter what the terrors of life may have been, some forms of psychic or social reconciliation can be achieved through the ritual of a proper burial, is a widespread cultural norm.[7] In Sophocles' play *Antigone*, the dramatic fulcrum is provided by the refusal of Creon to allow Antigone to bury the body of her brother as ritual requires. Everything else in the play, which is about the conflict between authority and individual conscience, flows from this one decision. The powerful need of families to accord a loved one a proper burial, irrespective of the circumstances of death, or even if the death happened many years before and the remains have only recently been recovered from some makeshift burial (as has often happened in the sectarian killings in Northern Ireland) suggests that the grave site has enormous symbolic power of emotional closure and longed-for finality. This is why the presence, or absence, of a body almost entirely determines the nature of the ritual and the architectural aesthetic of the setting.

THE SANCTITY OF THE GRAVE

The physical and moral inviolability of the grave was reinforced in the eighteenth and nineteenth centuries with the increasing individualization of burial (itself reflecting the deepening belief in the sovereign identity of each human being). Furthermore, it was the widespread horror of graverobbing, principally to provide bodies for the early dissection trade, that consolidated the notion of the sanctity of the grave. The return to earth was regarded as everlasting and final; or at least until the Resurrection.

The unlawful removal of bodies occurred in order to meet the needs of the anatomy departments of hospitals, and is the subject of Ruth Richardson's seminal study, *Death, Dissection and the Destitute*.[8] Until the Anatomy Act of 1832, newly interred bodies were often stolen from the graves in which they had been buried and sold to hospitals. Such was the public horror towards this business, which derived as much from the mutilation and dissection of the body itself as its appropriation, that in many churchyards measures were taken against the possibility of new graves being re-opened and the bodies removed.

In some cemeteries a great stone or slab of metal would be placed over any new grave to prevent re-opening, until such time as the body had deteriorated beyond use for anatomical purposes. In other places a 'mortsafe' or metal cage would be cemented into place over the grave. The bodies of paupers buried in quicklime in large pits, which were left open until full, were obvious targets for the grave-robbers, or 'resurrectionists' as they were sometimes called. Bodies buried in Jewish cemeteries were especially favoured for stealing, as Jewish custom requires the burial of the dead within 24 hours, and as a result such bodies were especially useful to the anatomists. After the passing of the 1832 Act, the bodies of paupers and workhouse inhabitants were used.

As Richardson notes: 'In the course of the first century of the Anatomy Act's application, almost 57,000 bodies were dissected in the London anatomy schools alone. Less than *half a percent* came from anywhere other than institutions which housed the poor.'[9] Those who entered upright, left in a box, and many were destined, against all norms of cultural justice, not for the grave but for the dissecting table. The horror of dissection was felt deeply in working-class communities, where perhaps even more importance was attached to a 'decent' burial, and the sanctity of the dead person, than in other parts of society. Though poor in life, many families subscribed to 'coffin clubs', as many friendly societies were called, in order to afford, at the end, a proper funeral and interment.

The power and mystery of the dead body is nowhere better described than in D. H. Lawrence's story 'Odour of Chrysanthemums' (1914).

A woman waiting for her husband to return from his shift at the mine suddenly apprehends that something has gone wrong. News comes that he has been injured in an accident: a fall of coal had cut off the air to the underground seam and suffocated him. The corpse is carried home from the mine, and the wife and the miner's mother share the task of washing it and clothing it afresh. At the beginning of the story, one of the miner's young children had picked a chrysanthemum to give to his mother, who wears it in her apron that day. In a way this choice of flower unwittingly anticipates the tragedy, as the chrysanthemum is a flower that in many cultures is associated with death and cannot be given as a gift to the living.[10] The smell of the chrysanthemums gives a sensual, bitter edge to the story.

A deep respect for the integrity and wholeness of the body after death is a constant theme in popular culture, with or without its resurrectionary element. While the injunction to allow the dead to remain undisturbed in perpetuity seems anthropologically clear-cut, the belief has at times conflicted with other cultural imperatives. An equally deep wish to map the past and find out more about previous lives and cultures – represented by archaeology, for example – has often involved the excavation of burial sites. After all, as the Italian historian Carlo Ginzburg has noted, 'The attempt to attain knowledge of the past is also a journey into the world of the dead.' This dilemma has become a contentious issue in North America, along with many other parts of the world, where archaeologists often come into conflict with indigenous or 'Native' peoples over the excavation of sites where remains may be discovered that are many hundreds of years old, but which local people insist must remain undisturbed.

In Britain, a 'Survey of Jewish Built Heritage in the United Kingdom and Ireland' is making a systematic record of all Jewish cemeteries, in the process discovering that possible medieval Jewish burial sites have been excavated without due process, in contradiction to the long-standing Jewish law that forbids the disturbance of the dead, no matter how long ago they were buried.[11] In response to similar pressures against such past forms of disrespect to the dead, a number of British museums are now in the process of returning bodies and bodily remains that were once exhibited to their countries of origin for burial according to local ritual. One museum specialist has decried the Western exhibition mentality whereby so many tourists and museum visitors forget 'that these specimens were once living people with their own cultural beliefs about death and the afterlife which, in most cases, would not include public spectacle or a storage cupboard in a Western museum'.[12] Even at the time these bodies were collected, those doing the collecting often knew that they were violating cultural taboos and undertaking activities that were forbidden in the home culture. The fact was that 'Racism and colonialism allowed a double standard, as bodies were taken from the Americas, the Pacific, Africa and Asia, in ways that would have been unacceptable at home.'[13] In May 2002, the Royal College of Surgeons in London began to return all of its Tasmanian collection of human bodies and body parts, and other institutions that house similar collections in Europe are beginning to do the same.

There is both a long and a short history to this belief in the talismanic or sacerdotal status of the grave. Grave sites have usually been accorded particular status within most belief systems, but in modern society, as we know it, this status was further consolidated by its association with the rise of individualism, so that by the end of the nineteenth century the individual grave plot had gained a personalized, sacrosanct character of its own. Not only was there a gravestone with an individual name on it, along with dates of birth and death, but there were often other family or personal details inscribed, delineating the character of the person interred beneath. Furthermore, many gravestones literally took on the attributes of a human body, with head-, body- and foot-stones distinctly arranged, with some gravestones being coffin-shaped or even body-shaped.[14] The personal grave therefore took on the character of a shrine, a place to be visited, a focal point for meditation and memory.

A belief that the grave itself continued the personality of the deceased might also be assumed from the common practice of grave visiting, during which many people literally

At its most fully developed, the Victorian tombstone not only embodied an effigy of the deceased, but told the story of a life. The tomb of Devereux Plantagenet Cockburn in the Protestant Cemetery, Rome.

continue a conversation that had begun in life but was interrupted by the other person's demise. In a UK study of attitudes to death, cremation and burial published in 1995, it was found that a larger percentage of women than men favoured burial over cremation, specifically for the reason that it created a meaningful place to visit and consequently was a means of maintain a connection with the deceased.[15] The survey showed that the grave sites of those buried received more visits than the places where cremated remains were interred. The same study also found that those interviewed who had suffered the death of a child, had overwhelmingly chosen burial rather than cremation. The authors of the survey suggest that this was because it was felt that those who had died 'before their time' needed a more permanent memorial than that offered by cremation, and there is a sense that cremation erases bodily identity more thoroughly and irrevocably than burial (echoes here perhaps of residual resurrectionary hopes).

The custom of large-scale grave visiting on All

A coffin-style tombstone in a Suffolk churchyard, which doesn't pretend to hide the shape of death.

Souls' Day is an example of this wish to maintain a relationship with the dead, in which the gravestone or tomb comes to represent the person interred beneath or within.[16] This continuity between the living individual and that of their grave site or memorial stone comes across in a remark once made by Kafka. In a fit of depression, the Czech writer was reported to have said 'I am the same as my gravestone . . . Only a vague hope survives, no better than the inscriptions on gravestones.'[17] This strange reversal – in which at the same time as the body decomposes to become a husk or empty shell, the carapace of the gravestone becomes the permanent embodiment of the one who has disappeared within – is evident in the way in which the headstone eventually becomes synonymous with the person it represents.

This is evident in Mark C. Taylor's essay 'Ghost Stories', which prefaces his and Dietrich Christian Lammerts' collection of photographs of headstones, in which Taylor asserts enigmatically that, 'The graveyard is where we keep the dead *alive as dead*.'[18] In his essay, Taylor admits to a lifetime's travels in pursuit of grave rubbings from the headstones of the writers, philosophers and intellectuals he has most admired. These facsimiles are then framed and hung in his living-room, along with a potted ivy grown from a cutting taken from Hegel's grave in Berlin. For Taylor, these provide a material connection to the once embodied individuals whose graves he has visited, mediated through a physical transliteration of the headstone, along with the occasional transposition of its lichens, mosses and ivy growths.

It is during the Victorian era in Britain, in com-mon with the mid-nineteenth bourgeois culture of much of Europe, that the high point of funerary architecture and culture occurred, as we have already seen: elaborate tombstones, expensive headstones and sculptures from then onwards mark the individual or family grave, along with detailed inscriptions and professions of faith. During this period, even greater symbolic importance is attached to the family grave. The elaborate, monumental family mausoleums to be found in London's Highgate, Père-Lachaise and Brooklyn's Green-Wood all attest to the belief that the family grave or mausoleum was a means of cementing the notion of the family as the principal social and affective institution in the wider culture. In Britain, legislation still allows for as many as six people – invariably members of the same family – to be buried within the same, usually enlarged, grave ; 're-openings', as they are called in the funeral trade, are today often the only burials still allowed in the historic cemeteries, as last surviving members of families claim a space in an otherwise 'closed' cemetery.

OUR TOWN

The individual grave became legally inviolate in the USA at the end of the nineteenth century, and burial similarly assured in perpetuity.[19] The result was that the cemetery quickly assumed a key role in American civic memory and identity. The moral power of the individual grave extended its collective reach through the form of the cemetery to become a moral centre of the community. Such traditional cemeteries continue to remain a crucial neighbourhood institution, according to the contemporary American undertaker (and poet) Thomas Lynch, who has written of the cemetery in his own town,

> The dead were put, properly, out of our homes but not out of our hearts, out of sight but not out of town. Thus Oak Grove always seemed a safe extension, a tiny banishment of the dead from the living, a kindly stone's throw away – a neighbourhood of its own, among whose stones the living often spent their Sunday afternoons picnicking among the granite suburbs . . . The distance between the dead and the living seemed no greater than the river.[20]

This American attitude is also evident in Thornton Wilder's still powerful, play *Our Town*, a moving evocation of small town America, in which the cemetery provides one of the two principal stage settings – though this play being in the early modern style, the props and scenery have to be imagined by the audience. *Our Town* opens with teenage schoolchildren gathered outside the Main Street soda-store backdrop, laughing and talking. A few scenes later we see them as adulthood beckons and relationships form. In between we have met their parents and grandparents, gossiping, arguing and getting by with the daily stuff of life. Great hopes are raised, and then dashed, small comforts achieved, hearts broken, and the brief span of life is shown to be even more fragile than any of them in maturity would ever have believed. By Act Three, the final one, some are already dead but sit comfortably on stage as ghosts. Throughout the play, Main Street and the town cemetery are set in counterpoint to each other: a townscape and a landscape interlocked within one other's envelope of meaning.

Act Three comes as a shock. The dead are on stage sitting in rows of chairs, as if upright in their coffins, when they see a cortege approaching. They, like the audience, are anxious to learn who is to join them, and it turns out to be young Emily, the main character in Act One, who has just died in childbirth. The rest of Act Three is about Emily's induction into the company of the dead on the day of her funeral, as her fears are allayed by the easy-going banter of the long dead, now comfortably at rest. This low-key discussion is intended to make the audience understand how indifferent the living are to the value of living itself, only realizing too late how pregnant with meaning each moment of daily life is.

CONVERSATIONS WITH THE DEAD

Our Town is a small but affecting play, at the heart of which is the notion that the dead listen, an idea as old as funerary culture itself. Within many belief systems the landscapes and buildings of the dead also act as confessional spaces, places in which the living can communicate with those who have gone before. This is what the architecture of death is most certainly meant to accomplish. For their part, the dead are thought to sit in judgement on the living, and act as a sounding-board for the moral debates of the living community. When Perikles gave his famous funeral oration, he assumed that he was speaking to the dead as well as the living, since the ghosts or 'shades' of the dead remained 'powerful forces of good and bad fortune'.[21] The same judgemental or interrogative role is played within many cultures by ghosts or ancestral spirits: the opening scenes of *Hamlet* provide a textbook example.

·

The historian Keith Thomas has suggested that this belief in ghosts – and the attribution of great significance to the messages they bring, the questions they ask, the approval or disapproval they express – functions as a symbolic way of representing the cultural need to respect the wishes of the dead. Thus in modern societies, he argues, 'The main reason for the disappearance of ghosts is that society is no longer responsive to the presumed wishes of past generations.'[22]

For many who have chosen burial for their loved ones, the grave site remains 'a valid place of communication', in the words of sociologist, Peter Jupp.[23] His interviews with a small group of bereaved people in rural settings confirmed that the grave site is still an important place in which conversations begun in life can be continued. 'I often go up to the grave to talk to my husband', said one widow. 'Whenever I needed help with anything, I went up and talked to my husband about it.' Another specifically mentioned her dislike of cremation for precisely these reasons: there was neither body nor grave to which one could direct one's attentions. 'I don't like cremation', another woman asserted. 'It's all out-of-sight, out-of-mind. I go down to the cemetery and I talk to my Mum.'[24] Grave sites also act as shrines, particularly those of children. In the children's section of the beautifully maintained Crooswijk Cemetery in Rotterdam, many of the graves are surrounded by toys and soft animals; balloons are tied to nearby bushes and trees. In the City of London Cemetery, according to its Director, at Christmas-time some bereaved parents and relatives set up Christmas trees and lay out presents: in doing so, the symbolic world reasserts its moral power.[25]

Even so, the wishes of the dead still come down to us with both great moral power and legal effect on occasion. One well-known example is J.M.W. Turner's expressed will when he donated many of his paintings to the British nation, that this gift was made on the condition that they would be exhibited for free, a condition that has caused galleries, museums and Government departments no end of difficulty ever since, especially in relation to the issue of gallery charges. The conservative (and conservationist) philosopher Roger Scruton attaches great importance to the idea that the ideas, wishes and judgements of the dead should still exert a moral pressure on contemporary discussions with regard to the historical landscape and townscape, arguing that living generations only have limited rights to sweep away the past in order to meet their contemporary needs. It is the felt legitimacy of the rights of past generations and cultures not to be lost from public memory and presence – notably in the buildings and landscapes they have left behind – that underpins heritage and conservationist movements around the world. Likewise, today's environmentalists increasingly place great importance on the needs and interests of generations as yet unborn, whose future rights should also impinge on present-day political decision-making.

Both views support the claim made at the outset of this book that the cemetery remains a moral force-field in society, acting as a meeting-place of past and future aspirations, as well as a reminder of the transience of human wishes and actions. In this function, it provides a rather longer time-frame for the way the living might think about their temporary appropriation of the institutions of power. Thus the landscapes of the dead are not just elements in the topography of place, but also act as amphitheatres, or echo chambers, in which the conversation of men and women is continued, generation after generation. As at Cerveteri, the city of the living and the city of the dead need to remain in constant touch with each other, through the processional flow of people, artefacts, ideas and memories.

THE RISE OF CREMATION

The rise in popularity of cremation was swift in many countries, sweeping in on a tide of twentieth-century rationalism and scientific orthodoxy. The first public cremations in Europe were carried out in Breslau (now Wroclaw) in 1874; in Dresden and Milan in 1876; in Gotha, Germany, in 1879. One of the first unofficial cremations in Britain took place in 1877, when the bodies of the wife and mother of a Captain Hanham in Dorset, which had been stored in a mausoleum, were cremated privately in an orchard by the Captain. In 1884, rather more notoriously, was the case of the singular Dr William Price of Glamorgan, South Wales. Price, a Chartist, Druid, vegetarian and advocate of free love, attempted to publicly cremate the body of his son, whose name was Jesus Christ and who had died at the age of only a few months. Price was forced to abandon the attempt by angry parishioners. However, attempts to prosecute Price for his attempted cremation failed, as there was nothing on the statute book that construed cremation as a legal offence, and this refusal to prosecute gave the cremationists further room to manoeuvre. The first public crematorium in Britain was established at Woking, and the body of a woman was cremated there in 1885, despite there

being no legislation in effect to warrant this. By the 1890s, however, crematoria were established in a number of cities in Great Britain, as they were also elsewhere in Europe and North America.

If attitudes towards death, and the disposal of the dead, are key rites and symbolic acts in the organization of any culture or social structure, then the very different rates of cremation in otherwise similar modern European and North American nations and cultures remains something of a sociological or anthropological mystery, not simply attributable to religious belief or other national cultural characteristics. Consider the figures in the box below.[26]

Percentage of Deaths Resulting in Cremation in 1999

Austria 21
Belgium 30
Czech Republic 76
Denmark 71
Eire 5
Finland 25
France 16
Great Britain/UK 70
Hungary 30
Italy 4 (in 1998)
The Netherlands 48
Norway 31
Portugal 14
Spain 13
Sweden 68
Switzerland 69
USA 25

The continued – though weakening – opposition to cremation by the Catholic Church largely explains the low rates in Eire, Italy, Spain, Portugal and France. Yet the great differences amongst the Scandinavian countries are not so easily explained, neither are those between ex-Communist countries such as the Czech Republic and Hungary. Similarly, one may wonder why Austria, Belgium and, to a lesser extent, The Netherlands, continue with low rates of cremation compared with other equally secular societies, such as the Czech Republic, Denmark, Great Britain, Switzerland and Sweden. It is clear that more than religion is involved, as the distinct case of the relatively low cremation rate in the USA (another modern, Protestant culture) suggests.

The sociologist Tony Walter believes that it is because so many Americans were immigrants. These immigrants regarded a burial in American soil as the ultimate symbol of occupying their new homeland. Getting cremated possibly seems a strangely disembodied or 'unearthed' form of disposal.[27] Getting buried is perhaps the most effective way of setting down roots into the native soil. It is for this reason, perhaps, that American military culture – and by implication the wider public culture – is still more resolute on repatriating the remains of armed forces personnel killed overseas for burial at home. The other exception to the popularity of cremation in the more Protestant or secular societies of the developed world is Finland, where, again, historical circumstances, such as lengthy Swedish and then Russian occupation, gave the Finnish churchyard or cemetery a particular national resonance and form of identity with the native soil. Even in a country as secular as

Finland, the cultural symbolism of 'homeland' represented by the church, the churchyard and the cemetery is still regarded with great importance.

Britain is now one of the countries where cremation is by far the most common means used in the disposal of the dead, though there is evidence that this is not always necessarily from choice, since cremation is usually much cheaper than burial, and this may be the deciding factor for many. Furthermore, now that burial space in many towns and cities is no longer available at close distance, or within the affective or imagined boundaries of an assumed geographical community (as in Wilder's play, or that evoked by Lynch), those who might have chosen burial as a way of expressing their commitment to place and community no longer have this option; in which case, one form of disposal becomes just as good as any other. Furthermore, those who leave the decision to others about their disposal after death are, according to research, most likely to be cremated.[28]

Yet, in recent years the seemingly inexorable advance of cremation towards becoming the universal form of disposal in developed societies, may have been arrested. Some religions still oppose cremation: a survey of religious attitudes to cremation undertaken in Britain in the 1990s found that 84 per cent of Catholics, 90 per cent of Muslims and Buddhists, and 96 per cent of Jews continued to assert the wish to be buried.[29] Other sensibilities still regard the quasi-industrial character of cremation as representing the worst aspects of a mechanized, over-rationalised culture (in which echoes of mass incineration in Nazi concentration camps in the Second World War still reside). For Jews, burial is a part of a long history of creating sacred places of memory and atonement, and it was the large-scale cremation of Jews that added further atrocity to the crime of genocide. The concentration camp survivor André Schwartz-Bart wrote at the end of his account of the camps:

> So this story will not finish with some tomb to be visited in pious memory. For the smoke that rises from the crematoria obeys physical laws like any other: the particles come together and disperse according to the wind, which propels them. The only pilgrimage, dear reader, would be to look sadly at a stormy sky now and then.[30]

Furthermore, environmentalists, having discovered that cremation is not so ecologically benign as it was once thought to be, today increasingly favour 'natural' or 'woodland' burial. But woodland burial is land-hungry; on the other hand, unlike a formal cemetery, the eventual return of the designated burial ground to natural woodland in the course of only a few generations gives it high ecological status, if not great cultural or aesthetic value. A number of single people are now choosing woodland burial, realizing that with nobody to look after their grave, nature alone is capable of solving the issue of subsequent maintenance and care.[31]

COMMEMORATING THE WAR DEAD

A number of those who have addressed the subject of mortality in the twentieth century regard the calamitous scale of death during the First World War as marking an irrevocable change in public attitudes to the relationship between the sovereign body and the continuation of personality after death. Resurrectionary beliefs suffered a grievous blow, as so many of the hundreds of thousands of bodies – or what remained of those bodies after gunfire and bombing had done their work – simply disappeared beneath the mud, or were buried at random where they fell. The attachment to the individual grave as the symbolic site of identity could no longer be sustained, hence the symbolic role played by the Tomb of the Unknown Soldier. In such conditions, the ideal of remembrance, in the form of a new kind of national, collective memory, emerged to fill the eschatological vacuum. While most of the following paragraphs relate specifically to the commemoration of twentieth-century wars involving Britain, in former Commonwealth countries, such as Australia, the seriousness with which both the people and the political culture took the commemoration of the war dead amounted to what has become, according to K. I. Inglis, a modern 'civil religion'.[32]

The Commonwealth War Graves Commission (formerly the Imperial War Graves Commission), founded in 1917 by Royal Charter and representing the governments of the United Kingdom, Australia, Canada, India, New Zealand and South Africa, continues to commemorate over one million Commonwealth dead of the First World War, over half of whom were finally buried in marked graves in war cemeteries throughout the world, the rest buried anonymously, with their names recorded on memorial plaques and stones. It is also responsible for the upkeep of over 170,000 graves in the UK.

The sheer scale of death and the physical

obliteration of so many of the bodies of the dead during the First World War meant that new ways of responding to burial were required. The suggested repatriation of bodies was quickly but agonizingly refused, as it was thought that this would raise public concerns that matters of wealth, status and influence were being exercised unevenly to honour some of the war dead more than others. The debates about this astonishingly bold policy are recorded in a rewarding and moving study, *Courage Remembered: The Story behind the Construction and Maintenance of the Common-wealth's Military Cemeteries and Memorials of the Wars of 1914–1918 and 1939–1945*. Despite the quasi-Governmental status of this report, the debates and issues it records remain affecting.[33] Likewise, the decision to mark all graves with an identical headstone, irrespective of rank or religion, was firmly advocated by the War Graves Commission in its published declaration that servicemen and -women 'In death, from General to Private, of whatever race or creed, should receive equal honour under a memorial which should be the common symbol of their comrade-ship and of the cause for which they died.'[34]

The founding architect of the War Graves Commission, Fabian Ware, has been described by the military historian John Keegan as 'a modest man who deserves to be recognised as a major semiologist of British culture in the twentieth century'. This is principally for his efforts in creating a uniquely British collection of landscape and architectural styles and symbols for war cemeteries, which, when taken together, created one of the most powerful and enduring cultural landscapes of all, and which are now found throughout the world.[35] There are today British

The serried rows of uniform headstones in the British War Cemetery in Rome.

war cemeteries in 134 countries, reflecting the far-flung extent of hostilities in the two World Wars. All of these cemeteries contain identical head-stones made of Portland stone, 2 feet, 8 inches high, 1 foot, 3 inches wide, engraved with a regimental badge and a symbol representing the known religion of the person commemorated. The cemeteries are carefully maintained, formal enclosed gardens, often with imposing entrance pavilions. Ironically, the modest, uniform headstones advocated by Ware are very similar to those found in the churchyards of the pacifist religious sect, the Quakers.

The simple, uniform style of headstones common in Quaker churchyards appears to have been emulated in the headstones adopted by war cemeteries.

The American Cemetery and Memorial at Meuse-Argonne, distinguished by its monumental design, propriety and sense of order.

While it has always been American policy to repatriate the remains of soldiers killed abroad, the scale of casualties in the First and Second World Wars meant that this was not always possible. American war cemeteries in Europe are equally distinguished in their monumental design and sense of propriety and order, as is evident at the Meuse-Argonne Cemetery, northwest of Verdun. Indeed, their form, according

to one historian, was 'part of a concerted effort to use these new monumental works of design to project a new image of America in the global arena'.[36] These 'enclaves of America' were 'wholly ordered constructions governed by . . . a rigorous and rigid application of Beaux-Arts principles of geometry, hierarchical order, and symmetry'.[37] Every American war cemetery abroad contains a chapel, a space for the inscription of the names of the missing and the dead, along with maps, murals and reliefs of the battlefields to which the cemeteries relate. They combine landscape, architecture, museum and artistic commemoration in one ordered and impressive whole.

The majority of British war cemeteries were designed, developed and maintained by British gardeners, many of whom had been trained at the Royal Botanic Gardens in Kew, and who were deeply familiar with the landscape designs and horticultural palettes developed by Gertrude Jekyll and Edwin Lutyens. The sensibility that informed their design is well described by garden historian Jane Brown:

For the cemeteries that Lutyens and Miss Jekyll designed in detail (which set the pattern for all the others) there is the enclosing evergreen (holly or yew) hedge, the symbolic fastigiate oak or Lombardy poplars, massings of the workaday shrubs of the English countryside – blackthorn, whitehorn, hazel, guelder rose and honeysuckle – with the Virgin's flowery meads ushered into soft borders where the headstones stand, hellebores, narcissus, forget-me-not, fritillaries, foxgloves, columbines, London Pride, begonia, nepeta and roses. These are Arts and Crafts gardens, outdoor rooms of green walls, their vistas ordered and closed by the most sublime stone works, most with book-room pavilions and shelters, all of them laced and imbued with meaning and double meaning, all the mannerist notions of their seventeenth-century forebears.[38]

British war cemeteries maintain the same landscape aesthetic wherever they are in the world, and it is the open, modest aesthetic of a formal garden, rather than a cemetery: consolatory, rather than gloomy and tragic. The writer Geoff Dyer, in one of the best contemporary reflections on the battlefields of the First World War, describes one of the smaller cemeteries in Flanders, Redan Ridge Number One, as 'one of the most beautiful places on earth . . . Standing here, I know that some part of me will always be calmed by the memory of this place, by the vast capacity for forgiveness revealed by these cemeteries, by this landscape.'[39] Those who doubt the power of landscape to console should visit some of these cemeteries, the design and care of which successfully embody and integrate so many nuances of public and private emotion.

These designs did not emerge fully formed. In 1917, when Lutyens was asked to visit war-torn France to report on what might be done in the form of military cemeteries and memorials, his first instinct was to let the devastated landscape speak for itself, with time and vegetation doing most of the 'grief-work' leading to topographical and emotional recovery. In a passage from a letter he wrote to his wife during that visit, Lutyens commented that

The battlefields – the obliteration of all human endeavour and achievement of destruction is bettered by the poppies and the wild flowers that are as friendly to an unexploded shell as they are to the leg of a garden seat in Surrey . . . a wilderness of annuals and where one sort of flower has grown the effect is charming, easy and oh so pathetic. One thinks for a moment no other monument is needed.[40]

Nevertheless, Lutyens, along with a small number of other architects, 'established the architecture, language and landscape of remembrance which were to become ubiquitous symbols for post-war British society: the headstones, the Cross of Sacrifice and the Stone of Remembrance within a landscaped garden'.[41] These cemeteries continue to evoke the scale of loss and desolation caused by the First World War more than any official history, or other form of documentation.

The influence of Lutyens's ideals and designs on the British imagination should not be under-estimated. He believed in an 'elemental mode' of ornamental art, and it is the plainsong austerity of the design of many of the war cemeteries, and, most notably, of the Cenotaph in Whitehall, London, that distinguishes British funerary design and culture of the First World War from most others. Lutyens's own personal character was formed through a strongly geometrical approach to design and architecture, influenced by certain pantheistic beliefs, as well as an underlying belief in spiritual universalism. The design of the Cenotaph, which at first sight seems to be a series of stepped plinths in the form of a rectangular monument, in fact

The ubiquitous Cross of Sacrifice, designed by Reginald Blomfield, found in British war cemeteries.

Lutyens's religious beliefs were more complex than most others at the time. According to Winter, he was 'a pantheist who moved in theosophist circles'. In the design of the Cenotaph, in the layout of the war cemeteries with their simple, common headstones, in Reginald Blomfield's Cross of Sacrifice, the British eschewed the rhetorical, religiose symbolism of many war memorials found elsewhere in Europe, where it was more common to employ the form of the Pieta or Crucifixion to give the sacrifice a religious meaning and consolation. Winter

The Cenotaph in Whitehall, London, designed by Edwin Lutyens: it dominates this part of London with its sombre presence.

contains no straight lines whatsoever, but is coordinated to form part of a vast, invisible sphere, whose vertical lines converge upwards to a point exactly 1.801 feet, 8 inches from the ground.[42] The effect of the Cenotaph, partly due to its location in Whitehall, bisecting this great street at the heart of British governmental power, managed, in the words of Jay Winter, 'to transform the commemorative landscape by making all of "official" London into an imagined cemetery'.

ascribes this simplicity to 'Anglican iconophobia', a deeply formed suspicion of any kind of Baroque or Marian sensibility. Even the adoption of the poppy as a symbol of remembrance was viewed with great disapproval in some quarters because of its pagan associations.[43] Likewise, a strong resistance to 'the pantomime of allegory' was expressed early on in the discussions as to the tone, style and aesthetic of remembrance that was already being discussed well before the Great War ended.[44] Simplicity, directness and a sober kind of English epiphany marked the cumulative mood.

Furthermore, the controversial British decision not to repatriate the bodies of those killed in the War was not adopted elsewhere in Europe, particularly in Catholic countries. In such places, large-scale public and private efforts were made to identify and bring back the remains of dead soldiers to their village or town of origin, usually with a great deal of civic and religious ceremony. In other ways the British response was more spontaneous and vernacular: there is evidence that in the more densely populated, poorer parts of London, for example, street shrines were hurriedly improvised, perhaps in the form of a wooden board with the names of local men killed inscribed on it, placed on a street corner, and where others could place flowers or other tokens of remembrance.[45]

After both world wars, however, many elaborate war memorials were constructed throughout Britain, usually listing the names of all those who had served and died abroad. It is estimated that the UK now has between 50,000 and 70,000 war memorials standing in 'churches, parks, private gardens, village and town halls, scout huts and railway offices', for many of which, according to one MP speaking in Parliament on the subject in 1998, 'no arrangements were made for their future upkeep'.[46] As a result a number are now in disrepair, overgrown, and in some cases artefacts have been found in antique shops, for sale. Even so, probably the majority are still maintained and cherished, particularly in those rural communities where demographic change has not been so rapid.

Such memorials and gardens quickly became one of the new defining features and coordinates of the local townscape, as well as the focus for a processional, memorializing culture that still exists today. In the summer of 1986, in the course of a cycle journey the length of Britain, from John O'Groats to Land's End along back roads and narrow lanes, my overwhelming impression was of a village life and culture that had been indelibly marked by the impact of the First World War. Not even the smallest settlement was without a war memorial of some kind. These were, most commonly, an obelisk set in its own immaculately maintained landscaped setting, sometimes a garden of remembrance, a memorial hall, a designated area in the village churchyard or cemetery, even a drinking trough or a public bench. Though the First World War was hardly ever visited upon civilian Britain, the commemoration of it changed the British landscape and townscape for ever – as it did in so many other countries, including 'faraway' Australia, as described in Inglis's detailed and moving history of that irrevocable change.[47]

A typical, and beautifully maintained, village war memorial in Batcombe, Somerset, erected at the end of the First World War.

PERPETUITY AND DECLINE

While *that* culture of memory remains strong, the wider memorial culture in Britain is badly neglected.[48] Furthermore, a number of commentators have compared the state of British cemeteries with those elsewhere in Europe, and found those in Britain to be among the worst.[49] In North America, many cemeteries in run-down urban and rural areas are equally suffering from lack of care and maintenance.

The neglected condition of many Victorian cemeteries in Britain is largely the result of an unhappy combination of poorly thought-out legislation combined with unsustainable economics.

In 1846, when the British government was openly faced with a burial crisis of major proportions, it responded by promising a series of Burial Acts in the 1850s, which made burial issues a matter for local decision-making and policy, but with one proviso: this was the insistence that once buried, 'human remains could never again be disturbed without special licence from the Home Office'.[50] This reversed a long tradition of re-using graves in churchyard cemeteries, and enshrined the principle of burial in perpetuity.

Estimates as to how many bodies the average English rural churchyard contains range from

5,000 (Kenneth Lindley)[51] to Oliver Rackham's assertion that 'the average English country churchyard contains at least 10,000 bodies'.[52] Within London it has been estimated that the churchyard of St Martin-in-the-Fields, while only 60 metres square, contained the remains of between 60,000 and 70,000 people.[53] Bunhill Fields, in the City of London, 'the *Campo Santo* of the Dissenters' according to the poet Robert Southey, contained some 120,000 corpses in just four acres by the time it was closed in 1852.[54] It is quite common to notice when visiting many ancient churches that the surrounding ground level is actually much higher than the floor level of the church itself, the result of so many burials. In Sylvia Townsend Warner's *The True Heart*, a novel set in rural Essex at the end of the nineteenth century, the local churchyard is described as 'so old that the dead who lay there had raised the level of the ground by six or seven feet, and in the flatness of the marsh this elevation was something considerable'.[55] Certainly some churchyard ground levels have risen as high as the surrounding walls, as at Kilpeck, Herefordshire. If you visit the beautiful cemetery at Te Vraag in Amsterdam, you will find that new retaining walls of woven branches have recently been inserted to reinforce the existing walls needed to keep the raised ground from spilling over into the surrounding paths and ditches. At Trinity Church in New York, the historic churchyard there contained the remains of over 100,000 New Yorkers by 1800, raising the level of the churchyard 'by several yards', according to one commentator.[56] The sheer accumulation of headstones in the Jewish Cemetery in Prague is evidence of the density to which these small religious or parochial cemeteries were packed.

Government policy in Britain at this time rejected Utilitarian ideas gaining credence in the same period about how to deal with burial on a large scale. Such ideas were exemplified in a report by the eminent Government adviser and social reformer Edwin Chadwick (1800–90). Chadwick was asked to provide a supplementary report to his enormous *Report on the Sanitary Condition of the Labouring Classes in Britain* (1842), which he did the following year in *A Supplementary Report on the Results of a special Enquiry into the Practice of Interment in Towns*. This uncovered evidence of horrific conditions relating to the care and interment of bodies in working-class areas, of enormous financial exploitation by ruthless funeral companies, and of serious health hazards posed by poorly managed cemeteries. Chadwick's proposals to deal with this situation were radical, some would say ruthless, in the extreme. He argued for a series of 'national cemeteries' (one imagines something along the lines of the schemes dreamed up by Boullée) run by the state, at some distance from the towns and cities, each with a 'corpse house' for the safekeeping of the body between death and interment, supervised by public health officers. Furthermore, all graves would be re-used after ten years, and the remains re-interred in a common grave, as was already common in many cemeteries in Europe. Not one of these ideas was ever adopted.

In practice, once even the largest of the great nineteenth-century cemeteries approached near-capacity, and as income dwindled, the companies either went bankrupt, or relinquished ownership of the cemetery into other hands. In either event, this nearly always meant the hands of the local authority (or elected city council). Since many of these already had so many other financial priorities, especially in regard to the care of the living, they allowed the quality of horticultural and architectural maintenance to be reduced to a minimal level – and sometimes even worse. In 1988 there was a public outcry in Britain when journalists reported that Westminster City Council (in London), keen to be rid of such a heavy revenue obligation with regard to the maintenance of its cemeteries, quietly sold three of them to a property company for just 15 pence. The sale was rescinded after vigorous protests by families of people who had been buried in these cemeteries, who suspected that in time the sites would be used for redevelopment. Similar development pressures have emerged in other parts of Britain, not always successfully resisted.

In looking for solutions to what appears to be an intractable economic problem – the long-term funding of expensive public assets that have no direct functional use any more, and in some cases little amenity use either, certainly in their present neglected state – people have looked towards other countries where the right to burial in perpetuity has never been commonplace, in law or in practice. For where re-burial has been allowed, cemeteries seem able to flourish, and maintain their position within the urban townscape and culture. If the historical cemeteries cannot be maintained to a decent standard, then in future new cemeteries should be costed and financed to allow for proper care.

This means considering the re-use of graves after an agreed period. In Australia, a number of cemeteries have gone ahead with the re-use of grave space in order to keep cemeteries in use, though this has not occurred without controversy.[57]

The idea of digging up the dead remains abhorrent to many, and often for good reason. In the past it has usually been the bodies of the poor – particularly the anonymous poor – that have been the first to be cleared for re-use, a situation many regard as an offence to social and natural justice. But there is also the issue of respecting the conditions under which people were buried originally, often in the strong belief and understanding, especially among loved ones, that this was an arrangement made in perpetuity. A number of commentators on such matters insist that such agreements – possibly contracts even – cannot be retrospectively rescinded to meet modern, changing priorities.[58] Few, however, would now oppose the idea that in future this might become accepted practice if it is undertaken by consent, though British and North American sensibilities may take some persuading.

THE RE-USE OF GRAVES

The re-use of graves is common in many parts of Europe. In Vienna's Central Cemetery (the one so loathed by Thomas Bernhard), the basic agreement for burial takes the form of a ten-year lease, which can be renewed again and again for a fee, but if not forthcoming, the remains are taken up after the initial lease runs out, re-interred along with many others in a much smaller space, and the original grave space sold

One of the burial fields at La Certosa, Bologna, in which previous interments have been excavated and the remains put in an ossuary, in order to re-use the site for new burials.

to the next buyer.[59] The practice clearly discriminates against the less wealthy; on the other hand, it also means that the cemetery continues in use, and funds continue to be provided to maintain it in good condition. On All Souls' Day every year, the cemetery in Vienna is packed with visitors bringing flowers and candles and paying respect to the dead, even to strangers who are unknown to them. More than three million people have been buried in the cemetery since it opened. At La Certosa in Bologna, as has already been observed, the re-use of graves is common, with whole sections being excavated and the remains removed for secondary burial after an agreed period – usually ten years – for earth interments.

In Greece, where cremation is prohibited by the Greek Orthodox Church, and where space is sometimes at a premium, burial in perpetuity is a luxury few Greeks can afford. Some families

transport the bodies of their loved ones abroad to be cremated, and bring the ashes back for interment surreptitiously. Others are obliged to rent a grave for as little a period as three years, after which the remains are taken up and buried elsewhere. Even large marble masonry used to adorn the original grave is re-used elsewhere.[60] The Greek practice of burial for a limited period before re-interring the remains elsewhere, has been sensitively documented by an American anthropologist, Loring M. Danforth, with photographs by Alexander Tsiaras, in an extra-ordinary ethnographic study of the subject.[61]

Danforth went to study the tiny village of Potamia in northern Thessaly, a village of just 600 inhabitants. The opening chapter describes the imminent exhumation in the village cemetery of the body of a young woman killed five years previously in a hit-and-run car accident, and whose bones, her anguished mother knew, were ready to be dug up from the grave. These would then be finally laid to rest, wrapped in a white cloth, in the small ossuary building, along with those of others who had gone before. This cemetery-keeping and exhumation work was women's work, along with the nightly gathering in the cemetery, where women sat on the graves of their loved ones, wept, shouted, and talked to the departed.

The exhumation of the remains of the young woman, in Danforth's words,

had to be done, according to custom, before she had completed five full years in the ground. She would be exhumed because her family wanted to see her for the last time and because she would not have to bear the weight of the earth on her chest for eternity. She would be exhumed so that she could see once more the light of the sun.[62]

It was the job of the younger women in the village to open up the grave and dig down until signs of the remains were encountered; and the job of an older woman, or the mother herself, to complete the task with a small hoe. This was a great ritual occasion, accompanied by much wailing and singing. This intimate culture of grave-watching, grave-care and the practice of re-burial, effectively kept the cemetery at the centre of village life, especially for the women.

However, legislation to allow the re-use of graves is not likely to solve the problems of existing cemeteries now poorly maintained or neglected. In such cases there are often competing claims as to what can be done to halt their decline, if not restore them to their former

glory. For some environmentalists, as I mentioned, the lack of public use and horti-cultural maintenance over many years has inadvertently created valuable urban micro-habitats for rare lichen, flora and fauna; as a result, they claim that this is their most appropriate function in modern circumstances, in support of bio-diversity, as we have already seen in the case of many historic churchyards. On the other hand, heritage enthusiasts are keen to see many of the original Victorian architectural features, such as chapels, mausoleums, sculptures and tombstones preserved and refurbished, weaving these great open-air galleries of past architectural and sculptural styles back into the urban fabric.

To further complicate matters, modern amenity and leisure interests offer yet another option: make such cemeteries safe to the public (which may include levelling and getting rid of bulky and dangerous monuments and head-stones, clearing all existing vegetation, and replanting them with grasses and wild flowers), and so turn these sites into new kinds of parks and open spaces. Such decisions in the end – which are about attempting to reconcile very different sets of interests and perspectives – are likely to be solved on a case-by-case basis, to meet local circumstances.

Issues of scale are crucial. It is surely right that the great Victorian cemeteries be brought back into use as public gardens with as much of their original buidings and statues restored as is possible. These are enormously original and important parts of the cultural heritage of any city, region or nation. Yet there is no reason why the smaller redundant churchyards and cemeteries should not be cultivated as small gardens or wildlife sites to fulfil other purposes.

BURIAL ECONOMICS

But such debates still do not address the question of how to finance, manage and maintain new cemeteries. In the twentieth century, a relative decline in belief in the afterlife, alongside the growing popularity of cremation, has meant that the economic underpinning of large-scale landscaping, architecture and maintenance has been undermined or compromised. The role of the cemetery in modern urban life and culture is a minority concern, too rarely addressed in public discussion or debate.

The rise of the grand Picturesque cemetery, or of the elaborate family tombs and memorial sculptures to be found in nineteenth-century cemeteries, reflected a rise in individual wealth and inherited prosperity, which, along with a powerful belief in life after death, and burial in perpetuity, meant that an expensive tomb in an exquisitely landscaped cemetery came to be regarded not as a cost but as an investment. As Victor Hugo once said, to be buried in Père-Lachaise was like having mahogany furniture. Even in working-class cultures, saving for a 'proper funeral' was regarded as one of the more important priorities of the household economy. But these attitudes are no longer so common.

Today, increasing numbers of people prefer to spend their savings in this life. Such concerns matter less where there is a strong political commitment to the civic meaning and culture of the cemetery, seen as an expression of collective values, such as may be found in many municipal

cemeteries in the larger and wealthier cities of Europe. Here the costs of maintaining a cemetery are regarded as a justifiable element in sustaining a local civic culture and civic pride. Yet at the other end of the political scale, where economic individualism holds sway, and it is private wealth alone that provides the only guarantee of landscape or architectural integrity, then the poorer end of the burial culture may end up reverting almost to a brute naturalism. This was certainly the case as represented in the shocking story of the Tri-State Crematory in Georgia, USA, when in February 2002 it was discovered that several hundred bodies that were supposed to have been cremated had been dumped in the woods or left to rot in outhouses, due to broken-down equipment and inadequate management and public regulation of facilities.

The early controversies over the financial and corporate structure of the new cemeteries were, and remain, a particularly American affair. In most of Europe the provision for burial resides almost entirely in the hands of the church or the municipal authorities. Not so in America, where the private sector dominates all aspects of funerary culture. And while many American cemeteries are exemplars of careful management and sympathetic design (and private family funeral firms, deeply imbued with the best of small-town communitarian sentiment), lack of public regulation has also meant that there have been serious irregularities and a signal lack of respect and basic humanity in the services offered to poorer communities at times. Furthermore, in America, as in Britain, the funeral business is increasingly subjected to takeovers, resulting in the domination of the industry by a few very large companies.

Writing about the role of the cemetery in twentieth-century North American culture, David Sloane, perhaps provocatively, has suggested that the decline in the cultural importance of the cemetery has coincided with the growing interest in other cultural institutions, such as museums, local history societies, sculpture parks and botanical and wildlife gardens. In his view, the symbolic intensity of the cemetery has been diluted within a burgeoning *museumization* of culture, including many versions of fake authenticity. The dead seem to be losing their moral power within a culture of ersatz history. It is possible that the non-secular, civic cemetery is being marginalized in North America today, either by the formidable cultures of the marketplace or revealed religion. Meanwhile, in some parts of Europe at least, attitudes are beginning to move the other way, towards a strengthening of the civic cemetery or public memorial garden.

The burial park at Colney Wood near Norwich, Norfolk.

chapter eight

A Place at the End
of the Earth

Thus the modern architecture of death is an

eclectic reflection of the pluralism of the

late-twentieth century and of the uncertainty

which death brings in its wake.

Modernism has always had a deep

and profound problem with the

architecture of death.

Edwin Heathcote, *Monument Builders*[1]

THE ARCHITECTURE OF DEATH IN THE
MODERN WORLD

The difficulties faced by architects and designers in responding to the matter and the mystery of death have been compounded by the unprecedented impact cremation had in Europe in the twentieth century. It has been profound, yet it has been relatively little discussed as an ethical or architectural issue. Without a body to provide the focal point around which the grave or the tomb is to be designed or articulated, it is not surprising that there has been an understandable retreat to a kind of polite formalism. Thus many countries have witnessed the rise of the neatly ordered rose gardens of remembrance, mathematically precise rows of columbaria, and modest cremation chapels, none of which seem capable of possessing the moral power of the embodied space represented by the traditional grave or tomb, let alone the historic landscaped cemetery.

As a result, it has been very difficult to produce a robust, let alone grandiloquent, architectural response to the housing of very small amounts of human ash. Perhaps those who choose cremation prefer it this way: cremation is, after all, an anti-monumentalist impulse in a non-Heroic Age society. Yet throughout history it has been the measure and form of the human body, from the emblematic role played by 'Vitruvian Man' in Renaissance architecture to Le Corbusier's hypothetical London policeman, that has provided the fundamental measure on which architecture is based, and from which it derives its basic morphology. Without a body it is unlikely that there can ever be a fully realized funerary architecture. In future it is more likely that there will be a range of architectural responses to the material fact of death and disposal, a number of which are considered here now.

This will be quite different to earlier periods when a single great development captured the public imagination, as happened with the opening of Père-Lachaise at the beginning of the nineteenth century, and when in the early years of the twentieth century Stockholm's Woodland Cemetery did the same. Both were strikingly original and influential new models of landscape and funerary architecture, which were visited, admired and emulated throughout many parts of the world. To a lesser degree, Forest Lawn – admired and execrated in equal parts – has also proved influential in the twentieth century, most particularly in North America.

The renewal of interest in cemetery architecture and landscape aesthetics would probably not have been anticipated as recently as a decade ago, when attention to funerary cultures seemed to have reached an absolute low. Today, however, there is a resurgence of concern with matters of death, ritual and applied design across the world. These trends, however, show a clear divergence in attitudes and styles, notably in differences between northern and southern European cultures, as well as differences with North America. Yet this renewed interest takes

place in something of a vacuum of analysis, description or debate, for though there are many books and monographs on twentieth-century gardens, there are remarkably few on cemeteries. Those that exist are largely local monographs, or gazetteers of famous graves.

Similarly, while books on twentieth-century architectural Modernism continue to be added to the shelves, still too few treat the war memorial, cemetery or mausoleum at length, or with any degree of intellectual seriousness. In his introduction to one of the rare exceptions, *La última casa* (The last house), the Spanish architect Pedro Azara writes that 'The absence of monographs on modern tombs, and the fact that contemporary architects do not mention – or wish to single out – the tombs and vaults they have constructed . . . might well collaborate Panofsky's judgement (that modernism has nothing to say about death). Most histories of modern architecture no longer allude to funerary art.'[2] Edwin Heathcote makes the same point in his recent study, *Monument Builders*, writing that 'the subject of death in modern architecture has been largely avoided'.[3]

Yet, as was observed at the outset of this book, architecture emerged from the setting of the grave. Death has shaped architecture in many other ways too. For example, in his richly detailed monograph on the design and enduring influence of the Pantheon in Rome, William MacDonald is adamant that 'Circularity in architecture derives in no small part from the tomb.'[4] The early stone circles, barrows, pyramids, round tombs and terraces all helped create the templates for many future architectural and monumental forms. Indeed, the revival of neo-Classical architecture

Circularity in architecture derives from the tomb: the Mausoleum of Augustus in the Field of Mars, Rome.

in the sixteenth century took many of its models from the monumental and funerary architecture of the Greeks and Romans.

Likewise, the nineteenth-century landscaped cemetery itself became the setting for many beautifully designed buildings and monuments, so much so that a recent survey of historic cemeteries in Britain noted that 'All the cemeteries had at least one building of architectural merit, with the majority having two or three.'[5] In fact, the historic cemeteries of Europe and North America are treasure-troves for all those interested in changing architectural styles and genres. It is not unreasonable to argue, therefore, that up to the beginning of the twentieth century, there had been 300 years of continuous interplay between the rituals of death and the design and architecture of appropriate settings and artefacts. In the past century that architectural impulse to commemorate death in works of great formal elegance has been increasingly rare.

Today, many architects seem silent on the matter of death; landscape designers only slightly less so. Spiritual matters don't come easily to professions and practices that are increasingly computer-scored, technology driven, and which too often stand aloof from the quotidian forms of life and ritual. In an increasingly competitive global economy and culture, the big statement has replaced the thoughtful one, and size has often trumped suitability. The human scale of design – and its attentiveness to the cycles and rituals of human life and vulnerability – has been squeezed to the edges.

Even the materials of modern architecture, notably concrete, steel and glass plus vast areas of hard-paving, seem inappropriate to a tradition in which stone, earthworks, crafted metals, wood and water have been the principal elements of assembly and commemoration. The void between corporate architecture and vernacular architecture seems to have become almost unbridgeable. Furthermore, as Edwin Heathcote has argued, it was one of the intentions (conscious or otherwise) of a certain style of modern architecture to forswear any contact with the landscape, let alone the ground beneath:

> Modern architects, and more specifically functionalist architects sought to disassociate buildings from the earth. Pilotis, walls of seemingly frameless plate glass, were intended to lighten the building's contact with the ground, to do away with the need for a cellar, the repository of repressed Freudian evils and the darkness below and to create an international style which was not bound to the earth but could quite easily sit anywhere.[6]

One of the few critics who has attempted to elaborate the principles of the funerary landscape, and the architecture within it, has been the anthropologist Louis-Vincent Thomas. He in turn based many of his propositions and prescriptions on themes first promulgated by the architect R. Auzelle.[7] These are summarized schematically (in translation) thus:

> architectural inscription in the site, centred on, emphasized by, the vegetation (solemnity) or drowned in vegetation (integration, disappearance, discretion); a command of volumes: the horizontal (rest), the vertical (resurrection), a combination of both (opposition, reflex action); horizontal lines (stability), vertical lines (spiritual longing), oblique lines (sadness), and a combination of all these (oppositions); naturalness of the materials: stone (strength, durability), concrete (flexibility, resistance), brick (colour, cleanliness), wood (warmth, ease of use); a sense of proportion in the modelling of forms: vigour and sobriety (perenniality), refinement without affectation (spirituality); finally, openness: narrow openings (seclusion, intimacy), wide openings (admittance, communion).[8]

This is a rich and productive taxonomy of properties, attributes, and symbolic motifs, many of which have been detailed and noted in the course of *Last Landscapes*. The taxonomy also makes clear that within the long history of funerary architecture and landscape, both hard and soft, architectural and natural, enduring and transient qualities are interdependent. The architecture of death has both to remind us of the longevity of memory and human culture, as well as the brevity of the individual human life; to reflect on and respond to the febrile and at times explosive concatenations of history as well as the more reassuring temporalities of the seasons and the natural world generally. It has also to articulate the connection between the world above ground, and the world below. This is why it is always difficult to separate out architectural and landscape issues from each other (though they still too frequently are), and ask why the successful integration of both is still so rare?

There are of course exceptions, notably in a number of beautifully designed memorial sites and parks that have caught the public imagination in recent years. One is the Kongenshus Mindepark in Jutland, designed by C. Th. Sørensen and Hans Georg Solvgaard between 1945 and 1953 to commemorate the early farmers who tried to make an inhabitable and productive landscape out of this bleak part of northern Denmark.[9] The overall design here was on the use of a large number of inscribed large boulders (in the tradition of rune stones), rearranged in the landscape to create paths, circles and ship-shaped funerary settings. Here the landscaping refers back to pre-Christian memorial cultures in its attempt to memorialize the sacrifices of a hardy group of agricultural pioneers.

Other successful and publicly appreciated memorial landscapes of recent years include Maya Lin's Vietnam Veterans' Memorial in Washington, DC (1981), which since it was completed has become a site of national gathering and reconciliation. Lin's imaginative decision to create a memorial that is both above and below ground level, its formidable use of inscription and strong

The Kongenshus Mindepark in Jutland, Denmark, designed to commemorate the efforts of the early farmers who colonized this bleak region.

axial lines, appears simple, but has proved robust and powerful in its effects. It also successfully integrates landscape design with monumental and laipdary traditions.

A final example is the Thames Barrier Park in East London, on the north bank of the River Thames. Designed by the French landscape architect Alain Provost of Groupe Signe (the principal design team for Parc André-Citroën in Paris), it incorporates a riverside promenade, sunken garden, water fountains, café and play area, along with a striking Pavilion of Remembrance commemorating the civilian victims of East London's Docklands communities who died during the Second World War. It was

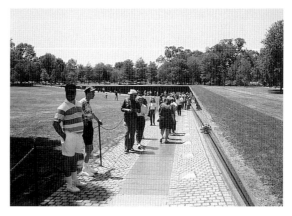

The Vietnam Veterans' Memorial in Washington, DC, designed by Maya Lin, one of the most successful memorial landscapes of recent times.

The Pavilion of Remembrance at Barrier Park in East London, commemorating the civilian victims of bombing during the Second World War. Designed by Alain Provost of Groupe Signe.

The Monument Hall designed by Gunnar Asplund at the Stockholm Woodland Cemetery.

The Golders Green Crematorium designed by Sir Ernest George in London in 1901, in what was then described as a 'Northern Italian, Lombard-Romanesque style', with elegant arcades, striped brickwork, and with the furnace chimney disguised as a campanile.

opened on 22 November 2000. The sunken, formal gardens make reference to the docks that once formed part of the site. The Park opens up magnificent views of the river and the Thames Barrier, and the memorial Pavilion is particularly affecting in its airy simplicity, based on slender columns supporting a roof with a central opening to the sky, and showing clear affinities to Gunnar Asplund's Monument Hall in Stockholm.

Memorial parks have provided some of the more successful examples of modern place-making, as these examples demonstrate, though there have been many others. However, since the principal concern of this book has been with actual burial sites themselves, in the concluding part of this chapter I shall concentrate on three areas of innovation in respect of the places of the dead: first, new architectural responses to cremation, its buildings and landscapes; second, the powerful response to the communal mausoleums and wall niches that dominate

cemetery design in southern European cultures; and, finally, the rise in preference for natural burial, particularly in northern Europe.

CREMATORIA AND GARDENS OF REMEMBRANCE

When Sir Ernest George came to design Golders Green Crematorium in London in 1901, he noted that 'Crematoria were, after all, a building type for which there was no architectural precedent.' It might have been thought, therefore, that here was a blank sheet on which architects and landscape designers could really 'make it new', producing designs that would make this emergent new building type clearly of its age and spirit. In fact, what happened was that the majority of architects in this early period simply chose to work in the Gothic style, because of an assumed relationship of these buildings to ecclesiastic architecture, though this assumption was pre-emptory and perhaps ultimately self-defeating. Things have changed little, for despite the popularity in Britain of cremation, and the proliferation of crematoria buildings and associated gardens of remembrance in the twentieth century, little has been written or published about this particular architectural form since then, a clear indication of the lack of innovation or architectural interest.[10]

Golders Green itself turned out to be one of the better crematoria buildings to be found in Britain, designed in what was then described as a 'Northern Italian, Lombard-Romanesque style', with elegant arcades and striped brickwork, and with the furnace chimney disguised as a campanile.[11] Despite this early attempt to make a bold architectural gesture towards the seriousness of purpose of such buildings, what has resulted since has been mostly disappointing. James Stephens Curl is adamant that 'Most crematoria in Britain are distressingly banal and poorly designed, and are composed of disparate elements that are uncomfortably resolved.' Another critic, Edwin Heathcote, has described the design of crematoria as 'largely a field of wasted opportunities'.[12]

Furthermore, Curl points to the critical problem that arises from the fact that the act of cremation remains without a proper liturgy of its own, or indeed an agreed order of service or processional. Usually when people are buried, the coffin is followed to the grave for the final act of committal; yet with cremation, fewer and fewer people are prepared to see the process of cremation through to completion.[13] In earlier periods, especially when the churchyard or cemetery was close to where people lived, mourners would follow the coffin or the hearse,

or join the cortège from the home to the burial place. The procession that accompanied the burial of a local dignitary, sports personality or admired community leader could literally bring the town to a halt. Some years ago I interviewed a parish priest in a northern industrial town in the course of some research into local civic life. When I asked him what the main difference was between when he had first arrived in the town and how life was today, he replied that, 'We don't have any big funeral processions any more.'

With cremation there is a gathering, but no subsequent processional to a final resting-place, which, in anthropological terms, has always been one of the principal features of funerary rite. This is not the case in North America, as has already been noted in respect of the Tri-State Crematory, where bodies due for cremation can be stored for an unspecified period after the service in conditions that may lack dignity, and which certainly don't offer the finality that same-day cremation at the place of the service offers.[14] Without an agreed set of ritual practices, then both architecture and design are without the unifying elements or imperatives that link ritual, plan, processional and built form in one coherent whole.

Another problem surrounding the ritual of cremation is that there is only the weakest of connections between building and landscape. While many crematoria are set within their own grounds, consisting of lawns, walkways and gardens of remembrance, the act of interment of the cremated remains is usually undertaken by professional staff at a time and occasion separate from the service. For those attending a funeral service, all of the important ritual takes place

The gardens of remembrance at Putney Vale Cemetery and Crematorium in London, one of the better landscapes associated with cremation.

inside a single room. The surrounding landscape is sometimes over-decorative, and often without long sightlines or landscapes that stretch to the horizon. This is not to say that such gardens are without merit: Heather Blackett gives the ornamental garden at Putney Vale Cemetery and Crematorium in London (1938) special mention, a garden that makes its mark by successfully using an incline to create interesting and successive changes of level, with Gardenesque paths and steps, bordering sloping lawns and memorial beds shaded by trees.[15]

The brick, oak and stained glass 'compound' design of many British crematoria buildings, with waiting-rooms and chapels designed as deep, hushed interiors, cuts ritual off from the open landscape and fails to employ any of the many consolatory effects that landscape can bring. The Iranian-born architect Mohsen Mostafavi has made some particularly valuable remarks on this subject, in discussing some of the qualities that Islamic architecture might bring to Western design, especially to places of ritual, remarking that,

The Alhambra is not just a high point of Islamic architecture, it is a pointer to one of the ways forward for architecture in cities worldwide. It reconciles architecture and landscape in a profound and very beautiful way. There is a powerful tradition in Islamic architecture of designing buildings in which outdoor and indoor space are blurred, in which water and light and shade play essential and life-enhancing parts. We are beginning to see this kind of architecture emerging again.[16]

Few crematoria buildings and landscapes have achieved anything like this level of aesthetic and ritual integration.

Of crematoria buildings in Europe worthy of architectural note, most critics include Golders

Green by Ernest George and Alfred B. Yeates (1905), C. Holzmeister's Vienna Crematorium (1922), Nymburk Crematorium in the Czech Republic by Feuerstein and Slama (1923), Ernst Wiesner's Crematorium at Brno, also in the Czech Republic (1925–30), Erik Bryggman's crematorium at Abo, near Turku (1938–41), Gunnar Asplund's Woodland Crematorium in Stockholm (consecrated 1940), Bushbury Crematorium, Wolverhampton (1954) by Lavender, Twentyman & Percy, Imre Makovecz's Farkasrét mortuary chapel in Hungary (1975), Lilla Aska Crematorium and chapel (Ove Hidemark (1990), Sweden, Peter Behrens' crematorium in Hagen, north Germany and the Treptow Crematorium in Berlin (built 1996–8), designed by Axel Schultes and Charlotte Frank.[17]

The last-named building, only very recently completed, has won many plaudits for its dignified design and ambience. At the centre of a complex of three chapels is a communal 'grove hall' in which concrete columns 'rise from the ground like trees at irregular intervals . . . their tops crowned by circular capitals of daylight where they break through the ceiling'. Once again we are in the 'forest space' beloved in northern European architecture. This interior has been compared by one critic with the effect of Stonehenge, the stone circles at Carnac in Brittany, and even the Mosque at Cordoba, while another finds that its 'nobility lies in its tenderness: its gentle conflation of archetypes of grove, tomb and cave'.[18]

Regrettably, there are too few other crematorium buildings in Europe or North America that are so distinctive or distinguished, though Catherine Merridale tells the story of two

Russian artists, Vladimir Mel'nichenko and Ada Rybachuk, who won a competition to design a new crematorium in Kiev in the 1960s.[19] Since cremation was then still regarded as culturally unacceptable, the two designers had to strike out on their own with the support of a few loyal followers, who over seven years created a new set of buildings, with landscaping, lakes and even diverted rivers. 'We wanted to create a ceremonial complex. We took over the whole space. We wanted to describe the route through life, to explain that death is not the end.' Although the work was eventually completed – only with the help of volunteers in its final stages – the municipal authorities have since let the complex deteriorate and become neglected, and while still functioning, many of the original features, murals and artworks have been vandalized, painted over or removed.

Perhaps it is because a number of people find the design of conventional cemeteries and gardens of remembrance so lacking in atmosphere that they are making their own arrangements for the final scattering or interment of ashes. This often involves an informal ceremony, at which the ashes of the loved one are buried or strewn in a place particularly associated with that person, or even requested by them: a favourite hillside, a childhood haunt, even the home ground of a beloved football team. This is precisely what my brother and I did with the ashes of our father, on a day which many years later is as memorable for the Downland views, spring flowers and prospect of the distant sea as it was for the poignancy and seriousness of the occasion. Such arrangements would not be tolerated in Sweden and Germany, for example, where the public or ecclesiastical authorities retain all burial rights, and insist that even cremated remains be interred formally in recognized burial grounds under their own watchful jurisdiction.[20]

THE NEW MONUMENT BUILDERS

While cremation will continue to be one of the most common forms of disposal in Europe, some form of inhumation of the whole body, above or below ground, will continue, and may be restored to widespread practice once again. Both the cemetery and the tomb certainly have a future, though this may take a different form in northern Europe compared with southern Europe, while Americans will continue to develop other styles and ritual arrangements, even while these share many affinities with European practices.

In Mediterranean Europe and certain parts of North America the beginnings of a new kind of architectural monumentalism and formalism are now evident, notably in the creation of large, regular volumes for housing wall tombs and columbaria. Aldo Rossi's rationalist architectural designs for the mausoleums at San Cataldo have already been mentioned, and they constitute perhaps the first great work in this new era of neo-Classical formalism. Elsewhere in northern Italy, Carlo Scarpa is responsible for one of the most distinctive twentieth-century tombs, that of the Brion family at San Vito di Altivole near Treviso (1968–78), erected in a plot or 'sanctuary' for family graves with a water garden, chapel and a marble and stone sarcophagi for Giuseppi and Onorina Brion in linked, individual tombs joined together by an arched concrete canopy.[21] This sanctuary takes the form of an L-shaped addition

The tomb of the Brion family at San Vito d'Altivole, near Treviso, Italy, designed by Carlo Scarpa, completed in 1978.

to the existing public cemetery, and also contains a cypress grove for the burial of local clergy (as well as Scarpa's own grave). The double sarcophagi rest in a small amphitheatre within a raised lawn surrounded by a concrete wall. In a lecture he once gave in Madrid about the project, Scarpa stated that in this particular design he was less interested in traditional lines and perspectives commonly associated with Italian formal garden design, and more interested in 'figures and atmospherics'.[22] In this his designs were at a distinct remove from those of Rossi's strict formalism.

Another astonishing work of cemetery design is the Igualada Cemetery (1986–90), sited in the suburbs of Barcelona, by architects Enric Miralles and Carme Pinós.[23] This stands at the opposite end of the aesthetic spectrum to the Stockholm Woodland Cemetery in every way. Whereas in Stockholm the visitor is led uphill from the

The cemetery at Fisterre (Finisterre) on the west coast of Spain in Galicia, designed by César Portela.

entrance, with views of the over-arching sky and hills ahead, at Igualada the visitor descends a path into a buried concrete city, where rows of formal niches in repeated patterns crowd in from both sides. If anything the Igualada Cemetery closely resembles the very first streets of the necropolis at Cerveteri, excavated below ground level. The architects have, however, used gabion walls (walls constructed from loose stones and boulders tightly bound into blocks with wire netting)

in construction, as does, interestingly, the Colney Wood Natural Burial Park in England. Perhaps the gabion wall is the one linking architectural feature between the monumentalist and the woodland cemetery.

More recently, the Spanish architect César Portela has designed a cemetery at Finisterre (from the Roman *finis terrae* or 'end of the earth'), in Galicia, a region of Spain. The town itself is located on what is known as the Costa da Morte

The new mortuary at León, a 'tomb of tombs', designed by Jordi Badia and Josep Val of BAAS Architects, completed 2001.

('coast of death'), so called because of the many ships that have been wrecked there. A more propitiously named place for a cemetery could not be imagined. It is spectacularly sited on a promontory reaching out into the Atlantic, with a series of granite cubes – set at random angles to each other – overlooking the sea, each cube containing twelve burial niches.[24] Above the burial chambers, at a small distance, are three other buildings in the same style: a chapel, a morgue and a forensic laboratory. Portela has said that

> I had the idea in the beginning that the cemetery would be a spectacle reserved for the dead and the gods. Situated in this magic place, these stones houses, dispersed across the slope like small cubic temples, take possession of the landscape. Like the Greek temples at Delphi, they listen to the infinite echo of the horizon . . . (and) reaffirms

architecture as a sacred space in our relation to the world.

These are above-ground vaults, with a pronounced solidity, which face the sea in a challenging, almost embattled way, as if in defiance of natural danger or the processes of erosion.

Elsewhere in Spain, BAAS Architects have designed a new mortuary in León, which is as equally assertive as the mausoleums at Finisterre in its protruding elements, which consist of concrete chutes acting as roof-lights clustered around the entrance, though the building itself is underground. Instead of a roof it has a large reflecting pool, so what the residential neighbours see is not an obtrusive building of sinister intent, but a ground-level formal lake with trees. The mortuary is for public use and has ten 'vigil rooms', where family and friends go to sit with the body or attend wakes, in advance of the funeral.

It is, according to its principal architect, Jordi Badia, a 'tomb of tombs', which, though appropriately underground, delivers light below and reflects the sky above, and thus connects both worlds in counter-harmony. Although much skill has gone into the way in which the building integrates into its locality, it retains all the qualities of a serious architectural statement about the place of death, with its many subterranean rooms reminiscent of those carved out of the rock at Cerveteri: equally minimalist, equally – but serenely – austere.

In Italy, the English architect David Chipperfield has won a public commission to expand the existing island cemetery of San Michele in Venice, as well as construct an entirely new island of the dead adjacent to the original one, connected by bridge. This will principally take the form of a series of courtyards made up of wall tombs, with extensive formal gardens and views of the city across the narrow waters. While much of the new island will consist of formal gardens, the constructed elements will consist of large rectangular buildings containing wall crypts and columbaria, with very high urban densities, as befitting the city of Venice itself. At the Green-Wood Cemetery in Brooklyn, home to so many great family mausoleums, a new four-storey mausoleum campus designed by Platt Byard Dovell Architects will provide space for several thousand new bodies. Elsewhere in America it is the large-scale communal mausoleums that are now a focus for architectural ingenuity and imagination, often, because of the purposes they serve, engineered and built in a fortified style. These new houses of the dead, consisting of endlessly repeating rows of vaults like bank-deposit boxes, are no longer part of the public or civic domain.

These large collective mausoleums, both in Europe and North America, are designed for single bodies, breaking with the tradition of the family grave. As the living city itself becomes increasingly home to one-person households, so in death the project of individualization is completed. Above-ground inhumation in such mausoleums remains rare in Britain and other parts of northern Europe, and is likely to remain so. Some people dislike the overly morgue-like associations suggested by this form of wall burial, and cling to the belief that burial is, and must be, somehow a return to earth.

The tension between monument-building and other forms of memorialization – through landscaping, story-telling, the graphic arts, or even music – is not new. James E. Young's book on Holocaust memorials deals with this subject at length, not surprisingly in view of its subject-matter and the central issue of how one attempts to remember a whole network of European Jewish cultures and peoples almost entirely destroyed. Jewish culture has always had a strong tradition of formal memorialization: the first mention in the Bible of a tomb refers to the *matzevah* which Jacob erected on Rachel's grave (Genesis 35:20).[25] Yet Young acknowledges the problems associated with monumentalism, observing that the 'extent to which we encourage monuments to do our memory-work for us, we become more forgetful'.[26] Young, like Lewis Mumford before him, believes that sometimes cultures that over-rely on monumentalization, including an attachment to excessive forms of funerary architecture, give a false sense of permanence and continuity and are in danger of being quickly eradicated, especially when compared to those that place 'their faith in powers of biological regeneration'. Finding a balance between monumentalism and more tenacious and resilient forms of memory-holding, poses a genuine dilemma for societies and cultures in the modern era.

A RETURN TO EARTH

Which is why the recent but growing preference for natural burial, is particularly pronounced in Britain and northern Europe. Natural burial is not only anti-architectural, but also refutes the long tradition by which the places of the dead are also the subject of particular kinds of human disruption or rearrangement of the landscape. Advocates of natural burial seek to create cemeteries that meld into the uncultivated landscape as quickly as possible, returning to a 'state of nature' as if the human presence on earth had never been.

This is a presumption of astonishing radicalism. For the past 2,000 years at least, one of the principal functions of burial and funerary ritual – from the inscriptions and epitaphs in the Roman catacombs through to the cult of the headstone in the era of the Enlightenment – has been to leave, where possible, a permanent record for posterity of each individual life lived. Natural burial denies this function, at least with regard to any kind of design or inscription at the place of interment, though other forms of commem-oration or record may take place elsewhere. This suggests that the strong desire to 'be at one with nature' and to leave no sign of burial behind is an unexpected and late-modern phenomenon, at least within Western culture, part of a new and unique kind of ecological consciousness, rather

than a trace element of pre-historic or pagan belief systems. It may be that many older Europeans who survived until the end of the twentieth century now feel that there has been too much history in their lives, and that some kind of reconciliation with nature is more important than adding to the burden of human self-aggrandisement, or providing even more work for the recording angel of history.

An exceptionally fine example of such a woodland burial park can be found at Colney Wood near Norwich in England, opened in 2000. The site, set on a high sandy ridge in 12 acres of mature woodland, takes its over-arching meaning from being 'a haven for wildlife and natural plant growth, reinforcing the concept of renewal of life'.[27] Neither stone nor rare hardwood memorials are allowed, and everything involved in the interment must be biodegradable. The burial plots are contracted on a lease that ends in 2099, at which point the whole site reverts to natural open woodland, intended to be held under the long-term protection of a Trust. Only certain trees are allowed to be planted adjacent to the grave – those that integrate with the natural ecology of the area – and a record of plant and bird species is kept by the park manager. There are no religious signs or symbols anywhere, and services can be held in accordance with any religion, or none. The cemetery is part of a publicly accessible landscape.

Although this mature woodland seems completely 'natural', it has been the subject of judicious landscape planning, and the cemetery has its own dedicated landscape architect.[28] The landscaping takes the form of repairing decades of past mismanagement, which included

The woodland burial park at Colney Wood near Norwich in England is a private venture, but marked by fine landscaping and a serene sense of place and reconciliation with the natural world.

Colney Wood near Norwich, Norfolk.

inappropriate felling along with the introduction of unsuitable commercial tree species. Instead the site is managed in order to enable a greater diversity of indigenous flora and fauna to flourish. Colney Wood is already known for its extensive bluebell woods, its wide variety of bird-life (and, therefore, birdsong), as well as a rich woodland undergrowth alive with frogs, toads and other small creatures. It is as much a function of the cemetery to encourage greater and more diverse wildlife as it is to bury the dead. The human animal is not given sovereign status in this landscape.

The design principle that informs the layout of the graves is admirably simple, though still imbued with ritual significance. Particular trees are chosen for their distinctive shape, form, height or other outstanding characteristic, and around these trees the plots are laid out in a circle, like the spokes of a wheel. Each grave is simply marked by two stout logs laid each side along the length of the earth mound. Over time the graves sink back to ground level and the logs crumble back into the earth. Some people elect to have a tree planted adjacent to the grave itself, while others have small, carved wooden grave markers that over time return to ground mulch, like everything else. Likewise, no glass vases or flower containers are allowed. It is accepted on all sides that the point of this kind of burial is that the grave site reverts to the very form and structure of the surrounding woodland as soon as possible. This 'return to nature' is often specifically mentioned as being the ultimate desire in the wording on the simple wooden grave markers. One, marking the grave of an 85–years–old man, reads: 'In this green quiet place / I give myself to rest and peace'.

The burial park is not in the least frightening or morbid. The forest itself – a mixture of pines, firs and broad-leafed trees, such as beech, oak and birch – is beautifully structured, with light breaking through the tree canopy and on to the paths and ground cover in cathedral-like slants and golden rays. The hilly terrain allows for a meandering network of main and subsidiary paths through the forest, with occasional outlooks from the escarpment through the trees on to the lakes and other distant vistas beyond. This cemetery – which is what it is technically, though it feels nothing like any other cemetery one has been in before – is a woodland in its own right, and the graves themselves are subsumed within this greater landscape structure. Any visitor could find peace and tranquillity here, for it is not the grave site that provides the focal point of meaning but the woodland itself, which orchestrates and resolves the deeper emotions.

Of equal importance to the landscape are the buildings. These have been designed by Graham Brown, a designer specializing in wooden structures using a 'reciprocal frame', his own invention, which creates buildings with large, unimpeded roof spans, all with window openings in the centre of the roof, providing the main source of natural light. The roof supports are based on a spiral principle, commonly found in natural structures, and can be adapted to produce buildings with three or more beams, their tepee-like roof openings giving them a distinctive, immediately recognizable style that fits in well with their forest surroundings, including a number of conical timber stacks that provide habitats for birds and small mammals.

This kind of woodland burial park seems infinitely more responsive to landscape than some of the newer cemeteries (or churchyard extensions) to be found in Europe and North America, often located on flat, featureless sites, already noted and deplored. Many such places, which can often be seen from the windows of suburban trains passing through the hinterlands of modern cities, bring to mind a remark in Kenneth Frampton's celebrated essay on modern architecture, *Towards a Critical Regionalism: Six Points for the Architecture of Resistance*.[29] For Frampton, 'the bulldozing of an irregular topography into a flat site is clearly a technocratic

gesture which aspires to a condition of absolute *placelessness*.' Drawing on Heidegger – as so many writing in this field do, despite deep political reservations – Frampton has argued for a new form of what he terms 'critical regionalism': that which restores topography to the centre of design.

Critical regionalism (the concept and term have been widely accepted and supported) implies, in Frampton's words, that the

specific culture of the region – that is to say, its history in both a geological and agricultural sense – becomes inscribed into the form and realisation of the work (with a) capacity to embody, in built form, the prehistory of the place, its archaeological past and its subsequent cultivation and transformation across time. Through this layering into the site the idiosyncrasies of place find their expression without falling into sentimentality.[30]

The woodland burial park attains to this condition of placefulness, very much more than the standardized lawn cemetery of the modern era. Certainly, Colney Wood is folded lovingly into the distinctive landform and woodland characteristic of that part of East Anglia, and though it appears in the first instance to be anti-architectural, it is not. The landscaping and the design and siting of the buildings are highly conscious 'interventions' in the setting, and thus need to be taken seriously by architectural writers and critics, particularly those who still pay far too little attention to context and the art of undemonstrative aggregation and assembly.

Death is surrounded by metaphor and illusion. Because it appears at times so arbitrary and meaningless, a negation of everything that human identity and culture appears to stand for, even the most hardened rationalist cannot avoid ameliorating the impact of death with comforting or redemptive vocabularies: the 'words against death' mentioned earlier. Though people endeavour to respect the wishes of the dead – which in all cultures still continue to embody a degree of residual moral power – the dead themselves are oblivious to the rituals and forms of consolation that follow their demise. Of all the metaphors in use, in both religious and secular societies and cultures, the notion that death is a return home is still one of the most powerful in Western culture, in both its architectural and cultural meanings.

Yet from time to time it is asserted or assumed that the home and the tomb stand at opposite ends of the architectural continuum. The domesticity of the former is supposedly non-monumental, the latter by definition embodies everything that monumentalism represents: an unexpected proportion or scale, great public resonance, power, oppressiveness, and even an element of fear. The differences can also be expressed, according to one recent critic, by asserting that the domestic building 'suggests *heimlichheit* (homeliness), which in turn implies that monuments might be *unheimlich*, or uncanny: the disturbing or worrying are themselves among the qualities which might be considered monumental'.[31]

It is worth remembering that the German word for monument, *Denkmal*, means 'think-mark', or object that makes you think, rather than something you might inhabit. This ambivalence as to whether the tomb is a home or a place that cannot be inhabited, and which is there to register an absence, continues to haunt architecture and art, perhaps most successfully in Rachel

This remarkable sculpture, *House* by Rachel Whiteread, was made from a cast of a 19th-century house in East London due to be demolished. The work captured the public imagination in 1993, before it too was demolished to make space for a park.

The Mikado sculpture was designed by Dutch landscape architect Adriaan Geuze for a housing and landscape exhibition at Malmö in 2001 to celebrate the relationship between the Swedish forest and the falun-red wooden houses, so typical of the Swedish landscape.

Whiteread's act of memorialization, 'House' (1993). In this extraordinary work, Whiteread made a concrete cast of a house in East London due to be demolished, the last surviving building in an area flattened by wartime bomb damage and post-war reconstruction. For many, Whiteread's 'House' is a work that has uniquely helped redefine the nature of public memory in the second half of the twentieth century, by its very subtlety in evoking this inhabited / uninhabited quality of architecture. Her more recent 'Holocaust Memorial' (2000), to the murdered Jews of Vienna, an inverted cast of a study or private library full of books, shaped like a mausoleum, not only confirms her originality, but again addresses this particular and critical conjuncture of inhabitation and vacation, presence and loss, in an unsettling and thought-provoking way.

The Dutch landscape architect, Adriaan Geuze, designed a memorial, 'Mikado' (2001), for the Swedish Design exhibition BO01, held in Malmö, commemorating Swedish timber and forestry workers. This exquisite construction, in very much the same spirit as Whiteread's 'House', was also only temporary, but it was greatly admired, and captured both the spirit of the memorial woodland grove as well as the collective strength of the workers who have devoted their lives to the forest.

It is also appropriate to see earth burial as a form of a return to an elemental, organic home: just another rearrangement of matter in the great thermo-dynamic scheme of things. It is no coincidence that the Portuguese-Jewish cemetery at Ouderkerk is called Beth Haim, the 'House of Life', nor that so much of cemetery planning, design and construction echoes that of the streets, boulevards and terraced houses or mansions of the living. Indeed, one historian of the cemetery has insisted that 'Implicit in the landscaping of a cemetery is the ability of users to locate a specific grave. Thus, internally, the site will be divided by roads and paths: each grave will have an established "address", registered as such in the site's documentation and so giving each family a sense of ownership of and control over a particular plot.'[32] As we saw at Cerveteri, the Etruscan cemetery there has long been regarded as one of the first great exercises in town planning; in addition to the full-size houses of the dead, even the ashes of those cremated were stored in urns modelled as miniature houses.

This 'return home' is often more than metaphorical. When I and my family first moved to the district of north London where we now live, it was already a place of settlement for the city's growing West Indian population, who had been arriving since the early 1950s. Along with the identifiable grocery shops that served the neighbourhood, prominent also were a number of travel agencies that specialized not only in air transport to the Caribbean, but also in the repatriation of bodies for burial 'back home'. Talking to some older West Indian neighbours at the time, several said that while they had managed to build a more prosperous life in Britain for themselves and their children, they still hoped to return to the island of their birth at the end of their life, if not to retire there, then at least to be buried in a cemetery on the island of their birth, possibly where their own parents' graves were to be found. This was, in their terms, 'going home'.

In this wish, they are not alone. In an era of global migration, increasing numbers of people have today travelled and settled far from their original place of home. In doing so they have often had to relinquish their original language, as well as the cultural and religious rituals of the cultures they have come from. It is not surprising that this may have deep psychic consequences. The vital symbolic role played by a sense of home

and community in a highly mobile, endlessly changing, world has been explored at length by the cultural critic David Morley in *Home Territories*, which deals with almost every aspect of the contemporary symbolism of home, community and nationhood and how these operate today, differentially, as crucial elements of identity in the modern, globalizing world. Morley specifically mentions how many migrants continue to cling to the hope of an eventual return to the place of their birth, if not in the course of their life, then at least for final burial.[33] The importance therefore of creating new symbols of habitation, settlement and community are now among the most important tasks of modern political cultures, one in which it has to be said, the USA has been particularly successful.

Yet, as noticed earlier in the case of so many immigrants to America, the decision to be buried in the new country also marks an equally important moment when choices about identity become irrevocable. One sociologist who has studied the Serbian community that established itself in Sweden after the break-up of the Yugoslavian federation has concluded that 'It is only since the recent war in Yugoslavia that the Serbs in Sweden have ceased to bury their dead in Serbia. Today most Serbs [there] are buried in Sweden. The decision to bury in Sweden indicates that the bereaved no longer wish to, or believe they will, return to Serbia. The grave becomes a mooring in Sweden.'[34] This notion that the grave itself becomes a 'mooring' for familial identity can pull survivors in different directions. A study of cemetery visitors in England in the 1990s described the plight of one Greek-Cypriot couple, resident in Britain, who had returned to Cyprus after their daughter had died. However, they found it impossible to cope emotionally with living in a different country to that in which their daughter was buried, and so returned to Britain, a place that now commanded their greater loyalty because it had become the location of their loved one's grave.[35]

Thus the grave can become an important locus of attachment, a fixed point in a changing and sometimes turbulent world. We must remember that the Egyptians built the pyramids and mausoleums of their most powerful dead to last for ever: the house in which one came to dwell at the end of life was regarded as far more important than the house in which one dwelt, temporarily, on earth. The architecture of the house, therefore, is common to the beginning of life and its end. As we have seen throughout this book, from the Etruscan terrace dwellings, the Roman mausoleums, the great nineteenth-century bourgeois family mansions of the dead, to the exclusive 'gated communities' of vaults for the rich at Forest Lawn, or even the high-rise houses of the dead designed by Aldo Rossi at San Cataldo, much – though not all – funerary architecture is in some form related to the domestic architecture of its time. No wonder then that the Spanish Mónica Gili called her book of photographs of twentieth-century tombs designed by architects, *La última casa* (The last house).[36] But houses are also homes, and the last house is also the last home.

For this reason, in a world in which geographical ties with the place of birth have been severed for so many people, the significance of that 'second' home at the end of life, gains in symbolic meaning and importance.

The importance attached to burial in American earth – as a confirmation of citizenship and acceptance for many immigrants to that country – is related to this sense of ultimate belonging or earthly destiny. There is no reason why such sentiments might not be growing elsewhere in a diasporic global culture. All the more reason, then, to think anew about the design and meaning of cemeteries, if they are increasingly going to take this weight of expectation, as a final home.

EPILOGUE

In the course of writing this book, the places and narratives encountered have not all been those of remote and haunting island earthworks, serene churchyards, and highly polished forms of cerebral, modernist monumentalism. Death is not only a mystery, but in many of the forms in which it has arrived – no less in the twentieth century than in any century before – it has come with a savagery and unconscionable cruelty that is hard to absorb or even dwell on for any length of time. This is why a writer and historian such as Catherine Merridale, in her book about death in Russia in the modern era, felt obliged to conclude that

> Despair like this is not to be comforted. The heart of this book, in the end, is absence and loss. Silence, and not an answer, lies at its core . . . There are always diversions – tomb architecture, peasant naivety, mafia funerals, the absurdities of the epitaph. But if we remain at the centre of the issue, if we stare at the object – death – without blinking, there is nothing to see.[37]

Is there really nothing to see? Is it really the case that death is simply and wholly a negation? A void? In the end a writer can only write from the place and times which he or she inhabits, and in my case, this world has been one of relative security and prosperity, within a culture in which individual human sovereignty has been legally secured and generally respected, though such rights were often hard won. In such a world death can, at least, be faced with a degree of equanimity. While it is true that I shall never directly experience my own death – a thought which gave great comfort to both Wittgenstein and Sartre – like everybody else I have experienced the death of others, even in the course of writing this book.

It is precisely this – the death of others – that originally inspired the first attempts to create a meaningful ritual, architecture and landscape for the disposal of the dead. It is the death of others that still remains the motive force for creating landscapes and forms of architecture that temper the loss and hopelessness felt at such times. Death does not stand only at the end of life, a thing apart, but is present with us every day, and shapes our deepest sense of life and identity. Death is embodied within us, like a fatal flaw: it is our teleology and destiny. Viewed in this way, it deserves a dignifying aesthetic of its own. It should always be remembered that the last landscapes of human culture were also among the very first. For it was when people began to mark the passage and place of death that they discovered their humanity.

References

INTRODUCTION

1 Lewis Mumford, *The City in History* (Harmondsworth, 1966), p. 18.
2 This phrase appeared in a review by Peter Stothard (*Times Literary Supplement*, 27 September 2002) of a biography of the British politician William Whitelaw; Stothard has kindly confirmed in a personal communication that the coinage is his.
3 Cited in Sarah Tarlow, *Bereavement and Commemoration: An Archaeology of Mortality* (Oxford, 1999), p. 6.
4 See Mario Erasmo, 'Among the Dead in Ancient Rome', *Mortality*, VI/1 (2001), which deals with this morphological aberration.
5 I am aware that James Stevens Curl, whose expertise in historical funerary matters exceeds most others, still insists on 'mausolea' as the correct plural form of mausoleum. In this instance, I prefer the vernacular 'mausoleums'. The *New Shorter Oxford Dictionary* allows both.
6 James E. Young, *The Texture of Memory: Holocaust Memorials and Memory* (New Haven, MA, 1993), p. 3.
7 Christopher Daniell, *Death and Burial in Medieval England 1066–1550* (London, 1998), p. 109.
8 Clifford Geertz, 'Blurred Genres: The Refiguration of Social Thought', in *Local Knowledge* (London, 1993),
p. 19.
9 James Stevens Curl, *The Victorian Celebration of Death* (Stroud, 2000), p. 25.
10 James Stevens Curl, 'Nunhead Cemetery', private research paper, undated.

11 This citation was most recently cited by Dr Ian Hussein on becoming President of the Institute of Burial and Cremation Administration (IBCA) in 2001. See *City of London Cemetery and Crematorium Newsletter*, 6 (Winter 2001/2002), p. 8.

12 Edwin Heathcote's fine book, *Monument Builders: Modern Architecture and Death*, Chichester, 1999), details some important twentieth-century architectural achievements in former East European countries. Likewise, *Folk Art in Hungarian Cemeteries* by Corvina Kiadó and Ernö Kunt (Budapest, 1983) offers a rich glimpse of a distinctive aesthetic at work, which ought to be more widely known and investigated.

13 One writer who records an occasional sense of sadness, if not despair, caused by the nature of the subject-matter is Sarah Tarlow in *Bereavement and Commemoration*. She rightly distinguishes between dealing with the subject in general, which is usually without any deep existential problems, and the very different matter of making a close study of individual epitaphs, inscriptions, personal outpourings of grief on the loss of children and other loved ones. In the case of the last mentioned, she recorded an occasional but nevertheless real challenge to her own emotional well-being.

ONE: LIVING WITH THE DEAD

1 Regina Barreca, 'Writing as Voodoo', in Sarah Webster Goodwin and Elizabeth Bronfen, eds, *Death and Representation* (Baltimore, 1993), p. 174.

2 Cited in Lindsay Prior, *The Social Organisation of Death: Medical Discourses and Social Practices in Belfast* (London, 1989), p. 111. This is an extraordinarily good book, a closely observed sociological study of all aspects of dying, death and funerary culture in contemporary Northern Ireland.

3 Françoise Dastur, *Death: An Essay on Finitude* (London, 1996), p. 5.

4 I am indebted to the ideas and suggestions of Richard Hill on many counts, but in this particular instance to his discussion of 'Aesthetic Experience' in Chapter 4 of *Designs and their Consequences* (London, 1999), pp. 87–108.

5 Dr Tony Walter, 'Ritualising Death in a Consumer Society', *RSA Journal* (April 1996), p. 36

6 Christopher Tilley, *Metaphor and Material Culture* (Oxford, 1999), especially pp. 177–84.

7 Howard Colvin, *Architecture and the After-Life* (London, 1991), p. 1.

8 Gaston Bachelard, *The Poetics of Space* (Boston, MA, 1994), p. 88.

9 Hilary Lees, *English Churchyard Memorials* (Stroud, 2000), p. 20.

10 Brian Bailey, *Churchyards of England and Wales* (London, 1987), p. 21.

11 Heinrich Härke, 'Cemeteries as Places of Power', in *Topographies of Power in the Middle Ages*, ed. Mayke de Jong and Frans Theuws, with Carine van Rhijn (Leiden, 2001), p. 20.

12 David Charles Sloane, *The Last Great Necessity: Cemeteries in American History* (Baltimore and London, 1995), p. 14. This excellent book sensitively and carefully delineates the very different attitudes towards death, burial and landscape that emerged in North America, in comparison with Europe, and which even today continue to develop in quite different directions.

13 The ideas of Yi-Fu Tuan are especially important to this book, especially those contained in Yi-Fu Tuan, *Space and Place: The Perspective of Experience* (London, 1977).

14 Christopher Tilley, *Metaphor and Material Culture* (Oxford, 1999), p. 181.

15 The reference to Malinowski's views and their implications is suggested by Tony Walter, 'Sociologists Never Die: British Sociologists and Death', in David Clark, ed., *The Sociology of Death* (Oxford, 1993), p. 273.

16 Mary Douglas, *Purity and Danger: An Analysis of the Concepts of Pollution and Taboo* (London, 1984), p. 39.

17 Françoise Dastur, *Death: An Essay on Finitude*, trans. John Llewelyn (London, 1996), p. 39.

18 W. G. Sebald, *Austerlitz*, trans. Anthea Bell (London, 2001).

19 W. G. Hoskins, *The Making of the English Landscape* (London, 1977), p. 12.

20 The Newham figure is contained in *Burial Space Needs in London* (London Planning Advisory

Committee, 1997), p. 54. The Boston figure is cited in Anne Whiston Spirn, *The Granite Garden: Urban Nature and Human Design* (New York, 1984), p. 219.

21 Phillipe Ariès, *The Hour of Our Death* (London, 1981), p. 64.

22 Sir Thomas Browne, *The Major Works* (London, 1984), p. 310.

23 See Population Reference Bureau website: www.prb.org

24 Browne, *Major Works*, p. 310.

25 D. H. Lawrence, 'Etruscan Places', in *D. H. Lawrence and Italy* (London, 1997), p. 12.

26 George Children and George Nash, *Neolithic Sites of Cardiganshire, Carmarthenshire and Pembrokeshire* (Hereford: Logaston Press, 1997).

27 Gustaw Herling (-Grudzinski), *Volcano and Miracle: A Selection of Fiction and Non-Fiction from The Journal Written at Night*, ed. and trans. Ronald Strom (London, 1996), p. 146.

28 In the former GDR, there has been a reaction against the use of large cemeteries in favour of reopening the historic, smaller ones. See Leif Arffman, 'Whose Cemeteries?', *Mortality*, V/ 2 (2000), p. 125.

29 Environment, Transport and Regional Affairs Committee, *Cemeteries*, vol. II, House of Commons, 21 March 2001, London, p. 156.

30 Jan Neruda, *Prague Tales* (London, 1993), p. 184.

31 Catherine Merridale, *Night of Stone: Death and Memory in Russia* (London, 2000), p. 381.

32 Robert Pogue Harrison, 'Hic Jacet', in W.J.T. Mitchell, *Landscape and Power* (Chicago, 2002), p. 351.

33 Marc Treib, 'Designed Restraint: The Urban Landscapes of Thorbjörn Andersson', in *Platser, places, Svensk Byggtjänst* (Stockholm, 2002), p. 65.

34 Bohumil Hrabel, *Cutting It Short and The Little Town Where Time Stood Still*, trans. James Naughton (London, 1999), p. 296.

35 Merridale, *Night of Stone*, p. 174.

36 Monika Krajewska, *A Tribe of Stones: Jewish Cemeteries in Poland* (Warsaw: Polish Scientific Publishers, 1993).

37 Environment, Transport and Regional Affairs Committee, *Cemeteries*, Vol. I, House of Commons, 21 March 2001, p. xxiv.

38 *Burial Spaces Needs in London*.

39 Lucinda Lambton, 'To Paradise By Way of Kensal Green', *The Independent* (3 March 1993).

40 National Funerals College, *The Dead Citizen's Charter* (1996). There is also now a *Charter for the Bereaved* in the UK, produced by the Institute of Burial and Cremation Administration (www.ibca.uk.co).

TWO: LANDSCAPES AND MEANINGS

1 Raymond Williams, *The Country and the City* (St Albans, 1975), p. 149.

2 This point is made by Tony Walter in his fascinating study, *The Eclipse of Eternity: A Sociology of the Afterlife* (London, 1996), p. 70.

3 An excellent, recent publication on this phenomenon is *American Sublime*, exh. cat., Tate Britain (2002).

4 Hugh Brody, *The Other Side of Eden: Hunter-Gatherers, Farmers and the Shaping of the World* (London, 2001), p. 242.

5 Annie Dillard, *Pilgrim at Tinker Creek* (New York, 1998), p. 123.

6 This point is made by, among others, by Hilary Lees, *English Churchyard Memorials* (Stroud, 2000), p. 31.

7 See, for example, Ian Cooke, *Antiquities of West Cornwall: Guide Three* (Penzance, 1996), p. 5.

8 Caroline Constant, *The Woodland Cemetery: Towards a Spiritual Landscape* (Stockholm, 1994), p. 99.

9 Simon Schama, *Landscape and Memory* (London, 1995), pp. 214–26.

10 Neil Leach, 'Vitruvius Crucifixus: Architecture, Mimesis and the Death Instinct', in George Dodds and Robert Tavernor, *Body and Building: Essays on the Changing Relation of Body and Architecture* (Cambridge, MA, 2002).

11 'Resting Place', *Architectural Review* (December 2001), p. 56.

12 Robert Pogue Harrison, *Forests: The Shadow of Civilization* (Chicago, 1992), p. 178. A modern tree cathedral is to be found at Whipsnade in England, part of a National Trust property, planted by an ex-soldier, E. K. Blyth, shortly after the First World War as a symbol of peace and hope for the future. The Tree Cathedral is still well looked after, and is still

used for religious services. See:www.nationaltrust.org.uk/whipsnadetreecathedral/history/htm

13 Joseph Leo Koerner, *Caspar David Friedrich and the Subject of Landscape* (London, 1990), p. 133.

14 Françoise Dastur, *Death: An Essay on Finitude* trans. John Llewelyn (London, 1996), p. 11.

15 Nigel Everett, *The Tory View of Landscape* (New Haven, MA, 1994), p. 12.

16 Mary Midgeley, *Gaia: The Next Big Idea* (London, 2001).

17 Jay Appleton, 'Towards an Aesthetic for Norbury Park', in *Arcadia Revisited* (London, 1997), p. 69.

18 Brody, *The Other Side of Eden.*

19 David W. Orr, *The Nature of Design* (Oxford, 2002), p. 14.

20 Raymond Williams, *The Country and the City* (St Albans 1975), p. 154.

21 Kenneth Woodbridge, *The Stourhead Landscape* (London: The National Trust, 2001), p. 19.

22 Marc Treib, 'Must Landscape Mean?: Approaches to Significance in Recent Landscape Architecture', *Landscape Journal*, XIV/ 1 (Spring 1995), pp. 47–62.

23 Horace Walpole, *The History of the Modern Taste in Gardening*, intro. J. D. Hunt (New York, 1995).

24 Nina Lübbren, *Rural Artists' Colonies in Europe, 1870–1910* (Manchester, 2001).

25 Lübbren, *Rural Artists' Colonies*, p. 110.

26 Ernst van Alphen, 'Touching Death', in Sarah Webster Goodwin and Elizabeth Bronfen, *Death and Representation* (Baltimore, 1993).

27 The best current guide to the 'land art' movement is Jeffrey Kastner's edited collection of essays and projects, *Land and Environmental Art* (London, 1998).

28 These thoughts owe much to an essay by Thorbjörn Andersson on 'The Functionalism of the Gardening Art', in *Sweden: 20th Century Architecture*, ed. Caldeerly, Lindvall and Wang (Munich and New York, 1998). [AQ: complete editors' names]

29 Andersson, 'The Functionalism of the Gardening Art', p. 230.

30 See, for example, Vito Fumagalli, *Landscapes of Fear: Perceptions of Nature and the City in the Middle Ages* (Cambridge, 1994).

31 I am grateful to Jan Woudstra, whose original article, 'Landscape: An Expression of History', *Landscape Design*, 308 (March 2002), first alerted me to this debate, and whose personal communications since have been very helpful. See also Joachim Wolschke-Bulmahn, ed., *Places of Commemoration: Search for Identity and Landscape Design* (Washington, DC, 2001), for Sibyl Milton, 'Perilous Landscapes: Concentration Camp Memorials between Commemoration and Amnesia'.

32 Woudstra, 'Landscape: An Expression of History', p. 48.

33 Joachim Wolschke-Bulmahn, 'The Landscape Design of the Bergen-Belsen Concentration Camp Memorial', in Wolschke-Bulmahn, ed., *Places of Commemoration*, p. 298.

34 Woudstra, 'Landscape: An Expression of History', p. 49.

35 Andrew Charlesworth and Michael Addis, 'Memorialization and the Ecological Landscapes of Holocaust Sites: The Cases of Plaszow and Auschwitz-Birkenau, *Landscape Research*, XVII/ 3, (2002), pp. 229 - 251.

36 See James E. Young, *The Texture of Memory: Holocaust Memorials and Memory* (New Haven, MA, 1993).

37 James Stevens Curl, *The Victorian Celebration of Death* (Stroud, 2000), p. 2.

38 Martha Schwartz, 'Landscape and Common Culture since Modernism', in Marc Treib, ed., *Modern Landscape Architecture: A Critical Review* (Cambridge, MA, 1993), p. 260.

39 Treib, 'Must Landscape Mean?', pp. 47–62.

40 Richard A. Etlin, *The Architecture of Death: The Transformation of the Cemetery in Eighteenth-century Paris* (Cambridge, MA, 1984), p. 238.

41 Chris Brooks, 'English Historic Cemeteries: A Theme Study', English Heritage unpublished report, London, 1994.

42 Nancy Gerlach-Spriggs, Richard Enoch Kaufman and Sam Bass Warner, Jr., eds, *Restorative Gardens: The Healing Landscape* (New Haven, MA, and London, 1998), p. 9.

43 *Derek Jarman's Garden*, with photographs by Howard Sooley (London, 1995), p. 12.

1 Philippe Ariès, *The Hour of Our Death* (London, 1983), p. 44. But for a sparing necessary critique, with a tribute to this book's historic reach and greatness, see Roy Porter, 'The Hour of Philippe Ariès', *Mortality*, IV/ 1 (March 1999).

2 Ariès, *Hour of Our Death*, p. 37.

3 Julian Litten, *The English Way of Death: The Common Funeral Since 1450* (London, 1991).

4 Ariès, *Hour of Our Death*, p. 91.

5 Ruth Richardson, *Death, Dissection and the Destitute* (London, 1988), p. 60.

6 Hilary Lees, *English Churchyard Memorials* (Stroud, 2000), p. 22.

7 Juha Pentikäinen, 'The Dead without Status', *Nordic Folklore: Recent Studies*, edited by Reimund Kvideland and Henning K. Sehmsdorf, (Bloomington, IN, 1989).

8 Monika Krajewska, *A Tribe of Stones: Jewish Cemeteries in Poland*, with an Introduction by Rafael Scharf (Warsaw: Polish Scientific Publishers, 1993), p. 19.

9 David Charles Sloane, *The Last Great Necessity: Cemeteries in American History* (Baltimore and London, 1995), p. 33.

10 Ann and Dickran Tashjian, 'The Afro-American Section of Newport, Rhode Island's Common Burying Ground', in Richard E. Meyer, ed., *Cemeteries and Gravemarkers: Voices of American Culture* (Ann Arbor, MI, 1989), p. 166.

11 Sloane, *The Last Great Necessity*, p. 24.

12 R. R. Stevens and R. K. Stevens, *North American Records in Italy: The Protestant Cemetery of Rome* (Los Angeles, 1981), p. 30.

13 Sloane, *The Last Great Necessity*, p. 18.

14 *Ibid*, p. 187.

15 Lindsay Prior, *The Social Organisation of Death: Medical Discourses and Social Practices in Belfast* (London, 1989), p. 116.

16 Prior, *Social Organisation of Death*, p. 117.

17 Yi-Fu Tuan, *Space and Place: The Perspective of Experience* (London, 1977), p. 35.

18 Sir Thomas Browne, *The Major Works* (London, 1984), p. 294.

19 Yi-Fu Tuan, *Space and Place*, p. 44.

20 Ralph Merrifield, *The Archaeology of Ritual and Magic* (London, 1987), p. 77.

21 Sarah Tarlow, *Bereavement and Commemoration: An Archaeology of Mortality* (Oxford, 1999), p. 60.

22 The information on Moravian Church burial practices is based on information kindly supplied by Paul Blewitt, the Moravian Church Archivist, in a private communication of 28 November 2001.

23 Michael Ellison, 'Garbo Goes Home to a Woodland Burial', *The Guardian* (18 June 1999), p. 16.

24 Eva Reimers, 'Graves and Funerals as Cultural Communication', *Mortality*, IV/2 (July 1999), p. 153.

25 Richardson, *Death, Dissection and the Destitute*, p. 270.

26 Seymour Slive and H. R. Hoetink, *Jacob van Ruisdael* (New York, 1981), p. 68.

27 Jane Brown, *The Pursuit of Paradise: A Social History of Gardens and Gardening* (London, 1999), p. 57.

28 Charles Dickens, 'The City of the Absent', in *The Uncommercial Traveller and Reprinted Pieces* (Oxford, 1978), p. 233.

29 Sloane, *The Last Great Necessity*, p. 13.

30 Erwin Panofsky, '"Et in Arcadia Ego": Poussin and the Elegiac Tradition', in *Meaning in the Visual Arts* (Harmondsworth, 1970), p. 366.

31 Italo Calvino, *Invisible Cities* (London, 1979), p. 89.

32 Caroline Constant, *The Woodland Cemetery: Towards a Spiritual Landscape* (Stockholm, 1994), p. 115.

33 Hilary Lees, *English Churchyard Memorials* (Stroud, 2000), p. 16.

34 This account owes much to Nigel Dunnett's brief essay, 'Tending God's Acre', *The Garden* (December 2000). However, it is not just historic churchyards that are developing a more ecological approach to landscape and maintenance. The City of London Cemetery – like Cathays Cemetery in Cardiff, Wales, both functioning municipal cemeteries – has published an excellent guide to the many trees to be found within its walls.

35 Information provided at the Museum of Garden History website: www.cix.co.uk/museumgh/garden.htm

1 Italo Calvino, *Invisible Cities* (London, 1979), p. 100.
2 Nigel Spivey, *Etruscan Art* (London, 1997), p. 34.
3 Hannah Arendt, *The Human Condition* (Chicago, 1958), p. 74.
4 Umberto M. Fasola, *Domitilla's Catacomb and the Basilica of the Martyrs Nereus and Achilleus* (Vatican City, Rome: Papal Commission for Sacred Archaeology, 1986).
5 Ada Cioffarelli and Maria Teresa Natale, *Guide to the Catacombs of Rome and its Surroundings* (Rome, 2000).
6 Cioffarelli and Natale, *Guide to the Catacombs of Rome*, p. 10.
7 Richard A Etlin, *The Architecture of Death: The Transformation of the Cemetery in Eighteenth-Century Paris*, (Cambridge, MA, 1984), and James Stevens Curl, *The Victorian Celebration of Death*, (Stroud, 2000), p. 25
8 Etlin, *Architecture of Death*, p. 239.
9 Philippe Ariès, *The Hour of Our Death* (London, 1983), p. 351.
10 Robert Williams, 'Vanbrugh's Lost Years', *Times Literary Supplement*, 5031 (3 September 1999), pp. 13–14; see also Williams, 'Vanbrugh's India and his Mausolea for England', in Christopher Ridgway and Robert Williams, eds, *Sir John Vanbrugh and Landscape Architecture in Baroque England, 1690–1730* (Stroud, 2000), pp. 114–30.
11 Bruce B. Lawrence, 'The Eastward Journey of Muslim Kingship', in *The Oxford History of Islam*, ed. John L. Esposito (Oxford, 1999), pp. 395–431. A detailed gazetteer to these and other sites is Philip Davies, *The Penguin Guide to the Monuments of India*, II: *Islamic, Rajput, European* (Harmondsworth, 1989): the Tomb of Iltutmish (p. 137), Humayun (pp. 132–3), the Mausoleum of Akbar, Sikandra (p. 197) and the Taj Mahal (pp. 192–6).
12 Williams, 'Vanbrugh's Last Years', p. 14.
13 Ariès, *Hour of Our Death*, p. 534.
14 Douglas Davies and Alastair Shaw, *Reusing Old Graves: A Report on Popular British Attitudes* (Crayford, Kent: Shaw & Sons, 1994).
15 William Lynwood Montell, in *Encyclopaedia of Vernacular Architecture of the World*, ed. Paul Oliver (Cambridge, 1997), p. 757.
16 Catherine Merridale, *Night of Stone: Death and Memory in Russia* (London, 2000), p. 355.
17 Gunnar Brands, 'From World War I Cemeteries to the Nazi "Fortress of the Dead": Architecture, Heroic Landscape, and the Quest for National Identity in Germany', in Joachim Wolschke-Bulmann, ed., *Places of Commemoration: Search for Identity and Landscape Design* (Washington, DC, 2001), pp. 215–56.
18 A good account of San Cataldo is to be found in Edwin Heathcote, *Monument Builders: Modern Architecture and Death* (Chichester, 1999), pp. 182–91.
19 Cited in Jonathan Glancey, *20th Century Architecture* (London, 1998), p. 304.
20 The Congrès International d'Architecture Moderne, founded in 1928, became the leading organization for promoting the ideals of modern architecture and town planning.
21 Cited in Mark C. Taylor and Dietrich Christian Lammerts, *Grave Matters* (London, 2002), p. 16.
22 Lindsay Prior, *The Social Organisation of Death: Medical Discourses and Social Practices in Belfast* (London, 1989), p. 117.
23 David Robinson, in his concluding essay to his book of photographs of funerary sculpture, *Beautiful Death: Art of the Cemetery* (London, 1996), makes this point well: that the strength of personal expression realized in memorial sculpture was in inverse proportion to the strength of religious feeling. Hence it was in the secular cemeteries that sculptural expressiveness developed to new heights.

FIVE: LIBRARIES IN STONE

1 Essay in Monika Krajewska, *A Tribe of Stones: Jewish Cemeteries in Poland*, intro. Rafael Scharf (Warsaw: Polish Scientific Publishers, 1993).
2 Thomas Hardy, *Tess of the D'Urbervilles* (London, 1978), p. 486.
3 Cited in Jean-Pierre Mohen, *Standing Stones: Stonehenge, Carnac and the World of Megaliths* (London, 1999), p. 144.
4 Cited in Peter Stansky and William Abrahams,

London's Burning: Life, Death and Art in the Second World War (London, 1994), p. 11. The punctuation is Moore's own, written on the back of a postcard.

5 Several of the most detailed recent books on European funerary sculpture are briefly described in the Select Bibliography.

6 Ada Cioffarelli and Maria Teresa Natale, *Guide to the Catacombs of Rome and its Surroundings* (Rome, 2000), p. 9.

7 Susan Stewart, *On Longing: Narratives of the Miniature, the Gigantic, the Souvenir, the Collection* (Baltimore and London, 1984).

8 James E. Young, *The Texture of Memory: Holocaust Memorials and Meaning* (New Haven, MA, 1993), p. 7.

9 Arnold Schwartzman, *Graven Images: Graphic Motifs of the Jewish Gravestone* (New York, 1993).

10 Schwartzman, *Graven Images*, p. 16.

11 Chaim Potok, in Schwartzman, *Graven Images*, p. 13.

12 The State Jewish Museum in Prague, *The Old Jewish Cemetery in Prague in the Works of Romantic Artists* (Prague, 1982).

13 Beth Haim is now the subject of an intensive restoration and maintenance programme organized by the David Henriques de Castro Fund Foundation. For more details go to www.cardozo.org/bethhaim/index.html

14 Schwartzman, *Graven Images*, p. 22.

15 Sarah Tarlow, *Bereavement and Commemoration: An Archaeology of Mortality* (Oxford, 1999).

16 I am very grateful to Roger Deakin, author of the delightful book, *Waterlog: A Swimmer's Journey through Britain* (London, 1999), for providing me with details of this touching example of gravestone biography in a personal communication.

17 Deepest thanks to Richard Hill for his fine pencil sketch of this heartbreaking inscription.

18 Douglas Davies and Alastair Shaw, *Reusing Old Graves: A Report on Popular British Attitudes* (Crayford, Kent: Shaw & Sons, 1994), p. 104.

19 Erik de Jong, in *Ian Hamilton Finlay: Et in Arcadia Ego*, trans. Donald Gardner (The Hague, 1999).

20 Andrew Mead, 'Garden of Memories', *The Architects' Journal* (31 January 2002), p. 29.

21 However, in his book, *Secure the Shadow: Death and Photography in America* (Cambridge, MA, 1995), Jay Ruby notes that despite the Jewish prohibition of graven images, he has found that many Jewish tombstones in American cemeteries carry photographs, mostly, though, of Jewish immigrants from European countries where this was common practice.

22 This story is told in James Langton, 'A Fallen Soldier Attains Immortality on the Net', *The Sunday Telegraph* (8 October 1995).

23 Gaston Bachelard, *The Poetics of Space* (Boston, MA, 1994), p. XVIII.

24 Bachelard, *Poetics of Space*, p. xxiii.

25 Edward Relph, *Place and Placelessness* (London: Pion Ltd, 1976), p. 16.

26 Gerard Seenan, 'Stunning Beauty of Deep Sea Grave', *The Guardian* (28 June 2001), p. 9.

27 Douglas J. Davies, *Death, Ritual and Belief: The Rhetoric of Funerary Rites* (London, 1997).

28 'Via Dolorosa', *The Guardian*, (27 February, 2002).

29 Philippe Ariès, *The Hour of Our Death* (London, 1983), p. 493.

30 William L. MacDonald, *The Pantheon: Design, Meaning, and Progeny* (London, 1976), p. 11.

31 Thomas Laqueur, 'In and Out of the Pantheon', *London Review of Books* (20 September 2001), p. 3.

32 Joseph Rykwert, *On Adam's House in Paradise: The Idea of the Primitive Hut in Architectural History* (New York, 1972), p. 27.

33 Edwin Heathcote, *Monument Builders: Modern Architecture and Death* (Chichester, 1999), p. 50.

34 Heathcote, *Monument Builders*, p. 50.

35 The subject of writers, artists, philosophers and their final, often contentious, resting places is the theme of an erudite, witty, but entirely fictional lecture given by the narrator of Malcom Bradbury's final novel, *To the Hermitage* (London, 2000).

36 Ian Cunningham, *A Reader's Guide to Writer's London* (London, 2001), p. 18.

37 Christopher Woodward, *In Ruins* (London, 2001), p. 144.

38 Woodward, *In Ruins*, p. 71.

39 Thomas Bernhard, *Cutting Timber*, trans. Ewald Osers (London, 1988), p. 119.

40 Christopher Zinn, 'Canberra puts Australia's most revered bones into contention', *The Guardian* (25 July 1995).

41 Lindsay Prior, *The Social Organisation of Death:*

Medical Discourses and Social Practices in Belfast (London, 1989), p. 186.

42 David Robinson states that he was told that Père-Lachaise 'represents the largest collection of nineteenth-century sculpture in the world'; see his *Beautiful Death: Art of the Cemetery* (London, 1996).

43 For more on this vociferous debate see John Morley, *Death, Heaven and the Victorians* (London, 1971), chap. 5: 'Sepulture and Commemoration'.

44 Gillian Darley, *John Soane: An Accidental Romantic* (New Haven, MA, and London, 1999). Darley's book finely captures the eccentric, and rather funerary, imagination of this strange architect.

45 Morley, *Death, Heaven and the Victorians*, p. 55.

46 There are a number of books that deal with this aspect of funerary sculpture, including Robinson, *Beautiful Death*, and Fabio Giovannini, *Guide al cimiteri d'europa* (Rome, 2000).

47 These comments on the statues and sculpture at Kensal Green Cemetery owe much to John Physick, 'Sculptors and Sculpture: A Supplement' in James Stevens Curl, *Kensal Green Cemetary* (Stroud, 2001).

48 K. I. Inglis, *Sacred Places: War Memorials in the Australian Landscape* (Melbourne, 2001), p. 82. Inglis also points out that the Australians largely eschewed the use of the cross in their war memorials, already seeing themselves as a country of many faiths and political points of view, where the state itself was a secular entity.

49 Cited by Douglas Crimp in 'On the Museum's Ruins', in Hal Foster, *Postmodern Culture* (London, 1985), p. 43.

50 Grey Gundaker, 'At Home on the Other Side: African American Burials as Commemorative Landscapes', in Joachim Wolschke-Bulmahn, ed., *Places of Commemoration: Search for Identity and Landscape Design* (Washington, DC, 2001), pp. 25–54.

51 Woodward, *In Ruins*, p. 212.

52 Ian Christie, in an online discussion forum on landscape at www.opendemocracy.net

53 Marshall Berman, cited in Camilo José Vergara, *American Ruins* (New York, 1999).

54 Alan Tate, *Great City Parks* (London, 2001), p. 118.

SIX: A WALK IN THE PARADISE GARDENS

1 John Dixon Hunt, 'Modern Landscape Architecture and its Past', in *Modern Landscape Architecture: A Critical Review*, ed. Marc Treib (Cambridge, MA, 1993), pp. 134–40.

2 Jean Pateman and John Gray, *In Highgate Cemetery*, Friends of Highgate Cemetery (London, 1992).

3 James Stevens Curl, *The Victorian Celebration of Death* (Stroud, 2000), p. 48.

4 Curl, *Victorian Celebration of Death*, p. 102.

5 John Fleming, Hugh Honour, Nicolaus Pevsner, *The Penguin Dictionary of Architecture and Landscape Architecture* (London, 1998), p. 353.

6 Quoted in Curl, *Victorian Celebration of Death*, p. 69.

7 This, and much other information about Abney Park Cemetery, was taken from the Cemetery's excellent website: www.abneypark.ground-level.org

8 James Stevens Curl, *Nunhead Cemetery*, private report.

9 David Cannadine, 'War and Death, Grief and Mourning in Modern Britain', *Mirrors of Mortality: Studies in the Social History of Death*, ed. Joachim Whaley (London, 1981), p. 193.

10 See also Sarah Tarlow, *Bereavement and Commemoration: An Archaeology of Mortality* (Oxford, 1999).

11 Richard A. Etlin, *The Architecture of Death: The Transformation of the Cemetery in Eighteenth-century Paris* (Cambridge, MA, 1984), p. 359.

12 Cited in David Charles Sloane, *The Last Great Necessity: Cemeteries in American History* (Baltimore and London, 1995), p. 44.

13 Leo Marx, *The Machine in the Garden: Technology and the Pastoral Ideal in America* (New York, 1967).

14 For a well-illustrated and more detailed account of New Orleans's cemetery history, see Peggy McDowell, 'J.N.B. de Pouilly and French Sources of Revival Style Design in New Orleans Cemetery Architecture', *Cemeteries and Gravemarkers: Voices of American Culture*, ed. Richard E. Meyer (Ann Arbor, MI, 1989).

15 See Blanche Linden-Ward, 'Strange but Genteel Pleasure Grounds: Tourist and Leisure Uses of Nineteenth-century Rural Cemeteries', in Meyer, *Cemeteries and Gravemarkers*.

16 Edmund V. Gillon Jr, *Victorian Cemetery Art* (New York, 1972), p. IX.

17 Philip Pregill and Nancy Volkman, *Landscapes in History: Design and Planning in the Eastern and Western Tradition* (New York, 1999), p. 460.

18 Cited in an editorial by Hannes Bohringer in *Daidalos*, 38 (December 1990), p. 17.

19 Sloane, *The Last Great Necessity*, p. 107.

20 Sloane, *The Last Great Necessity*, p. 167.

21 Sloane, *The Last Great Necessity*, p. 166.

22 Tony Walter, 'Dust Not Ashes: The American Preference for Burial', *Landscape* [Berkeley, CA], 32/1 (1993), p. 42.

23 Sloane, *The Last Great Necessity*, p. 218.

24 Sloane, *The Last Great Necessity*, p. 175.

25 Marc Treib, 'The Landscape of Loved Ones', in *Places of Commemoration: Search for Identity and Landscape Design*, ed. Joachim Wolschke-Bulmahn (Washington, DC, 2001).

26 Geoffrey and Susan Jellicoe, Patrick Goode, Michael Lancaster, *The Oxford Companion to Gardens* (Oxford, 1991), p. 102.

27 This discussion is dealt with in Caroline Constant, *The Woodland Cemetery: Towards a Spiritual Landscape* (Stockholm, 1994), which is full of intellectual riches and insights.

28 Thorbjörn Andersson, 'The Functionalism of the Gardening Art', in *Sweden: 20th Century Architecture*, ed. Claes Caldeerly, Joran Lindvall and Wilfried Wang (Munich and New York, 1998), p. 233.

29 Andersson, 'The Functionalism of the Gardening Art', p. 234.

30 Other European landscaped cemeteries noted as being of wider importance in this period would have to include those detailed by Jan Woudstra and Andrew Clayden in a recent appreciative essay, in which they acclaim the achievements of G. N. Brandt's Mariebjerg Cemetery in Copenhagen (1925–36), Wim Boer's General Cemetery at Doorn in The Netherlands (1952–8), Christian Zalm's Cemetery Almere-Haven, also in The Netherlands (1975), and the Igualada Cemetery in Barcelona by Enric Miralles and Carme Pinós (1986–90). See Jan Woudstra and Andrew Clayden, 'Some Approaches to Twentieth-century Cemetery Design: Continental Solutions for British Dilemmas', in *Mortality*, VIII/1 (2003).

31 Dieter Kienast and Christian Vogt, *Parks and Cemeteries* (Basel, 2002), p. 7.

SEVEN: THE DISAPPEARING BODY

1 Peter Jupp, *From Dust to Ashes: The Replacement of Burial by Cremation in England, 1840–1967* (London: The Congregational Memorial Hall Trust, 1978), p 3.

2 John Hooper, 'Riddle of the Sands', *The Guardian* (18 April 2002).

3 John Hooper, 'Briton Finds a Resting Place', *The Guardian* (7 August 2002). An equally poignant story was reported in *The Scotsman* newspaper (11 January 2003), under the title 'A Ghost Laid to Rest' by Stephen McGinty. This told of the body of a man who came to be known as 'Skye man' locally, who had travelled to the Isle of Skye, laid down by the water and waited to die. There was nothing about him or his clothing to identify where he came from, and apparently such suicides are not uncommon in the remoter parts of Scotland, 'chosen as the final destination of desperate people', according to the report. After several months of police enquiries, a woman came forward who believed the body to be that of her father. A local was reported as saying – in the same spirit as the people of Juist – 'it would be a tragedy to bury a man with no name in what would be a pauper's grave. I think he came here for a reason, he could have gone anywhere, but he came to die in this part of Skye and I think we should respect his decision. I hope he'll be buried here, but now with a proper headstone.'

4 I am very grateful to Richard Hill and Tanis Hinchcliffe for alerting me to this story. Further details are available in *The Corncrake* [Colonsay], 55 (13–30 April 2002).
A fuller account of the sinking of the *Arandora Star* is told by Alfio Bernabei, 'A Gold Watch is Missing', in *Italian Scottish Identities and Connections*, XV, Italian Cultural Institute (Edinburgh, 2001), pp. 53–9.

5 I am again grateful to Richard Hill for providing not only details of these graves, but of kindly giving me a sketch he made of the cemetery, the gravestones and some of the inscriptions.

6 The story of Finisterre Cemetery is given in detail in the final chapter.

7 None the less, the Romans, for example, were at times prone to mutilating and abusing the corpses of those regarded as public enemies. See Eric R. Varner, 'Punishment after Death: Mutilation of Images and Corpse Abuse in Ancient Rome', *Mortality*, VI/1 (2001), pp. 45–64.

8 Ruth Richardson, *Death, Dissection and the Destitute* (London, 1988).

9 Richardson, *Death, Dissection and the Destitute*, p. 271.

10 Jack Goody, *The Culture of Flowers* (Cambridge, 1993), p. 289.

11 The work of the Jewish Built Heritage project is described briefly in evidence given to the UK House of Commons Select Committeee report, *Cemeteries* (London, 2001), p. 51. See also: www.art.man.ac.uk/reltheol/jewish/heritage

12 Jane Morris, 'Bones of Contention', *The Guardian* (9 July 2002), p. 15.

13 Morris, 'Bones of Contention'.

14 This point is made by Philip Rahtz in 'Artefacts of Christian Death', *Mortality and Immortality: The Anthropology and Archaeology of Death*, ed. S. C. Humphreys and Helen King (London, 1981), p. 126.

15 Douglas Davies and Alastair Shaw, *Reusing Old Graves: A Report on Popular British Attitudes* (Crayford, Kent: Shaw & Sons, 1995), p. 25.

16 Whereas most European countries maintain some kind of cemetery rituals associated with All Souls Day, in Britain and North America people are now much more likely to make a point of visiting graves on Mother's Day and Father's Day, now that these two modern 'invented traditions' have taken hold so strongly, according to Ian Hussein, Director, City of London Cemetery, in a personal communication.

17 Pietro Citati, *Kafka*, trans. Raymond Rosenthal (London, 1990), p. 24.

18 Mark C. Taylor and Dietrich Christian Lammerts, *Grave Matters* (London, 2002), p. 23.

19 David Charles Sloane, *The Last Great Necessity: Cemeteries in American History* (Baltimore and London, 1995), p. 7.

20 Thomas Lynch, *The Undertaking: Life Studies from the Dismal Trade* (London, 1997), p. 123.

21 Richard Sennett, *Flesh and Stone: The Body and the City in Western Civilization* (London, 1994), p. 68.

22 I owe these references in the first instance to Tony Walter, who cites Keith Thomas in his *The Eclipse of Eternity: A Sociology of the Afterlife* (London, 1996), p. 188.

23 Peter Jupp, 'Cremation or Burial? Contemporary Choice in City and Village', *The Sociology of Death*, ed. David Clark (Oxford, 1993), p. 181.

24 Jupp, 'Cremation or Burial?', p. 186.

25 Ian Hussein, Director, City of London Cemetery, in a personal communication.

26 Source: The Cremation Society of Great Britain at http://members.aol.com/CremSoc4/Stats/Interntl/1999

27 Tony Walter, 'Dust not Ashes: The American Preference for Burial', *Landscape* 32/1 (1993), p. 45.

28 The most helpful guide to contemporary British attitudes to cremation, burial and the pattern of grave-visiting is contained in Davies and Shaw, *Reusing Old Graves*.

29 Cited in *Burial Space Needs in London* (London Planning Advisory Committee, 1997), p. 31.

30 André Schwartz-Bart, *The Last of the Just* (London, 1961), cited in James E. Young, *The Texture of Memory: Holocaust Memorials and Meaning* (New Haven, MA, 1993),

31 This point is made by one of the leading burial experts in the UK, Ken West, Bereavement Services Manager for Carlisle City Council, in his evidence to the UK House of Commons Select Committee Report, *Cemeteries* (London, 2001), p. 39.

32 K. I. Inglis, *Sacred Places: War Memorials in the Australian Landscape* (Melbourne, 2001), p. 470.

33 G. Kingsley Ward and Major Edwin Gibson, *Courage Remembered: The Story Behind the Construction and Maintenance of the Commonwealth's Military Cemeteries and Memorials of the Wars of 1914–1818 and 1939–1945* (London: HMSO, 1995).

34 Cited in Kate Berridge, *Vigor Mortis: The End of the Death Taboo* (London, 2001), p. 53.

35 John Keegan, 'England is a Garden', *Prospect* (November 1997), p. 22.

36 Michael A. Stern, 'The National Cemetery System: Politics, Place, and Contemporary Cemetery Design', in *Places of Commemoration: Search for Identity and Landscape Design*, ed. Joachim Wolschke-Bulmahn (Washington, DC, 2001), p. 110.

37 Stern, 'The National Cemetery System', p. 111.

38 Jane Brown, *Pursuit of Paradise*, pp. 71–2.

39 Geoff Dyer, *The Missing of the Somme* (London, 1995), p. 130.

40 Quoted in Mary Lutyens, *Edwin Lutyens* (London, 1991), p. 177.

41 Bob Bushaway, 'Name upon Name: The Great War and Remembrance', in *Myths of the English*, ed. Roy Porter (London, 1993), p. 144.

42 Jay Winter, *Sites of Memory, Sites of Mourning: The Great War in European Cultural History* (Cambridge, 1998), p. 103.

43 It was General Sir G. M. Macdonagh who opposed the adoption of the poppy, according to Bushaway, 'Name upon Name', p. 155.

44 The phrase belongs to the writer A. C. Benson in 1916, and is cited by Bushaway, 'Name upon Name', p. 146.

45 Bushaway, 'Name upon Name', p. 140.

46 Lucy Ward, 'MP's Plea to Save the Forgotten War Memorials', *The Guardian* (11 February 1998).

47 Inglis, *Sacred Places*.

48 The UK House of Commons Select Committee enquiry into *Cemeteries* (2001) is full of complaints about the shockingly bad, even derelict, state of many British Victorian cemeteries. This only endorses the principal assertion of Chris Brooks *et al.* in *Mortal Remains*, (London, 1989), particularly chap. 2: 'The Present State'.

49 For example, in evidence to the UK House of Commons Select Committee enquiry into *Cemeteries* (2001), a memorandum from the Commonwealth War Graves Commission noted that 'It is perhaps worth mentioning the Commission's experience in maintaining small numbers of graves in public cemeteries in other countries. In France and Belgium the preference is for hard surfaces with little horticulture and these can be kept clean by liberal applications of weedkiller. In The Netherlands cemeteries are more like those in Britain, although virtually all are well maintained. In Germany and Denmark standards are extremely high with horticulture often of a fine standard.'

50 House of Commons, *Cemeteries*, vol. I, Environment, Transport and Regional Affairs Committee, 21 March 2001, p. xi.

51 Hilary Lees, *English Churchyard Memorials* (Stroud, 2000), p. 23.

52 Oliver Rackham, *The History of the Countryside* (London, 1995), p. 344.

53 Victorian London Cemeteries at www.gendocs.demon.co.uk/cem.html

54 This acerbic quotation is recalled in James Stevens Curl, *The Victorian Celebration of Death* (Stroud, 2000), p. 33.

55 Sylvia Townsend Warner, *The True Heart* (London, 1985), p. 49.

56 Sloane, *The Last Great Necessity*, p. 19.

57 Davies and Shaw, *Reusing Old Graves*, p. 38.

58 In the UK, Ruth Richardson and Brent Elliott are among the most prominent opponents of re-use of existing burial spaces, principally for the reason that these were originally contracted to be secure and undisturbed in perpetuity.

59 Ian Traynor, 'A Fine and Privatised Place', *The Guardian* (29 May 1995).

60 Helena Smith, 'Greeks Fight for the Right to Rest in Peace', *The Guardian* (22 January 2000). See also Davies and Shaw, *Reusing Old Graves*, p. 100, which refers to Greek Orthodox attitudes and practices regarding the re-use of graves.

61 Loring M. Danforth, *The Death Rituals of Rural Greece*, with photos by Alexander Tsiaras (Princeton, NJ, 1982).

62 Danforth, *Death Rituals*, p. 15.

EIGHT: A PLACE AT THE END OF THE EARTH

1 Edwin Heathcote, *Monument Builders: Modern Architecture and Death* (Chichester, 1999), p. 12.

2 Pedro Azara in Mónica Gili, *La última casa* (Barcelona, 1999), p. 24.

3 Much of the spirit of this chapter is indebted to Edwin Heathcote's beautifully illustrated and thoughtful *Monument Builders: Modern Architecture and Death* (Chichester, 1999). The reference here

can be found on page 7.

4 William L. MacDonald, *The Pantheon: Design, Meaning, and Progeny* (London, 1976), p. 44.

5 Julie Dunk and Julie Rugg, *The Management of Old Cemetery Land* (Crayford, Kent: Shaw & Sons, 1994), p. 38.

6 Heathcote, *Monument Builders*, p. 12.

7 This summary in English relies on the translation from the French provided by Pedro Azara in his essay in Mónnica Gili, *La última casa* (Barcelona, 1999).

8 Pedro Azara, in Gili, *La última casa*, p. 36.

9 See Marc Treib, 'The Landscape of Loved Ones', in Wolschke-Bulmahn, ed., *Places of Commemoration*, pp. 95–101.

10 There were 242 crematoria operating in the UK in 2001, of which 193 were owned by local authorities, according to statistics supplied by the Cremation Society to the UK House of Commons Select Committee, London, 2001.

11 For an exceptionally detailed and thoughtful critique of a particular piece of crematoria architecture, see Hilary J. Grainger, 'Golders Green Crematorium and the Architectural Expression of Cremation', in *Mortality*, V/1 (2000), pp. 53–73.

12 Heathcote, *Monument Builders*, p. 38.

13 James Stevens Curl, *The Victorian Celebration of Death* (Stroud, 2000), pp. 190–93.

14 Until very recently, cremation in the UK was required to occur on the same day as the funeral service, though this has now been amended to 'within 24 hours' (Ian Hussein, Director, City of London Cemetery, in a personal communication).

15 Geoffrey and Susan Jellicoe, Patrick Goode, Michael Lancaster, *The Oxford Companion to Gardens* (Oxford, 1991), p. 104.

16 Cited in Jonathan Glancey, 'The Ideal Dome Show', *The Guardian* (17 June 2002).

17 Some of these are more fully detailed by Heathcote, *Monument Builders*.

18 The first comparison comes in the Internet City Guide to 'Berlin's Hidden Places': www.berlin-hidden-places.de. The second citation is from Peter Driver, 'Ritual of Death', *Architectural Review* (January 1999). However, not everybody finds the Treptow Crematorium quite as sublime. Two

English visitors to it (both cemetery professionals) told me that they personally found the interior gloomy and prescient with a sense of foreboding.

19 Catherine Merridale, *Night of Stone: Death and Memory in Russia* (London, 2000), p. 357.

20 I was told that up to 50 per cent of cremated remains are taken away by family or friends for disposal as they choose. Ashes are often interred in a private garden, or even in a plant pot that can be taken from one house to another, as and when people move home (Ian Hussein, Director, City of London Cemetery, in a personal communication).

21 A good description of the Brion Cemetery, amply illustrated with photographs, is to be found in Heathcote, pp. 204–13.

22 For a rather esoteric, art-historical explanation of the Scarpa sanctuary, see George Dodds, 'Desiring Landscapes / Landscapes of Desire: Scopic and Somatic in the Brion Sanctuary', *Body and Building: Essays on the Changing Relation of Body and Architecture*, ed. George Dodds and Robert Tavernor (Cambridge, MA, 2002).

23 A fine monograph is available on this extraordinary campus of the dead by Anatxu Zabalbeascoa: *Igualada Cemetery: Enric Miralles and Carme Pinós* (London, 1996).

24 David Cohn, 'Eyes to the Sea', *Architectural Record* [USA] (July 2002), pp. 108–11.

25 James E. Young, *The Texture of Memory: Holocaust Memorials and Meaning* (New Haven, MA, 1993), p.3.

26 Young, *Texture of Memory*, p. 5.

27 For more details about Colney Wood Burial Park: www.woodlandburialparks.co.uk

28 I am very grateful to John Dejardin, the landscape architect of Colney Wood, for his guided tour of the cemetery and his patient answers to my many questions. Thanks also to Donald Boddy, one of the progenitors of the burial park, and early designer.

29 Kenneth Frampton, 'Towards a Critical Regionalism', *Postmodern Culture*, ed. Hal Foster (London, 1985).

30 Frampton, 'Towards a Critical Regionalism', p. 26.

31 Jeremy Melvin, 'Monument: Antimonument', *Architectural Review* (October 2002), pp. 89–96.

32 Julie Rugg, 'What Makes a Cemetery a Cemetery?', *Mortality*, V/3 (2000), pp. 259–75.

33 David Morley, *Home Territories: Media, Mobility and Identity* (London, 2000).
34 Eva Reimers, 'Graves and Funerals as Cultural Communication', *Mortality*, iv/2 (July 1999), p. 152.
35 Doris Francis, Leonie Kellaher and Georgina Neophytou, 'Sustaining Cemeteries: The User Perspective', *Mortality*, v/1 (2000), p. 42.
36 Gili, *La última casa*.
37 Merridale, *Night of Stone*, p. 24.

Bibliography

Listed below are the writings which I have found most helpful and sympathetic to the argument of this book. Others will identify important omissions, for which I can only apologise. I have only included books and journals where the text is in English (or dual language texts), apart from those where photographs predominate. Nevertheless it is important to record that an increasing number of the most interesting essays and books on the funerary architecture, landscape and culture are now being published in Dutch, German, Italian, Spanish and Swedish.

ANTHROPOLOGY AND PHILOSOPHY

Albery, Nicholas, and Stephanie Wienrich, *The New Natural Death Book* (London, 2000)

Arendt, Hannah, *The Human Condition* (Chicago, 1958)

Hugh Brody, *The Other Side of Eden: Hunter-Gatherers, Farmers and the Shaping of the World* (London, 2001)

Calvino, Italo, *Invisible Cities* (London, 1979)

Clark, David, ed., *The Sociology of Death* (Oxford, 1993)

Danforth, Loring M., *The Death Rituals of Rural Greece*, with photography by Alexander Tsiaras (Princeton, NJ, 1982)

Dastur, Françoise, *Death: An Essay on Finitude*, trans. John Llewelyn (London, 1996)

Davies, Douglas J., *Death, Ritual and Belief: The Rhetoric of Funerary Rites* (London, 1997)

Dollimore, Jonathan, *Death, Desire and Loss in Western Culture* (London, 1998)

Douglas, Mary, *Purity and Danger: An Analysis of the Concepts of Pollution and Taboo* (London, 1984)

Gill, Sue and John Fox, *The Dead Good Funerals Book* (Engineers of the Imagination, Cumbria, 1996)

Herling(-Grudzinski), Gustaw, *Volcano and Miracle: A Selection of Fiction and Non-fiction from The Journal Written at Night*, selected and trans. Ronald Strom (London, 1996)

Lagerkvist, Pär, *Evening Land (Aftonland)*, trans. W. H. Auden and Leif Sjöberg (London, 1977)

Lynch, Thomas, *The Undertaking: Life Studies from the Dismal Trade* (London, 1997)

Merridale, Catherine, *Night of Stone: Death and Memory in Russia* (London, 2000)

Morley, David, *Home Territories: Media, Mobility and Identity* (London, 2000)

Morley, John, *Death, Heaven and the Victorians* (London, 1971)

Phillips, Adam, *Darwin's Worms* (London, 1999)

Prior, Lindsay, *The Social Organisation of Death: Medical Discourses and Social Practices in Belfast* (Basingstoke, 1989)

Richardson, Ruth, *Death, Dissection and the Destitute* (London, 1988)

Rorty, Richard, *Contingency, Irony and Solidarity* (Cambridge, 1993)

Sebald, W.G., *Austerlitz* (London, 2001)

Sennett, Richard, *Flesh and Stone: The Body and the City in Western Civilization* (London, 1994)

Stewart, Susan, *On Longing: Narratives of the Miniature, the Gigantic, the Souvenir, the Collection* (Baltimore and London, 1984)

Tarlow, Sarah, *Bereavement and Commemoration: An Archaeology of Mortality* (Oxford, 1999)

Walter, Tony, *The Eclipse of Eternity: A Sociology of the Afterlife* (London, 1996)

HISTORY AND ARCHITECTURE

Ariès, Philippe, *The Hour of Our Death* (London, 1983)

Brooks, Chris, et al., *Mortal Remains: The History and Present State of the Victorian and Edwardian Cemetery* (Exeter, 1989)

Colvin, Howard, *Architecture and the After-Life* (New Haven and London, 1991)

Constant, Caroline, *The Woodland Cemetery: Towards a Spiritual Landscape* (Stockholm, 1994)

Curl, James Stevens, *The Victorian Celebration of Death* (Stroud, 2000)

—, *Death and Architecture* (Stroud, 2002)

— , ed., *Kensal Green Cemetery: The Origins and Development of the General Cemetery of All Souls, Kensal Green, London, 1824–2001* (Chichester, 2001)

Davies, Douglas and Alastair Shaw, *Reusing Old Graves: A Report on Popular British Attitudes* (Crayford, Kent: Shaw and Sons, 1995)

Dodds, George, and Robert Tavernor, *Body and Building: Essays on the Changing Relation of Body and Architecture* (Cambridge, MA, 2002)

Dunk, Julie and Julie Rigg, *The Management of Old Cemetery Land* (Crayford, Kent: Shaw and Sons, 1994)

Dyer, Geoff, *The Missing of the Somme* (Harmondsworth, 1995)

Environment, Transport and Regional Affairs Committee, *Cemeteries*, Volumes I and II, House of Commons (London: HMSO, 2001)

Etlin, Richard A., *The Architecture of Death: The Transformation of the Cemetery in Eighteenth-century Paris* (London, 1984)

Gili, Mónica, *La última casa* [The last house] (Barcelona: Editorial Gastavo Gili, 1999)

Halsall, Guy, *Early Medieval Cemeteries: An Introduction to Burial Archaeology in the Post-Roman West* (Skelmorlie, Ayrshire, 1995)

Harbison, Robert, *The Built, The Unbuilt and the Unbuildable: In Pursuit of Architectural Meaning* (London, 1991)

Heathcote, Edwin, *Monument Builders: Modern Architecture and Death* (Chichester, 1999)

Holt, Dean W., *American Military Cemeteries* (Jefferson, NC, 1992)

Inglis, K.I., *Sacred Places: War Memorials in the Australian Landscape* (Melbourne, 2001)

Johansson, Bengt, O.H., *Tallum: Gunnar Asplunds and Sigurd Lewrentz skogskyrkogård I Stockholm*, with photographs by Fabio Galli (Stockholm: Byggförlaget, 1996)

Kiadó, Corvina, and Ernö Kunt, *Folk Art in Hungarian Cemeteries* (Budapest, 1983)

Krajewska, Monika, *A Tribe of Stones: Jewish Cemeteries in Poland* (Warsaw: Polish Scientific Publishers, 1993)

Lees, Hilary, *English Churchyard Memorials* (Stroud, 2000)

Meyer, Richard E., *Cemeteries and Gravemarkers: Voices of American Culture* (Ann Arbor, MI: UMI Research Press, 1989)

Nedoroscik, Jeffrey, A., *The City of the Dead: A History of Cairo's Cemetery Communities* (Westport, CT, 1997)

Panofsky, Erwin, *Tomb Sculpture: Four Lectures on Its Changing Aspects from Ancient Egypt to Bernini* (London 1992)

Piacentini, Guido, *La Certosa di Bologna* (Comune di Bologna, 2001) [principally photographs]

Renfrew, Colin, ed., *The Megalithic Monuments of Western Europe* (London, 1983)

Robinson, David, *Saving Graces: Images of Women in European Cemeteries* (New York, 1995)

—, *Beautiful Death: Art of the Cemetery*, text by Dean Koontz (London, 1996)

Schwartzman, Arnold, *Graven Images: Graphic Motifs of the Jewish Gravestone* (New York, 1993)

Sloane, David Charles, *The Last Great Necessity: Cemeteries in American History* (Baltimore and London, 1995)

Taylor, Mark C., and Dietrich Christian Lammerts, *Grave Matters* (London, 2002)

Ward, G. Kingsley and Major Edwin Gibson, *Courage Remembered: The Story behind the Construction and Maintenance of the Commonwealth's Military Cemeteries and Memorials of the Wars of 1914–1818 and 1939–1945* (London, 1995)

Winter, Jay, *Sites of Memory, Sites of Mourning: The Great War in European Cultural History* (Cambridge, 1998)

Worpole, Ken, *The Cemetery in the City* (Stroud, 1997)

Young, James E., *The Texture of Memory: Holocaust Memorials and Meaning* (New Haven, 1993)

Zabalbeascoa, Anatxu, *Igualada Cemetery: Enric Miralles and Carme Pinós* (London 1996)

LANDSCAPE

Augé, Marc, *Non-Places: Introduction to an Anthropology of Supermodernity* (London, 1995)

Bachelard, Gaston, *The Poetics of Space* (Boston, MA, 1994)

Brown, Jane, *The Pursuit of Paradise: A Social History of Gardens and Gardening* (London, 1999)

Everett, Nigel, *The Tory View of Landscape* (New Haven and London, 1994)

Harrison, Robert Pogue, *Forests: The Shadow of Civilization* (Chicago, 1992)

Hill, Richard, *Designs and their Consequences* (New Haven and London, 1999)

Jarman, Derek, *Derek Jarman's Garden*, with photographs by Howard Sooley (London, 1995)

Kienast, Dieter and Christian Vogt, *Parks and Cemeteries* (Basel, 2002)

Koerner, Joseph Leo, *Caspar David Friedrich and the Subject of Landscape* (London, 1990)

Lawrence, D. H., *D. H. Lawrence and Italy* (London, 1997)

Lübbren, Nina, *Rural Artists' Colonies in Europe 1870–1910* (Manchester, 2001)

Schama, Simon, *Landscape and Memory* (London, 1995)

Treib, Marc, ed., *Modern Landscape Architecture: A Critical Review* (Cambridge, MA, 1993)

Tuan, Yi-Fu, *Space and Place: The Perspective of Experience* (London, 1977)

Vergara, Camilo José, *American Ruins* (New York, 1999)

Weiss, Allen S., *Unnatural Horizons: Paradox and Contradiction in Landscape Architecture* (New York, 1998)

Williams, Raymond, *The Country and the City* (St Albans, 1975)

Wilton, Andrew, and Tim Barringer, *American Sublime: Landscape Painting in the United States, 1820–1880*, exh. cat., Tate Britain (London, 2002)

Wolschke-Bulmahn, Joachim, ed., *Places of Commemoration: Search for Identity and Landscape Design* (Washington, DC, 2001)

Woodward, Christopher, *In Ruins* (London, 2001)

ESSAYS AND PAMPHLETS

Andersson, Thorbjörn, 'The Functionalism of the Gardening Art', in *Sweden: 20th-Century Architecture*, ed. C. Caldeerly, J. Lindvall and W. Wang (Munich and New York, 1998)

Beck-Friis, Johan, *The Protestant Cemetery in Rome* (Rome, 1998)

Bohringer, Hannes, 'Places of No Return', *Daidalos*, 38 (December 1990)

Browne, Sir Thomas, 'Hydriotaphia: Urne-Buriall or, A Brief Discourse of the Sepulchrall Urnes Lately Found in Norfolk', in *The Major Works* (Harmondsworth, 1984)

Bushaway, Bob, 'Name upon Name: The Great War and Remembrance', in *Myths of the English*, ed. Roy Porter (London, 1993)

Cannadine, David, 'War and Death, Grief and Mourning in Modern Britain', in *Mirrors of Mortality: Studies in the Social History of Death* (London, 1981)

Charlesworth, Andrew and Michael Addis, 'Memorialization and the Ecological Landscapes of Holocaust Sites: The Cases of Plaszow and Auschwitz-Birkenau', *Landscape Research*, 27/3 (2002)

Cioffarelli, Ada and Maria Teresa Natale, *Guide to the Catacombs of Rome and its Surroundings* (Rome, 2000)

Fasola, Umberto M., *Domitilla's Catacomb and the Basilica of the Martyrs Nereus and Achilleus*, English edn by Frances Pinnock (Vatican City, 1986)

Francis, Doris, Leonie Kellaher and Georgina Neophytou, 'Sustaining Cemeteries: The User Perspective', *Mortality*, 5/1 (2000), pp. 34–52

Grainger, Hilary J., 'Golders Green Crematorium and the Architectural Expression of Cremation', *Mortality*, 5/1 (2000), pp. 53–73

Heinrich Härke, 'Cemeteries as Places of Power', in *Topographies of Power in the Middle Ages*, ed. Mayke de Jong and Frans Theuws, with Carine van Rhijn (Leiden, 2001)

Jupp, Peter, *From Dust to Ashes: The Replacement of Burial by Cremation in England 1840–1967* (London: Congregational Memorial Hall Trust, 1978)

Keegan, John, 'England is a Garden', *Prospect* (November 1997)

Lacqueur, Thomas, 'In and Out of the Panthéon', *London Review of Books* (20 September 2001)

Magnus, Bente, *Birka* (Stockholm: National Heritage Board, 2000)

Nagel, Thomas, 'Death', in *Mortal Questions* (Cambridge, 1983)

Naso, Alessandro, *Cerveteri: 3 Itineraries* (Rome, 1990)

National Federation of Cemetery Friends, *Notes on Saving Cemeteries* (York, 1991)

National Heritage Board, *Myth, Might, and Man: Ten Essays on Gamla Uppsala* (Stockholm, 2000)

Pateman, Jean and John Gay, *In Highgate Cemetery* (London: Friends of Highgate Cemetery, 1992)

Pentikäinen, Juha, 'The Dead without Status' in *Nordic Folklore: Recent Studies*, ed. Reimund Kvideland and Henning K. Sehmsdorf in collaboration with Elizabeth Simpson (Blomington, IN, 1989)

Reimers, Eve, 'Graves and Funerals as Cultural Communication', *Mortality*, 4/2 (July 1999), pp. 147–66

Rugg, Julie, 'What Makes a Cemetery a Cemetery?', *Mortality*, 5/3 (2000), pp. 259–75

Walter, Tony, 'Ritualising Death in a Consumer Society', *RSA Journal* (April 1996)

Woodbridge, Kenneth, *The Stourhead Landscape* (London: The National Trust, 2001)

Worpole, Ken, 'In the Midst of Life', in *Town and Country*, ed. Anthony Barnett and Roger Scruton (London, 1998)

Woudstra, Jan, 'Landscape: An Expression of History', *Landscape Design*, 308 (March 2002)

— and Andrew Clayden, 'Some Approaches to Twentieth-century Cemetery Design: Continental Solutions for British Dilemmas', *Mortality*, 8/1 (2003)

Acknowledgements

For her continuing enthusiasm and companionship, along with the wonderful photographs, I would like to express my deepest thanks and love to my wife, Larraine Worpole.
In addition, there are many other people to thank for their help in the making of this book, in the first instance four long-standing friends, Liz Greenhalgh, Richard Hill, Dave Morley and Jenny Uglow, who once again generously read early drafts of the text, and whose suggestions, though invisible to the reader, resulted in a book greatly strengthened in structure and more considered and elucidatatory in tone – or so I hope. Many thanks are also due to a number of landscape specialists who, in recent years, have been generous with their time and knowledge with me: amongst these I would especially mention Thorbjörn Andersson, David Lambert, Elizabeth LeBas, Laurence Pattacini, Marc Treib and Jan Woudstra. In addition I would like to thank Brent Elliott, Ian Hussein, Ruth Richardson and Tony Walter, who gave time to answer my questions early on in the development of this book.

For many small kindnesses in relation to the production of this book, knowingly or otherwise, I would also like to thank Sabrina Aaronovitch, Alan Barber, Alfio Bernabei, Ian Christie, Roger Deakin, John Dejardin, Jayne Engel-Warnick, Mauro Felicori, Debbie Fitzgerald (of *The Garden*, Journal of the Royal Horticultural Society), Alberto Formatger (BAAS Architects), Patrick Goode, Sten Göransson, Harm Grünhagen, David Hayes, Richard Hill, Tanis Hinchcliffe, Anneke van Kieft, Antonella Mampieri, Andreas Michaelides, Alice Naish, Ivan Nio, Julie Osborne, César Portela, David Solman, Diane Warburton, Stephanie Wienrich (Natural Death Centre), Jim and Rachel Wight and Ian Worpole.

Photographic
Acknowledgements

All photographs are courtesy of Larraine Worpole (whose general portfolio is represented by Edifice), with the following exceptions: page 34: photo Hannah Collins, reproduced by kind permission of Hannah Collins and Tate Enterprises Ltd; pages 39 (foot) and 187: photos A. C. Cooper/British Architectural Library, RIBA, London; page 46: Gemäldegalerie Neue Meister, Dresden; page 47 (top): Detroit Institute of Arts (gift of Julius H. Haas, in memory of his brother Dr Ernest W. Haas); page 47 (foot): Öffentliche Kunstsammlung Basel, Kunstmuseum (Depositum der Gottfried Keller-Stiftung); page 52 (top): photo by kind permission of Tanis Hinchcliffe; page 54: photo by kind permission of Jan Woudstra; page 94: photo by kind permission of Daniele De Lonti & Auroras; pages 143, 145, 181 (top): photos by kind permission of Marc Treib; page 165 (foot): photo by kind permission of the American Battle Monuments Commission, Arlington, Virginia; page 181 (foot): photo by kind permission of Laurence Pattacini; page 188: photo Hisao Suzuki, by kind permission of César Portela; page 189: photo by kind permission of Eugeni Pons and BAAS Architects.

Photographing cemeteries, places where public and private rights and interests overlap, is a delicate issue. Forbearance is kindly sought of any individual, family or organization whose rights may be felt to have been affected in any way; the photographs were taken in a spirit of respect, the principal theme of *Last Landscapes*.

Index